Voice of Triumph:
Hitler's Speeches at Nuremberg

1933, 1935–1938

Voice of
TRIUMPH

Hitler's Speeches at Nuremberg

Translated by David Kelly

ANTELOPE HILL PUBLISHING

First Antelope Hill edition, third printing 2024.

Translated by David Kelly, 2024.

Cover art by Swifty.
Edited by Harlan Wallace.
Proofread by Tom Simpson.
Layout by Sebastian Durant.

Antelope Hill Publishing | antelopehillpublishing.com

Hardcover ISBN-13: 979-8-89252-014-0
Paperback ISBN-13: 979-8-89252-013-3
EPUB ISBN-13: 979-8-89252-015-7

CONTENTS

The Führer's Speeches at the 1938 Party Congress of Greater Germany

THE FÜHRER'S SPEECHES
AT THE 1933 PARTY
CONGRESS OF VICTORY

THE COURSE OF THE NSDAP'S
FIFTH PARTY CONGRESS

An introduction

Thirteen long, hard years the Brown Army fought. Thirteen years, in all the districts, cities, and villages all across Germany, workers, farmers and burghers, old frontline soldiers and the young volunteers of the second freedom fight hoisted the blood-red flag of the German revolution, wrestled and fought for every single new comrade, every fellow German, every woman who joined the ranks of National Socialism's great community of destiny. Thirteen long years in which — like healthy cells in a sick body — fellowships of blood and ideas formed all over the German land, from which a new spirit flowed into a despondent and famished people; in which, despite being a time of bleakest decay, ideals became reality — ideals which loomed over the heads of a rotted ruling class like fiery beacons of a coming rebirth; in which there was devotion again and faith, in which there was purity and fellowship, in which lived *a Führer* and one holy duty: *Germany*.

The proud, bold breath of this fellowship of German revolution wafted into the Volk and into all corners of the German land. This breath took hold of those who were not yet hollowed out, but who were just tired from all the hopelessness and pressure of a dirty, dishonorable revolt and its dishonorable consequences. Suddenly they lifted their heads again, as from afar they could hear the defiant march step of the eternal Germany, as young fists took up a young flag bearing the ancient German symbol of victory and carried it through the slavering hatred of inferior humanity, all the while laughing and victorious, faithful and brave. They lifted their heads and became joyous and proud again, like those who marched — and then they marched with them. Anyone who was still healthy marched with them: the young and old factory workers marched along, who refuted Marxist slave morality with the *honor of their work*. The old and young farmers marched along, who with desperate doggedness wanted to defend their fields and birthright against foreclosure by bankers and capitalist interests. The burghers and their sons marched along, whose blood and hearts went out to their working comrades to build a new Germany. They all marched along. They numbered well over a hundred thousand and always kept growing — and today *one Volk, one destiny, and one age* marches behind the flag for which three hundred undefeated comrades fell. This flag is sanctified like no other piece of fabric by blood and selfless sacrifice; it is a flag for which a hundred thousand willingly and joyously took up hardship and misery. A Volk marches that has been called back home to itself by a man; a Volk that has found itself again through the enjoinders and calls, the struggles and action, of the Führer Adolf Hitler.

Bells called the National Socialist Party Congress into session. There was deep, stricken silence among the thousands of people who gathered in all parts of the city. The bells that tolled there were bells of thanksgiving, resounding over a nation saved from deep brokenness. They were bells of thanksgiving that told of the nation's dire wrestling against almost certain downfall and despair. They were bells of a promise, bells of a people's fidelity to its most beautiful tradition and noblest history.

And these bells resounded over a city in whose most distant corners and narrowest alleys the love and gratitude of the poorest and simplest often found their most touching expression. This city's streets and houses disappeared behind the forest of garlands and flags. Here every window announced the joy with which the whole people began these festive days. Here storms of jubilation, gratitude, and devotion accompanied every step of the Führer. And yet, all this was but a small slice, a quiet utterance, for there were not merely a hundred thousand, but millions — a whole people that wanted to express its ultimate love and faith. Nuremberg was only one heartbeat in the new life of the awakened nation — but this one beat gave an inkling of the power that this one man's call awakened.

Rudolf Hess, representative of the Führer, opened the great Party

Congress with these words: "I hereby open the fifth Party Congress of the NSDAP, the first Party Congress after National Socialism's seizure of power. I open the Party Congress of Victory." As he did so, and as the standards of the SA were carried in amidst the din of a march and under the welcome of the entire leadership cohort of the New German Reich, the celebration became a hundred times greater than the welcoming cheers of the population. More than a celebration, it became a consecration, and the magnitude of this victory was revealed more clearly and beautifully than ever before.

How many dreams were dreamt in silent hours among the brown comradeship of a coming third and eternal Reich? But no one could imagine it. Yet now it was reality, through the ancient, indissoluble bond between leadership and discipleship, a reality that burst through the confines of one party and grew to encompass the whole state. This reality now linked the highest wielder of state power with the unknown comrade of the brown front. With reverence, the giant assembly of the first men of the New German Reich greeted the old victory symbols of the SA, carried to their triumph by the same trusty workers' and farmers' fists that hoisted them through all the years of terror and persecution. A deep gratitude flowed through the hall and acknowledged the three hundred comrades, whose spirits accompanied the standards of victory to their place of honor.

At the same time these thousands turned their eyes toward the man whose greatness of leadership alone made this triumph possible. This man we saw and heard in hundreds and thousands of gatherings, years ago in smoke-filled rooms, then in Germany's largest halls, and finally in the final struggle for power. Every hour and with every word he fought and struggled for the sake of love and fellowship and the understanding of the whole German Volk. He never let the flag waver. He first appeared to us all in his full greatness in the hour when no one saw a path forward, when he himself was overstretched and overworked, and yet he always decided on the hardest path, for uncompromising struggle, for unmistakable and uncompromising fealty to the flag and the idea. He was ridiculed and scoffed at, hated and loved—but his word and his deed remained the same. His answer to every persecution and difficulty in those unspeakably difficult thirteen years was: "I believe in this Volk; I believe in Germany." This belief was given life and form in the faith of countless brown fighters, in the laughing love of a half million members of the Hitler Youth—boys and girls. Finally, it manifested in the fealty of the whole people, which shone forth best in the sacrifice and work of every individual for the well-being of the whole and for the renewal of the state.

The faith of the best and even the loyalty of the least now hung over the Party Congress like a silent blessing, like a covenant in which the sacrifices of countless generations came alive again and lent their strength to the newly awakened will to life of the nation. It was as if a million voices from every village and every living room in Germany intoned along with Rudolf Hess when, in his opening remarks, he turned to the Führer and said: "My Führer! As leader of the party, you were our guarantor of victory. When others faltered, you remained steadfast. When others looked to strike a compromise, you were unbending. When others let their courage wane, you showed new courage. When others left our ranks, you gripped our flag more determinedly than ever, until the flag became the flag of the state, thus signaling our victory—and again, you carry the flag forward! As leader of the nation, you are our guarantor of ultimate victory. We greet the leader and in him we greet the leader of the nation. Adolf Hitler, we greet you!"

The Party Congresses of the NSDAP were always a balancing act. They were a balance between discipline and the will of the movement, which found its symbolic expression in the marches of the SA, SS, and Hitler Youth. Likewise, it was a balance of the intellectual work that had been done in the years leading up, and the shaping and ramifications of the intellectual content of the movement. One never experienced a stagnant moment or a step backward at the National Socialist Congresses. Indeed, as the brown columns visibly grew in determination, discipline, force, and unity, so each Party Congress became a milestone of increased intellectual power, where the intellectual agenda was broadened and deepened, and the future's tasks became clear. The old parties of bourgeois Marxist liberalism were content to blather on about their ancient yet never realized program goals, but all could see that at the NSDAP's Party Congresses the worldview of National Socialism formed through the combined efforts of the men who heeded the Führer's calls for collaboration in the Congresses.

At the Party Congress of the NSDAP the crystal-clear summit of the idea grows, as it were, out of the march of the brown columns. Here the feel and rhythm that animates the march of the SA, SS, and Hitler Youth obtains its ultimate intellectual, self-conscious purpose. At the National

Socialist Congress, idea and power, purpose and will merge into an indissoluble, inevitable creative entity.

In the early years this entity was the core of both the intellectual and disciplinary resistance of a young Germany against the old system. Even then the festivities of the NSDAP were the strongest concentration of energy and political insight; however, then they were of necessity oriented against the state, which clueless partisans had turned into an instrument of despotism that threatened the life and future of the people. With Adolf Hitler's chancellorship, the great transformation of this center of resistance into the focal point of the new state will have occurred, as it was also in opposition, but now freed from all bonds and inhibitions. Thus began the interpenetration and cross-pollination of the state and the movement. However, the NSDAP remains what it was and should continue to be: the strongest expression of the nation's will to live; the eternal, continually renewed powerhouse that animates the new German state.

Thus, the Party Congress of 1933 became the noble celebration of the brown fighters' victory, as well as the most beautiful, liveliest expression of the German will for resurrection. It became the wellspring from which a new impulse proceeded into the whole national life—an impulse evident as much in the steady strength of the brown battalion's march as in the grave seriousness of the great Congress.

The discipline of the SA has in the last months become the leading principle of the whole people, and yet the unanimous force of the 120,000 brown shirts in Nuremberg challenges every individual to ever higher subordination and stronger commitment. In the speeches of the National Socialist Congress, we saw the exclusive way and will of the new state. With overwhelming force, we saw how today National Socialism is beginning to transform every area of the state and is giving each organ of the state its new tasks and goals.

Today, the party and movement belong to the state. They will only keep legitimacy so long as they use this power for the common good of the nation. In truth, as the NSDAP represents the most incomparable organization of the most unconditional devotion to the state, so it must also preserve its identity as constant critic, as eternal troubled conscience, which holds up in the face of every accomplishment an image of an even higher challenge, to every sacrifice the example of an even greater selflessness in service of the whole. In this sense, the fighting community of the NSDAP will be eternal, and its fighters will build the new German order, whose one law will be the undying spirit of the eternal German volunteer soldier.

The proud blessing of this volunteerism — this also ruled the festival days of Nuremberg. This was happily self-evident for all, as the hundreds and thousands of fighters, called by the Führer to take their place in the state, gathered at the Party Congress as the great army of National Socialism, and in place of the hierarchy of the state there was the leadership hierarchy of the movement. Men who may have been ministers and high officials in the state were again mere party officials here and took their place among the rank and file of the fighting community. But in the place of honor here were the men who were first in the meritocracy of the party, and who were the most accomplished fighters and therefore the foremost men of the state.

Out of this lively combination of state and party grew an agenda for the coming years. National Socialism spent these days solicitously, drawing another hundred thousand German-blooded and German-spirited people, with its mysterious strength and greatness, inspiring them to work with us. It spent these days effectively, remaking itself, fulfilling itself, giving strength to its spiritual breadth and depth. Similarly, it will have one day solicitously and effectively taken hold of the whole Volk, with National Socialism changing its form and mass, but always remaining what it was upon its foundation: the mission, the project, the formation, the ever-recurring rebirth of the eternal Germany.

This German rebirth found its tremendous expression in the Führer's six speeches. There was no one who, under the sheer force of these ideas, was not shaken by the dynamism of the National Socialist revolution and the creative power of its leader, who, even in victory, calmly and single-mindedly showed the way forward for the universally advancing new will of the nation.

The Führer's great proclamation at the start of the Congress lays forth several eternal laws and traditional truths for all to see and consider. The observation of these laws and truths is what made the NSDAP's rise and victory possible. It is a duty of the party to ensure that these laws will be observed in the future German state. The party will reach its goal through the elite, selected from among the people, as the Führer described them:

Among our tasks for the future is to craft a union between feeling and reason again, that is, to raise that untainted generation that will recognize the eternal lawfulness of development with a clear mind, and with this will deliberately find its way back to primitive instinct.

These words had to convince the nation that National Socialism's revolutionary will for the formation of a new undeformed man, a new normal generation, would never rest on the laurels of that attainment. Translated to the political, the demand for this new man means the will to break from all outmoded, artificially constructed forms in the national life: "The National Socialist movement is not the conservator of the states of the past, but their liquidator for the sake of the Reich of the future."

In his powerful speech at the cultural conference, the Führer widened the frame of this will for the reestablishment of the German political order to include the emerging meaning of National Socialism's worldview as the "heroic doctrine of the valuation of blood, of race, and of personality, as well as the eternal laws of selection." And at the end of this fundamental address, this sentence: "This new state will give a very different attentiveness to the nurturing of culture than the old did." This acknowledgement by Adolf Hitler rang out, past all the worry and workload of reconstructing the state, as the announcement of the new German idealism — and the Führer knows that he has the people's spiritual support in this appeal to idealistic forces, just as he won their support back then when he was preaching and practicing sacrifice for an idea from within the deepest swamp of materialism.

The Führer speaks to the party officials of their task of seeing to the political education of the people:

You, my party officers, are responsible before God and before our history for ensuring that a November 1918 will never again be possible in German history, through the political rearing of the German people toward one Volk, one idea, one expression of the will.

To his youth, Adolf Hitler speaks of the eternal fidelity of comradeship: "You must be true; you must build amongst yourselves one single, great, glorious comradeship." However, the SA hears of the joy of victory: "The debt of our Volk is erased, its sin atoned, its shame removed, the men of

November are deposed and their power is at an end." These proud and victorious words coming from the Führer are the greatest thanks for the Brown Army for their past struggle and risk. There on the Luitpoldhain,[1] before the vast brown columns of discipline, of self-sacrifice, there came also a word directed at the world abroad:

> We do not need to rehabilitate our Volk's historical honor on the battlefield, for no one took it from us there. Only one dishonor came upon us, and it came upon us not in the West, nor in the East, but on the home front. This dishonor has been rectified.

Finally, the great concluding remarks of the Congress about the political leadership of the nation; one final, gripping appeal to the fighters of the movement, to whom the Führer again gave the explanation of the National Socialist fight and the National Socialist mission:

> If the word socialism is to have any meaning at all, then it can only mean to assign to everyone — with iron fairness and deepest insight — that part of the preservation of the whole that accords to his inborn disposition and consequently his worth.

With this creed of ultimate service to the Volk and the state, the Party Congresses of the victory of the NSDAP ended. At no moment was the Congress at a triumphal and satisfied rest, but rather always a challenge and a call to new obligation.

"The future will one day weigh us in the same measure as we thought of it. Therefore, may our God guard us against making those mistakes founded in human self-interest." With these words from the Führer, National Socialism went forth out of Nuremberg into the continued fight.

— Dr. Walther Schmitt

---

[1] The park wherein the rally took place.

THE PROCLAMATION OF THE FÜHRER AT THE OPENING OF THE 1933 PARTY CONGRESS

When the National Socialist movement was called into life in 1919 to establish a new Reich in place of the Marxist democratic republic, this undertaking seemed utter foolishness. Thanks to their superficial historical education, those sophistical intellectuals could, at most, bring themselves to offer a sympathetic smile.

Most of them well recognized that Germany had run into hard times. The majority of the so-called national intelligentsia had quietly grasped that those who held power in the November Republic were partly too evil and partly too incompetent to successfully lead our Volk. The one thing they did not recognize was that the new regime would not be overcome by the same forces that for fifty years shrank from the attack of Marxism, only to wretchedly capitulate to it in the hour of greatest need. Maybe it also was in the nature of the personal decrepitude of the earlier political leadership. They were unable and unwilling to recognize the timescales necessary for the restoration of a people's strength.

That we National Socialists could see the requirements for overcoming Marxism, and also worked toward this overcoming, divorced us from the bourgeois intellectual world.

The first requirement revealed itself with the insight that a power that is determined to kill the mind through terror will not be broken by the polite opinion that terror can be overcome by the mind. It makes sense to employ purely intellectual tactics only so long as all segments of the population are ready to submit to the outcome of such an intellectual wrestling. The moment Marxism launched the mob slogan "If you won't be my comrade, then I'll smash in your head!" they declared the rule of force. The mind can either resist with equivalent weapons or else lose its influence and become historically irrelevant.

Furthermore, it is clear that one cannot expect anything different from a movement than what it held up to be engraved and innate through the course of its coming-to-be. Bourgeois parties could venture so little outside their traditional mentality; likewise, Marxism had to hew to Marxist dogma. This means it is a fallacy to believe that party structures that have been dueling for decades with more or less pitiful intellectual weapons can suddenly do heroic deeds. It is likewise a fallacy to expect that Marxism would ever renounce its terroristic inclinations.

This is also the reason that one must not think that old and stale organizations can be directed toward new ends, even if they are headed by new leadership. You cannot coax powers out of an organization that does not possess them. The spirit that birthed it and ruled its development searched, found, and gathered a people fit to its character. He who, like Clausewitz said, makes "false cleverness" the ruling law of his movement cannot hope to one day discover heroic fanatics among it. It was therefore folly when, in the years 1919, 1920, and after, men who recognized the distress of our Fatherland believed that a switch in the leadership of the bourgeois parties would suddenly lend these the strength to annihilate the internal enemy. Quite the opposite: every attempt to give the bourgeois parties leaders who were not characteristic of them lead to a split between leadership and party members. When for seventy years you glorify a false democracy, you cannot in the seventy-first year grasp for dictatorship. Such attempts lead to comical experiments. Seeking help, one borrows the principles of others without believing in them. Hence bourgeois parties that vote themselves a dictator, under the condition that he never dictates!

The opposition to Marxism therefore required from the beginning an organization whose entire being was made for and suited for this fight. But this required time to emerge. Just by looking at the aged political leadership of the bourgeois antipodes of Marxism, one can find the key to the consistent incomprehension of this class for the methods of the young National Socialist movement. With few exceptions, age kills not only physical, but also intellectual potency. Because everyone desires to experience the fruits of his fights himself, he seeks the easier (because quicker) methods of actualizing his ideas. Not comprehending any organic development, rootless intellectualism seeks to bypass the laws of growth through quick experiments. In contrast, National Socialism from its first day was ready to take on the dreary, long work of rebuilding the instrument with which we hoped to finally destroy Marxism. Because this path was not grasped by the superficial mentality of our politicizing bourgeoisie, the young movement could at first only develop through those classes that had stayed intellectually unspoiled, uncomplicated, and therefore closer to nature. What the wisdom of the wise could not see was understood by the soul, the heart, and the instinct of these primitively naive and healthy people! Among our tasks for the future is the necessity of crafting a union between feeling and reason again — in brief, to raise that untainted generation that will recognize the eternal lawfulness of development with a clear mind, and with this deliberately find its way back to primitive instinct.

While directing its plea for the formation of a new movement to the broad mass of our Volk, National Socialism had to first suggestively burn into the minds of the few people it had already won over that they can eventually be the saviors of the Fatherland. This problem of teaching self-confidence and faith in the self was as important a goal as it was a difficult one. People who, on the basis of their social and economic heritage, mostly occupied the lower and often hard-pressed classes had to be imbued with the political conviction that they would one day be the political leadership of the nation. The fight that the National Socialist had to engage in, against such a greatly superior force, obliged us to strengthen his trust in the movement and his self-confidence by all means available. The bourgeois world constantly found scorn and derision for our method of implanting what they called the "presumptuous megalomania" of one day leading the Reich. And yet, fanatic faith in the victory of the movement was the prerequisite for every later success. The most psychologically effective part of this upbuilding, besides the practice of the daily struggle and getting used to the enemy, was the visible demonstration of belonging to a great and strong movement! Therefore, our rallies not only won more adherents, but above all they solidified and morally strengthened those already won. While the ingenious leaders of our bourgeois world talked about the "work in secret," and at best delivered profound discourses at tea parties, National Socialism began its march into the

Volk. We held hundreds of thousands of rallies. A hundred and a hundred thousand times our speakers were in assembly halls, small smoky pub rooms, and the great sports arenas and stadiums. Each rally not only won us more new people, but first and foremost solidified everyone and filled everyone with that suggestive confidence that is the prerequisite for every great success. The others spoke of democracy but shunned the Volk. National Socialism spoke of authority, but fought and wrestled alongside the Volk like no other movement before it.

Hence, the Party Congresses of the National Socialist movement were never comparable to those squabbles of quarrelsome parliamentarians and party and union secretaries who gave their seal of approval to other parties' meetings.

The points of the National Socialist Party Congress were: firstly, for the Führer of the movement to once again have the opportunity for personal acquaintance with the party leadership; secondly, to renew the bond between the party members and their leadership; thirdly, to strengthen everyone's confidence in victory; and fourthly, to set forth the great spiritual and psychological impulses for the continuation of the fight.

In 1920, 1921, and 1922, the first Party Congresses took place. They were expanded general-membership meetings of the party, which was then almost exclusively limited to Munich and Bavaria.

It was also Munich that, on January 27th, 1923, experienced the first Party Congress, with representatives from the rest of Germany. By November of that year, the party was banned.

Three years later, we celebrated the memorable resurrection of our party in Weimar.

In 1927, the third Party Congress took place, and this time for the first time in Nuremberg, as did the fourth Party Congress in 1929.

Then, when for several years no Party Congress could take place, it was not our fault, but rather due to the conduct of others. The attempt to gather in Nuremberg again in 1930 ran aground against the resistance of our political opponents, who were then the Bavarian government. For three years this bourgeois conservative government sabotaged any further attempt at meeting. But for the movement and for all time henceforth, the place of our Party Congress shall be the city in which we first, with a powerful announcement, proclaimed the new German will.

September 2nd will mark ten years since, for the first time in Germany since the shameful collapse, there was in this city an overpowering march led by National Socialism. This march not only whipped up the cheering Franconian city, but was received by all of Germany as the sign of a coming turning point!

In order to give the movement a feel for the honorable tradition of our struggle, the Party Congress will for all time take place here in this city!

Thus, you were called here to the fifth Party Congress of the NSDAP, the first in the New German Reich!

A miracle has occurred in Germany. What we hoped for in the long years of struggle, what we believed within our breasts, what we were ready to give any sacrifice to achieve — even our own lives — has now become reality!

The National Socialist revolution has defeated the state of betrayal and perjury, and has in its place restored a Reich of honor, loyalty, and decency. The bulk of the people joined us, so we did not have to carry out this revolution as leaders of the "historical minority" against the majority of the German nation. We were happily relieved that the overwhelming majority of the German Volk came to recognize our principles already before the turning point of destiny. Thus, it was possible that one of the greatest upheavals of power could happen with almost no bloodshed. Thanks to the shining organization of the movement, the instrument of leadership at no moment slipped out of hand during this historic upheaval. Besides the Fascist revolution in Italy, no similar historic undertaking can be compared in its inner discipline and order to the National Socialist uprising. We feel it as a great fortune that today the overwhelming majority of the German Volk stands with us in loyal attachment to the new regime. It is good and advantageous to know there is power in one's fists, but it is better and happier to be able to call the love and assent of a people one's own!

And as you are gathered here in this hall, millions of German men and women and today's youth live with us. The National Socialist revolution has become the German Reich, the German state. Behind the flag of our former opposition, the German nation marches!

And this is also the surest guarantee of the ultimate success of our work.

Just as the sick man cannot be healed by the physician's arts alone if his body mounts no resistance to the death knocking at its door, if even the will to life is extinguished, so also a people cannot be spared of its destruction by political leadership alone if it either has become worthless in its inner substance, or if the political leadership does not succeed in awakening the will of all and enlisting them in this task. The joyful participation of the mass of the nation does not only regain its freedom, but economic problems are also unsolvable without the regime's measures having the trust and support of the whole Volk. The situation in which we find ourselves is clear to everyone. At the beginning of this year there were weeks in which we avoided the precipice of Bolshevik chaos by a hair's breadth. The threatening political situation arose from the more than slightly dangerous economic condition. The rapid crash last winter seemed like it would grow into a total collapse. When the great historian Mommsen described Judaism as a "ferment of decomposition" in public life, this decomposition was already far advanced in Germany. And as a single human can spread a sickness to a stadium, where it would be difficult or impossible to reverse, so it is in public life. So, with grim determination, National Socialism took up arms in defense against the creeping "decline of the West," carried by the belief in the not-yet-totally-destroyed great inner values that are inherent to the civilized people of Europe, and which are especially apparent in our German people. When Fascism gave the example with its great historic deed of saving the Italian people, National Socialism made it its mission to do this also for the German people. For this reason, we will not tolerate the enactors of our people's former destruction continuing to make our people spineless — or even just unsure — through their eternally negative operations of degradation, especially at a time when our people's whole will must help to avoid catastrophe and overcome the crisis. Therefore, it will be one of the most important tasks of our movement to declare a relentless war against the destroyers of our people's strength and to wage it until their utter annihilation or submission. As the sole wielder of state power, the party must recognize that from now on it alone carries the whole responsibility for the course of German destiny. In view of the international spread of the primary ferment of this decomposition and the special dangers to Germany resulting from this, we will all the more have to ensure that the spirit of doubt, of diffidence, or of self-indulgence is banished from within our people. We National Socialists went through too long a period of persecution and suppression to not recognize the actual value of the glitzy democratic slogans of our political enemies. We are determined to act accordingly! The educational work the movement will have to do is tremendous. For it is not enough to organize the state according to certain principles; it is also necessary to nurture them in the people. Only when the Volk inwardly takes part in the foundations and methods that carry and animate its state organization will a living organism arise, instead of a dead and merely formal and mechanical organization.

When necessary for self-preservation, only that which is filled with life will be able to lay claim to and issue life.

Among those problems brought to us to solve, the most important is the overcoming of unemployment. We do not see its danger as purely material. The effects of distress show themselves in the lives of the people in various ways. Weak-willed surrender alternates with desperate vigor. The material preservation of one part of the nation which cannot find work—at the expense of that part which can find work—can only have negative results in the long term. It is neither logical, nor moral, nor just to take away a part of the fruits of the labor of the working part of a people in perpetuity. Rather than take away the results of work, it would be logical to distribute the work itself. No one has the moral right to require that others work so that he himself does not have to work. Rather, everyone only has the right to demand their state organization to find the means and solutions to let work be available to everyone! We will have to exert ourselves tremendously to solve this problem in a responsible and useful way. Within just a few years we will have to set right the foolishness and recklessness of decades. We will do this when we succeed in forcing the nation to a lively participation in this tremendous undertaking. This is all the more necessary because numerous other projects have to step into the background so that all our strength can be focused on solving this one problem. We are traveling down roads that have hardly been trodden historically. All crises up to this point cannot be compared to our current economic deterioration, as they fail to live up to it either in their magnitude or their extent, or else they are too far from us in time, so that no detailed enough study can be made to get a clear picture of the methods used to correct them. Because of this, it is always a possibility that this or that measure we enact will not prove effective; but for this reason it is all the more necessary to prevent the nagging criticism that is forever bent on subversion! It is irrelevant if a thousand critics live, but it is not irrelevant if because of them a people collectively renounces its life and perishes. All those men who through their insane or criminal behavior since November 1918 thrust us into our present misfortune and who used the phrases "liberty," "fraternity," and "equality" as the leitmotif of their dealings do not today share in the fate and sorrow of the victims of their politics! Through them, millions of German comrades were delivered into the hardest bondage that there is. Their very being was raped by hardship, misery, and hunger. The seducers certainly enjoy their freedom in foreign lands to take foreign pay to slander their own people, to dole out hate; yes, they would like for them, if possible, to be mowed down on battlefields as defenseless cannon fodder! That these men's spirits once and for all disappear from Germany is one of the National Socialist movement's greatest duties, and a prerequisite for the convalescence of the German people. May our common sense and our determination for all time prevent our Volk from losing our unity of thought and will for the sake of the catchphrase of "the right to free criticism." With this it would be abandoning the best thing that it possesses. If we believe in the resurrection of the German nation, it is not because this type of rootless critic instilled confidence, but only because we believe in the healthy kernel of our Volk.

The average German has always been better than the most excellent of Marxist subverters!

This Party Congress, too, thus has the high duty to strengthen and cement the wonderful confidence of our people. The active party militant who had the good fortune to be able to take part in this conference must go forth with his newly strengthened confidence into his social circle and work as an apostle for the National Socialist idea and National Socialist action. The German people, having faithfully entrusted their fate to the movement, will be happy to see the firmness and self-assurance with which the movement determines the way.

The ascent and finally the stunning victory of the National Socialist movement never would have happened if we had tolerated the principle that in our ranks each can do as he wishes. This habit of democratic permissiveness can only lead to uncertainty, dissoluteness, and ultimately to the decline and deterioration of every authority. The argument our opponents make, that we ourselves once made use of these rights, is untenable. We made use of an unreasonable right, which was an inextricable part of an unreasonable system, in order to topple this system on account of its unreasonableness. Nothing falls which is not ripe for falling. When the old Germany fell, it proved its own internal weaknesses, just as the November Republic's fall makes its weaknesses plain for all to see. We would only lack the right to fight with these weapons if we planned to let ourselves succumb to the very same illogic and weakness!

Through its work of politically educating the German people, the Party will have to make the German man more and more spiritually immune against any relapse into this past. While we negate the democratic parliamentary principle, we most acutely represent the right of the people for the determination of its own life. We alone recognize that the parliamentary system does not actually express the will of the people, which, logically, can only be a will for the preservation of the people; rather we see in this system a distortion, if not a total inversion of the people's will. A people's will to assert its existence appears in its clearest and most useful form inside the heads of its best! They are the representative leadership of a nation, and they alone can be the pride of a people; never can it be the parliamentarian, whose birthplace is at the polls and whose father is the anonymous ballot. It will require years to build up the most capable minds into the future leadership of the nation. The corresponding education of the people will take decades.

If our movement's Party Congresses have so far been an exemplar of organization and discipline, this is only because the movement knows that it can require nothing of its followers that it does not do itself. Only in applying the principle of authority and discipline straight down from top to bottom in the party's organization does it win the moral right to ask the same of even the lowest comrade. And it must do this! For the greater the challenges that these times pose, the greater the authority that has to be commanded by whoever will have to solve them. It is important that our organization's leadership has such self-assurance in its resolutions that it instills unconditional confidence in party members as well as followers. For the people will rightly never understand it if its leadership, having failed to straighten out problems, suddenly lays these problems before the people for them to discuss and provide clarification. It makes sense that even very wise men may fail to reach complete clarity on especially difficult problems. However, it would be a capitulation of leadership as such if it opens up exactly these problems to public treatment and commentary. In doing so, it esteems the broad mass as having more power of judgment than the leadership itself. Then it should also go along with the consequences and, logically, turn over leadership to those whom it deems fitter to judge!

In opposition to this, the National Socialist Party must be convinced that it will be able to find and unite to itself the most politically talented people in Germany, thanks to a process of selection imposed by the vital struggle. This community has to follow the same law amongst itself that it wishes to see the mass of the nation follow. The party must therefore constantly nurture in itself the mental habits of respect, of authority, and the free adoption of the highest discipline if it wants to nurture the same within its following. It has to be hard and consistent. It is clear: our political enemies are defeated. Their own quality was unmasked as clearly inferior. The only thing they could hope for is, through their deft subversion, to loosen the national discipline and to shake our trust in each other and our leadership.

Let this Party Congress be a singular warning to all these tempters. This party stands here, with its organization more stable than ever, resolute in will, rigorous in self-correction, unconditional in discipline and in its respect for its responsible authority to those below, and its authoritative responsibility to those above.

Only with this spirit will we overcome all the alleged and real differences in economic and other aspects of life and solidify our Volk into one body. Only with this can you take burghers and farmers and workers and all the other classes and reconstitute one Volk!

Over the course of the thousand-year development of our Volk, German tribes and then governments started to form, and along with this development, there came to be certain entities that we still see today as our federal states. Their existence cannot be attributed to any national necessity. In weighing their pros and cons for the German nation, the former disappear in light of the latter. Even in the realm of culture, the emerging nation proved to be more creatively fertile ground. Only due to the preexisting correlations between political and cultural hotspots did we get the decentralization of German art, which has caused our Fatherland to appear so beautiful and rich. While we are determined to protect these and other valuable traditions, we must advance against these barriers to our national unity, which have done incalculable political damage to our people for centuries. What would Germany be today if past generations had done nothing against the appalling cacophony of so many little states, which never did the German people any good, but was always a boon to our enemies? One Volk that speaks one language, possesses one culture, and has experienced the formation of its destiny through one common history, can do no other than to also strive for unity in its leadership. Besides, it would lose the advantages of its numbers, while still having to suffer the disadvantages thereof. We saw at the January, February, and March conferences this year to what lows these circumstances can bring a people's character and strength, when the smallest party-egoists coldly combined their despicable party interests with provincial regional interests and thus sought to threaten the unity of the Reich. The German nation's first answer to these agitators against its unity and greatness was the Reich Governors Law. Fundamentally, however, the National Socialist Party must recognize the following:

The former German Reich at least ostensibly wanted to build itself up out of the individual states. But the states themselves could no longer build themselves up out of the German tribes, but perhaps at best out of individual German persons. Today's German Reich no longer forms itself out of the German states, nor out of the German tribes, but instead out of the German Volk and the National Socialist Party, which includes and encompasses the entire German Volk. The nature of the coming Reich will therefore not be determined by the interests and perceptions of the building blocks of what is past, but by the interests of the building blocks that have constructed today's Third Reich. Neither Prussia, nor Bavaria, nor any other state will be the pillars of today's Reich; rather the only pillars are the German Volk and the National Socialist movement. The individual German tribes will be happier to forge this mighty unity once more than they ever could have been in their only purported former independence. For a German state of six or seven million or even more people would never be independent, but only a plaything of the more powerful influences neighboring it. Therefore, the National Socialist movement is not the conservator of the states of the past, but their liquidator for the benefit of the Reich of the future. Because the party is neither North German nor South German, neither Bavarian nor Prussian, but *simply German*, all rivalries dissolve away as meaningless within it. The party's task then is to educate the German Volk, the German people in this spirit, and thus ensure that further legislation will win the joyful appreciation and the will of all. And if, despite all this, this or that person decides not to understand what we are doing, then we will know how to bear it. As long as the party champions principles that are theoretically sound and have stood the test of millennia, we should not let the criticisms of the present deter us. But woe to us if—even just theoretically—it would be possible for an opposition to form with better principles, better logic, and therefore with more right. Power and the brutal application thereof can do much, but a condition is only safe in the long term if it appears to be logically and theoretically unassailable. And this above all: the National Socialist movement must adopt that heroism that prefers every adversity and every hardship over even once forsaking a principle that it has deemed right. There is only one fear that may enter the movement's heart, and that is the fear that a day might possibly come that would find it untruthful and thoughtless. Whoever wants to save a people must think heroically. The heroic thought must constantly be ready to relinquish the assent of the present age when truth and honesty demand it. As the hero relinquishes his life in order to live on in the pantheon of history, so a truly great movement must see in the rightness of its idea and in the honesty of its dealings the talisman that will surely guide it from the passing present into the undying future.

It was only a few weeks ago that the decision was made to hold the first Party Congress in the same year as this, the year of our victory. This grand organizational improvisation was accomplished in hardly a month. May it serve its purpose to increase the manpower of the party as it shoulders the burden of German destiny, to strengthen our resolve to enact our principles, and to bring into greater consciousness the unique meaning of this phenomenon. Above all, let the nature of this rally reaffirm that the leadership of this nation may never ossify into a purely administrative machine, but that it must stay a living leadership — a leadership that does not see the Volk as an object for its manipulation, but a leadership that lives in the Volk, that feels with the Volk, and that fights for the Volk. Forms and establishments come and go. What stays and should stay is this living substance of flesh and blood suffused with its own essence, as we know and love our Volk. Both physically and spiritually, our continued existence is dependent on the endurance of our Volk. We wish for the endless earthly existence of our Volk, and we believe that by fighting for this we are obeying the Creator's command, who planted the drive for self-preservation deep within all beings.

Long live our Volk!

Long live the National Socialist Party!

THE FÜHRER'S SPEECH AT
THE CULTURAL CONFERENCE

On January 30th, 1933, the National Socialist Party was entrusted with the political leadership of the Reich. By the end of March, the revolution came to an end, on the surface — an end as far as the complete takeover of the reins of power. But only he without any inner understanding of this immense struggle could think that this means the end of the great struggle between competing worldviews. That would only be the case if the National Socialist movement merely had the same aims as all the other customary parties. These regard the takeover of political power as the zenith of their existence. But worldviews see the acquisition of political power as just a precondition for the completion of their actual mission. Within the very word "worldview" lies the solemn proclamation of the decision to view all things through the understanding that flows from within it. Such an understanding can be right or wrong. It is the basis for every opinion on all phenomena and occurrences of life, and it is a binding and obligatory law for every action. So, the more such an understanding places itself under the natural laws of organic life, the more useful its conscious application will be for the life of a people.

Consequently, the unspoiled, primitive Volk has the most natural worldview in its instincts, which lets it automatically take the most natural, and therefore most useful, stance on all relevant questions of life. Just as the healthy, unspoiled individual conjures up from his innermost self a totally unconscious natural reaction that gives him the most appropriate stance toward the questions that deeply move and challenge him, so also the healthy Volk will instinctively find within its drive for self-preservation the reaction to all of life's challenges, a reaction that is most appropriate to its needs. The equality of life-forms of a certain kind thus formally spares the formation of binding rules and compulsory laws.

Only with the physical mixing of inwardly diverse individuals do attitudes get confused. This necessitates rules and laws to let such a people speak with one voice, which otherwise has fragmented and diverse reactions to the influences and demands of life.

Because the types of people that Providence has willed and made different have not been given the same purpose, when these mix, it is decisive for the conduct and composition of the life of such a mixture which of the parts' inborn attitudes are made compulsory in the different areas of the struggle for existence.

All historically verifiable worldviews are only understandable in their relation to certain races' attitudes toward and purposes in life. Therefore, it is very hard to take a stance on the rightness or wrongness of such attitudes when you do not test their effects on the people to whom you would like them applied.

What would be the most natural and appropriate expression of life for one people, for whom it is inborn, for another alien people may become, under some circumstances, not only a serious threat, but even perhaps the end.

In the long run, there is no nation assembled from various racial nuclei that can hold two or three different points of view at the same time and use these to determine its life in all the most important areas or as a foundation on which to build itself up. Sooner or later this necessarily leads to the dissolution of such an unnatural union. If this is to be avoided, then *which* racial component will assert its character and worldview is crucial. This will determine the trajectory of such a people's further development.

Every race asserts its existence with the powers and values that are natural to it. Only the man suited to heroism will act heroically. Providence gave him the preconditions for it. Those who are by their nature purely matter-of-fact as well as physically unheroic beings express only unheroic traits in the course of their struggle for life. As much as the unheroic element of an ethnic community can drag the heroically disposed toward the unheroic and thereby make them renounce their innermost being, so also can the decidedly heroic purposefully subordinate contrary elements to its disposition.

National Socialism is a worldview. By gripping those people who by their innermost disposition also belong to this worldview, it becomes the party of those who, by their character, can actually be attributed to a certain race. It acknowledges the reality of the different racial substances in our Volk. It also is far from rejecting this mixture, which forms the overall pattern of our Volk's expression of life. It knows that this inner racial arrangement of our Volk determines the normal span of our capabilities. However, it wishes for our Volk's political and cultural leadership to preserve the face and expression of that race which, through its heroism alone (thanks to its inner disposition), turned a conglomerate of different components into the German Volk in the first place. National Socialism confesses a heroic doctrine of the valuation of blood, of race, and of personality, as well as the eternal laws of selection. With this, it stands in unbridgeable contrast to the worldview of pacifist international democracy and its effects.

This National Socialist worldview necessarily leads to a reorientation of almost all realms of national life. Today we cannot yet begin to estimate the magnitude of the effects of this tremendous intellectual revolution.

As the relationship between conception and birth became clear only after a long course of human development, so the meaning of the laws of race and its inheritance are today only beginning to dawn on humanity. This clear recognition and conscious consideration will one day serve as the foundation of future development.

Proceeding from the recognition that in the long run all created things can only be preserved by the same powers that once created them, National Socialism will ensure that the character of those components that formed the German national body over the course of many centuries will have the greatest influence and most visible effects within the German Volk.

If the National Socialist mission is to maintain its inner justification, then it will have to lift the German man out of the depths of a merely materialistic conception of life and into the heights of a worthy representation of what we are meant to understand by the phrase "human." Because if this phrase is really meant to apply to a higher life form, then he must raise himself above the animal. If all his striving had stayed within the bounds of primitive necessities, then he never would have elevated himself above the sphere of the animalistic. Here too, man must obey the law that Providence imposed on him. For it is just as natural for certain human types to fulfill their life purpose by the satisfaction of the lowest necessities of life, as it is unnatural for those races tasked by Providence with higher things to go against the admonishing voice of their conscience, yes, the burning urge of their being and devolve to this primitive conception of life, or — which would be the same — to let themselves be forced to adopt it.

In such cases, because nature's living dissent interjects, such a people bifurcates, and two different racial components try to live alongside each other, each according to its character. The man who needs nothing more than food and drink for his life's satisfaction and fulfillment has never possessed an understanding for the man who would rather spare his daily bread in order to sate the thirst of his soul and the hunger of his mind. It is also wrong to think that a man will ever be able to grasp what Providence did not put in his nature to grasp. Just as certain principles have to be championed for the maintenance of a human society without regard for whether every single individual gives his assent, so also the culture of a people must be fashioned after the image of its best components, who — thanks to their nature — are the born carriers of culture.

What those not born to this task lack in inner understanding, what their heart and soul will never grasp, conscious education must at least shift toward humble respect. Apart from that, all they have to do is to learn to appreciate the manifestations of life of the one side of their people, just as the other side must come to terms with this side's mentality.

Hence, worldviews have always determined not only the character of politics, but also the image of cultural life. Poets lauded heroes when heroic times allowed for such manifestations, or they sank to the nadirs of everyday life when the times were unheroic and unheroic men set the tone.

You can never separate art from man. The byword that art is international is hollow and dumb. Even if one can maintain some moderate level of skill in other sections of life through education, one must be born to art. That is, the fundamental disposition as well as aptitude that lies beyond the realm of education is of crucial significance. This disposition is a component of a genotype. This does not mean that everyone who, racially, belongs to the most talented type needs to be a creative artist, but it does mean that true genius will only arise out of this type and this race alone will really perceive and understand it.

It is a sign of the bleak spiritual decadence of former times that they spoke of styles without acknowledging their racial conditionalities. The Greek has never built "international"; he built Greek. That is, every clearly distinct race has its own handwriting in the book of culture, provided it is not without any artistic capacity of its own—as, for example, the Jews are. When people copy an alien art, it is not evidence for the internationality of art. Rather, it is evidence that something intuitively experienced and created can be plagiarized.

Only where there is the same racial root beneath all the distances of time and language can there really be an understanding of another people's art. The more a people maintains an external worldview and a certain racial nucleus has a dominating internal influence, the more easily and quickly will it be able to approach other racially similar peoples and states politically and culturally with no concern for historical distance. The inner disposition of the races does not change, no matter how much the external world changes. The passage of epochs is not influential so long as the genotype itself is not spoiled in its blood.

Hence, the ideal of beauty of the ancient Germanic peoples and states will be imperishable so long as people of the same disposition, owing to their shared origin, live on the earth. It is not stone or the inanimate form that is imperishable, but people—people who owe their heritage to the same root. It is also folly to think that a race's primal creative force directs its cultural expressions by means of some stylistic law, or regiments it. No: only the people that is insecure in its instincts, because it has become racially disunited, requires rules in order to not lose that wonderful thread that was once found by uncomplicated, natural representatives of a gifted race. It is laughable to think that you can find a new "life-, culture-, and art-style" without a renewal of worldview, and therefore a racial purification, just as it is laughable to suppose that nature entrusts any average bungler with this clairvoyant purpose.

Not every Greek man could have built a Parthenon. But when a Greek wrought this wonder, all of them knew that it was the most tremendous—because the most glorious—proclamation of the Greek character and spirit.

Thus, the inclinations founded in the race and the worldview of an age will also determine the inclination and psyche of art. The race that stamps its seal on the whole life of a people will then also see the tasks of art before it. It molds the artwork according to its own spirit, grasping in a sovereign manner all the circumstances and requirements of the function and of the material. But only the clearest human spirit can find the way to the loftiest beauty. The last measure lies in the recognition of a crystal-clearly fulfilled purposiveness. This has absolutely nothing to do with that supposed "objectivity" that cannot grasp that man should not confuse animal primitivity with harmonious beauty.[2]

Not every artist will find this final perfection; but all should seek it. Every race has its natural limits. The divinely gifted artist, being the concentrated tenacity of his nation made man, will always spur on the average general perception of his people and will unconsciously find the composition that will be perceived and seen as the highest and loftiest beauty, but its purposiveness will often only be proven after millennia.

Just as the noble human being has always been conscious of beauty in both sexes, only to recognize, perhaps after millennia, that the highest beauty of woman lies in the purposeful shaping and perfection of her body and essence (just as it does in man), so can the constructive and tectonic form of solving their two tasks succeed for the truly gifted artist, before so-called "exact science" can provide evidence for the actual static correctness of the solution found.

We know from our own experience that in antiquity as well as at present, the Aryan Nordic man has always found the compelling synthesis between the assigned task, the purpose, and the given material. His free creative spirit has always stayed the same. Even when, for centuries, certain worldviews, being the outward expression of another ethnicity, forced humanity under the yoke of laws of styles, which were worldview-correct in that time but were contrary to the true Aryan character, this spirit searched constantly for an escape to his own, even if bygone, world.

And so it is no wonder that every politically heroic age has immediately sought in its art the bridge to a no less heroic past. Greeks and Romans then suddenly seem so near the Germans because all their roots meet in a foundational race. For this reason, the immortal accomplishments of the ancient peoples always again work their magnetism on their racially related posterity. Because it is better to emulate the good than to create

---

[2] Here Hitler refers to the New Objectivity, a modernist movement in the arts that was dominant during the Weimar Republic and later officially condemned during the Third Reich as "degenerate art."

something bad, the existing intuitive creations of these peoples can today, as a style, certainly work their nurturing and guiding mission. But in the same measure that the Nordic spirit experiences his conscious resurrection, he will have to solve today's cultural tasks with no less clarity and beauty than that which was required as his racial forebears mastered the problems posed to them.

It is just as laughable, even childish, to want to fearfully avoid the already discovered classical forms and manifestations of artistic creative power, as it would be dumb to reject other insights and experience in life only because earlier generations had already found these truths.

Humanity would degenerate and culture would regress if it became afraid to continue nursing a usable genetic lineage on its greatest inheritances of life and culture only because decadent or racially alien elements—in their spiritual anarchy or their racially inherent rejection—would rather let lie the torch of all the past's accomplishments.

Conversely, a creative race should not elevate the sum of their ancestors' accomplishments into a style that becomes a tyrannical law, limiting and oppressing every further accomplishment of its own.

The future will only be built from both the past and the present. The given objective, the constructive prowess of the present, as well as the technical material, are the elements out of which the true creative spirit forms his works, without being afraid to use the traditional good found by his forebears. He is brave enough to combine it with his own newly found good!

For it is likewise pedantic with the construction of a theater to outwardly deny that we are here mere renewers and perpetuators of an institution that has already been essentially handed down for millennia, as it is conversely unbearable to want to glue on Greek or Gothic features to the exterior of a factory or electric plant. It is therefore also totally wrong to speak of a "new style" that has to be found. Rather, we can only hope that the best of our humanity might be chosen by Providence to pull out of their inner being, animated by their blood, a solution to the challenges posed to us today just as masterfully as, for example, the Aryan peoples of antiquity did. What this past, especially that part of it related to us, has delivered to us in constructive and creatively useful experiences, we will freely use and develop further, just as the art of the ancients was itself only the result of a long development. What is crucial, though, is that through the conscious singularization of the racial substance that carries our Volk, as well as through the sovereign proclamation of its being and its corresponding worldview, we form a kernel that for great spans of time will let its creative spirit operate.

It is no coincidence that in its liberalistic licentiousness — that is to say, uncertainty — the age blurriest in its worldviews was also uncertain in the realm of cultural creativity. In barely one century, the artistic accomplishments of almost every age and nation were tried out and again cast aside. This uncertainty finally found the only appropriate, because certain, expression in the Cubistic-Dadaistic cult of primitivity. This is the cultural manifestation of the cultureless dregs of all nations.

Marxism necessarily flows, not just politically but also culturally, into nihilism. While the official art scene at the outset of this age can only leave behind the most despicable impression, important intellectual, political, and cultural groundwork was being laid for the renewal of the nations.

Just as National Socialism in Germany is the fulfillment of numerous prophetic intimations and actual scientific insights, so at the same time the groundwork was unconsciously laid for a new artistic renaissance of the Aryan man.

This renaissance notably emerged out of the challenges for whose solution there no precedent obtained. Modern technology forced humanity to find its own way. From the purpose and materials of the age, only those forms which breathed more of the Greek or other spirit into the aesthetics of machinery were discovered and developed, rather than poorly conceived buildings. This tremendous new realm can claim as uncharted territory the landmarks of an equally modern and aesthetically satisfying creativity. From here on out, development will necessarily go down a path appropriate to the purposes of building and utilizing novel building materials like steel, iron, glass, concrete, and so on.

But even here, not every average man is called to achieve immortality. He who seeks newness for its own sake will all too easily lose himself in the realm of foolishness, because the dumbest thing expressed through stone and material will naturally and all the more easily be called the most novel, as indeed in earlier ages not every fool was permitted to offend his surroundings with the miscarriages of his sick brain. Under the watchword of "be new at any price," every bumbler can make something special. One must be careful in such experiments to look for a sign of meaning in a man and his work.

Only a few divinely gifted people have ever been called by Providence to the mission of really creating something new and immortal. But these people are the guides to a long future, and it is a part of educating a nation to instill in it the necessary reverence for men of such greatness, for they are the incarnation of a people's highest values. They did not create, possessed by a sickly imagination, to bring about something new at any price; rather they created something new because they wanted to create the best, and they had to create the best.

"Never before seen" is no sign of the worth of an achievement, but could just as well be a sign of its never-before-seen worthlessness. When a so-called artist sees it as his life's calling to create the most rambling and incomprehensible display possible out of the achievements of the past or of the present, then those achievements of the past remain achievements, while the artistic sputtering of such a charlatan of a painter, musician, sculptor, or builder will only be the sign of the greatness of a nation's decay.

It is also impossible for such a degrading man to suddenly unlearn everything and be able to create something better. He is worthless and stays worthless. He has failed because he lacked the calling toward the very highest, as well as natural excellence. For him to wrest attention by distinguishing himself through conscious craziness stems not only from an artistic failure, but also from a moral defect.

Art is an elevated mission that obliges you to fanaticism. He who is chosen by Providence to bare the soul of a people to the world – to play its tones or to let it speak in stones – he suffers under and is ruled by an almighty compulsion; he will speak its language even when the world does not want to understand him; he will rather take on any hardship than to even once be untrue to the star that guides him inwardly.

The National Socialist movement and regime cannot tolerate, in the realm of culture, incompetents and impostors suddenly switching their flag and so entering into the new state, as if nothing happened, in order to have their way once again in the areas of art and cultural politics. Whether Providence will bestow upon us all the men who could give a cultural expression equal to the political will of our time and all its accomplishments, we do not know. But one thing we know: that under no circumstances can the representatives of the decay that is behind us suddenly become the standard-bearers of the future. Either the miscarriages of their former production were a true inner experience – in which case, as dangers to the healthy spirit of our Volk, they belong in asylums — or this was just speculation; for this latter betrayal they belong in an institution appropriate to *that*. Under no circumstances do we want to let the cultural expression of our Reich be falsified by these elements; this is *our* state, and not theirs.

This new state will give a totally different attention to the nurturing of culture than the old did. So far as National Socialism recognizes the right of those components of our national body who first initiated and completed its formation, to receive a special primacy of their character, it also needs to justify this morally.

The satisfaction of animal necessities lies in the nature of all humans. No type could from this derive the special right to lead others, let alone to rule them. The only thing that makes people seem chosen for this is the obvious capacity to elevate oneself above the primitive and to ennoble the common traits of life. The political regime will always have to, in substance and in fact, deliver the prerequisites for the operation of art. Even if a people extinguishes and people keep silent, the stones will speak, so long as there are other peoples with similar cultural capabilities.

For this reason, every great political age in world history demonstrates its right to exist through the most visible record of its worth that there is: its cultural achievements.

The opinion that, in materially impoverished times, cultural issues have to retreat to the background is as foolish as it is dangerous. For he who wants to evaluate a culture by its material profits has no idea of its character or its purpose. But this conception is dangerous because it sinks all of life to a level where finally, at best, the quantity of the worthless decides.

It is especially important in times of economic hardship and worry to make it clear to all people that a nation also has higher tasks than to engage in mutual economic egoism. Mankind's cultural monuments were always the altars of reflection on its better missions and higher dignity.

When a people no longer cares to know this, then it has already lost the better component of its blood, and its downfall is only a matter of time. While we are convinced of the inner worth of the German Volk, we want to ensure that its political and governmental leadership gives it the opportunity to prove its worth.

For their part, let German artists be conscious of the task that the nation has assigned them. Though folly and injustice seem to rule the world, let us call them up to take on the proudest defense of our German Volk through German art.

THE FÜHRER'S CONCLUDING REMARKS AT THE 1933 PARTY CONGRESS

Only a few hours and the party's great demonstration is ended. Train after train rolls through the night into the German districts. Everyone returns to work, this one to his field, another to the factory, a third to his office. The struggle of life again ensnares him, and yet cannot erase the memory of the past days.

Someone who has not been gripped by the character of this movement, because he himself cannot grasp it, may ask himself the questions:

Firstly: why have such a demonstration? Secondly: why do people go to it? How is it possible that men drive far across the land to march around somewhere and sleep in tent camps, accepting meager fare, and all this without being paid? How is this possible?

I posed this question to myself and my party comrades before I began this work. I asked myself then: can one demand this of the German Volk? A very grave question, for on its answer depended not only the founding of a party, the possibility or impossibility of calling into life a movement, but indeed, on this answer depended the very fate of the German nation!

Had this question been answered with a no, then every attempt at a regeneration of our Volk would have been futile. If one believed it could be answered with a yes, then this audacious undertaking had to be ventured.

When for many years, in all situations, under all circumstances I believed in the victory of the National Socialist movement, this unshakable conviction came from fundamentally thinking through the laws of life and development. My political adversaries neglected to do the same.

Now, after the victory, if I speak freely about these thoughts instead of only with the leaders as it was until now, it is for two reasons. Firstly, now the adversary may just as well learn them. And secondly, the whole movement should see it as a perpetual duty to not forget these insights and to follow their lessons!

Nature has no unexplainable coincidences. What seems unregulated to man is merely beyond his understanding. Every development proceeds from the law of cause and effect. Because effects are the chiefly visible and sensible things, most people are only concerned with them. Humans have a deep-seated aversion to seeking and finding the causes, especially when their corrupted selves sense unpleasant, because obligating, realizations from the sudden uncovering of certain causes. But those truths that signify an attack on favorite accustomed vices are always unpleasant. That which contradicts sluggish habit—which opposes the leisureliness of everyday life, which friends do not understand and which aggravates neighbors, that which disturbs slothful somnolence—this is that which one would rather not discover. And yet one will only find an enduring healing of sick conditions when one addresses their causes. Only then will the course of events in the national life be comprehensible; only then will the mystifying comings and goings of the people lose its mystery. The individual fates made up of a hundred thousand supposed coincidences untangle and appear like countless stations on a clearly predetermined train track, which either leads down—that is, to the end of a people—or up to its enduring self-assertion, and therefore its perpetuation. No nation that has once proceeded down this uneven descending path has ever pulled itself back up from it except through a positive consideration of such insights. Whether this happens through reason or unconscious instinct is all the same. Happy the people that possesses in its natural instinct its admonisher and therefore its savior. Unhappy the people that believes it can do without instinct; its fate then hangs on the possibility that one day true reason might prevail over vain, superficial knowledge, with the humbling recognition of the eternal laws of life that are the foundation of instinct.

To recognize the sickness of the body of a people, it is first necessary to grasp its structure.

Today, almost every nation builds itself up out of diverse racial elements. These fundamental elements carry in them capacities that deviate from one another. Equality of all persons can be assumed only in the most primitive functions of life. Beyond that, they immediately begin to drift apart in their character, their disposition, and their capabilities. Many of the differences between the individual races can be outwardly (and of course inwardly) quite enormous, and they *are*. The gulf between the lowest still-so-called human and our highest races is greater than that between the lowest human and the highest ape!

If there were not a few races who, in their time, determined the cultural face of the earth, then one could hardly speak of human culture at all. Neither the climate nor nurture is responsible for this, but only the man to whom Providence has gifted this capability.

But even if this cultural ability is fundamentally peculiar to certain races, its effects are only played out under certain favorable conditions. A man as an individual (no matter what powers he holds within himself) will be incapable of high achievements if he cannot put the powers of the many into the service of an idea, a vision, a will, and unify them into one operation. A look at nature shows that the creatures of one pure race are more or less equal in their bodies, character, and abilities. This equality is the biggest obstacle to the formation of a higher association. For if the higher cultures are formed by achievements that can only be ascribed to the mustering of human manpower, then the majority of individuals must sacrifice a part of their individual freedom in order to subordinate themselves to the will of another. Regardless of how strongly reason dictates that this must be so, in reality it would be difficult to explain among equals the reasons why ultimately one of them must elevate his will above the wills of others. The two terms "command" and "obedience" gain a wholly new and compelling meaning the moment that people of different worths clash or collide, and then, through the stronger part, a new community of purpose is formed. In the most primitive sense of the word, this already happens in the moment when man asserts his dominion over the animals, wrests them out of the freedom of their former lives, and assimilates them into *his* way of life—all without concerning himself with the consent of his animal servants. Long before this, men did this amongst themselves. The higher race—initially higher in its organizational capacity—subjugates the lower one to it, and they enter into a relationship that now encompasses two unequal races.

With this, the subordination of a majority of people to the will of often only a few is first accomplished, simply by the right of the strong — a right that, seen from nature, is the only imaginable (because reasonable) right. As reluctant and unhappy as the mustang is to take on the yoke of humans, so is a people reluctant to take on the yoke of another. Despite this, in the span of a long development, this compulsion has often been a blessing for all. Some commonwealths form whose character is determined through the welding together of different races. This, however, always requires the subordination of the wills and agencies of many under the will and vigor of the one! To the extent that people discover the awe-inspiring results of this conglomeration of their abilities and manpower, they also recognize not only the usefulness, but also the necessity of such an endeavor. And so it is that Aryan cultures of greatness and meaning did not arise where Aryans lived purely and exclusively among themselves, but rather everywhere that Aryans engaged in a lively association with other races — not in the sense of a mixture of blood, but in an organizational sense, as a community of purpose. And what the conquered initially felt as a difficult coercion later became their blessing. In the master race, the recognition came into ever sharper focus, and came to be an ethic that it cannot exercise its lordship with arbitrariness, but rather with noble prudence. Providence did not give them the capacity to subjugate others for them to senselessly make their power felt or to torment; rather, they were given mastery so that through the association between their genius and the other's strength, a humane (because useful) common existence could be built.

As soon as this process of nation and state formation was introduced, humanity's communist age was ended. For communism is not a higher stage of development, but it is the most primitive of starting points.

People of totally equal character and equal type, and therefore also equal capabilities, will necessarily also be equal in their accomplishments. This premise is valid for totally racially uniform peoples. Under the assumption of this premise, the sole result of the activity of such creatures will only correspond to the common average. Because, as already mentioned, great accomplishments are impossible without the potential for an amalgamation of the many under the will of the one, those assets of life fashioned merely after the average will deal only with entirely primitive values. Without the necessary achievement gaps, this situation lacks the prerequisites for a clear emergence of the concept of property. For this concept loses its meaning if the outcome of a communal project can from the outset be equally shared due to totally equal contributions. In such a condition, communism is a totally natural and morally understandable order. With the meeting of people of different worths, the results of their labors will also be different — in brief, the qualitatively superior race will contribute more to the result of a common project than the qualitatively inferior. Most importantly, their capacities will be on different levels. The primitive capacity of the one race from the start creates different values than the more developed or different-natured partner race. From this, however, the distribution of the products of labor will inevitably accord to a consideration of achievement. In other words, that which is produced will be administered as property in the same measure in which it was created.

The notion of private property, then, is inseparably tied to the belief in the diversity of the types and worths of people's capabilities, and there-fore also the diversity of the types and worths of people themselves. One cannot now accept the different worths of people — which I would now like to call different dispositions — as a certain moral claim in one realm of life, only to dispute it in another and act thus illogically. For it is illogical to explain that private property is justified because people's abilities are unequal due to their different dispositions, and hence the results of labor land so unequally, and that in administering these results one must con-sider the merit of contributions, and then to turn around and claim that in the most important realm of public administration of all — in politics — all have the same capacity. It would be gainsaid that all people of a nation would be capable of managing a farm or a factory, or of deciding about its management. Only that they're all capable of managing the state, or of voting on its management, is solemnly attested to in the name of democ-racy.

It is a self-contradiction.

Either people are, due to their equal ability, equally entitled to manage a state — then adherence to a notion of property is not just an injustice, but foolishness — or people are really not in the position to put the communal-ly created material and cultural assets of a nation into communal owner-ship and communal management, because they are much less in a posi-tion to communally rule the state!

Communal judgment of values by all should not be possible for the reason that not all were equally engaged in the creation of those values. The communal management of the state is still much less possible because the state owes its existence to all even less than other things; rather it exists on the basis of a certain part of the nation, which is the pillar of the state and thus the preserver of the state, and it holds this place because it was the founder of the state.

This declaration is not an unjust one, and also not a tough one, but it is merely a declaration of the truth.

It remains, then, to clarify whether the formation of, say, the German Volk and the German state was a product of the universal will of all that took part in it, or not.

We can answer this very clearly: the German Volk came about no differently than almost all truly creative civilized peoples known to us. A small, organizationally capable, and culturally creative gifted race, through the course of centuries, eclipsed other peoples, partly absorbing them and partly assimilating itself. Of course, every separate component of our Volk brought its own special capabilities into this union. But it was created by only one Volk- and state-building kernel. This core Volk imposed its language, naturally not without borrowing from the conquered, and ultimately placed them all under a common destiny so long, that the life of the state-building Volk has become indissolubly connected with the lives of the other gradually assimilated components.

In that time, since long ago, the conquerors and the conquered have formed a community.

It is our contemporary German Volk!

And we love it and we depend on it the way that it is. In the course of its thousand-year history, all of its diverse customs have become familiar and dear to us. So great is this unity that we are happy about every contribution that accrues to us from it. We do not inspect to whom we owe the musicality of our Volk, or to whom the technical abilities, who gives us the art of fabulating, and who the coolness of thought, whence come our philosophers, statesmen, or generals.

We certainly do not inspect in order to then perhaps value them especially; at most, we inspect simply to know what type is the root out of which the German Volk draws its abilities. And we have become so united that our wish is for all our Volk's components to contribute their best to the richness of our entire national life. So long as every part gives where it has something to give, it will help and be of use to our life. We will be glad for it. And correspondingly, it is our concern that every part also takes charge of that which it contributed to our common assets. For it alone can the musically-gifted Volk work in the realm of sound, and also preserve their work as a patrimony by their steady care. And never in any event can one part take responsibility for something that some other part contributed.

Because this is natural, in life it will normally be ordered this way. For you can not only conclude the capability from the race, but you can also conclude the race from the capability. This means: it is not necessary to discover the musically-gifted people as a race in order to entrust them with the care of music; rather, music discovers the race that possesses the requisite capabilities.

On the day when one chooses a career, life poses to each person the question of their origin. All individuals of a people receive knowledge of all the different functions of life. But every function finds a special reso-nance in only one part. It is *that* part that, by reason of its origin, has been made capable of being, and has been called to be the special carrier of this function.

How little choice of career has to do with considerations of economic advantages or disadvantages can best be seen by the fact that we leave this choice to an age group that lacks the capacity for such insights. Be-yond that, we say explicitly that a boy "should be born to something." That is to say nothing other than that we let him decide unconsciously, and yet consciously. Unconsciously in that he could hardly estimate all the material effects; consciously in that he instead listens to an inner voice that advises him better than superficial human reason ever could. For what is more wonderful than when an eleven-year-old boy begins to whittle and draw in his farming village and can no longer pull himself away from his oh-so-impractical passion, and ultimately, as an Old Mas-ter, gives his nation immortal works! What fails to move thousands will enthrall hundreds because it speaks to their ancestral disposition. It can only ever be in the people's interest that this voice of ancestral disposition is always heeded. For this voice does not give to the Volk people who are oppressed and coerced because they were not inwardly born for a thing, but it gives the Volk people who are fulfilled in their passion and devoted to it.

Just as we cannot feel any envy in all the realms of life where those specially born to it — that is, those etiologically gifted — exercise the deci-sive influence, so also in the realm of the political preservation of what, over the course of millennia, became our Volk, we can likewise feel no envy.

Just as the unmusical person does not feel hurt or offended that he does not make music or conduct orchestras, while the musically gifted *do*, so in every other realm we cannot regard it as an affront that mastery and responsibility is given to those suited to the particular thing rather than to those not suited to it. In reality this is really never the case anyway. Only a conscious seduction can breed this insanity.

Following from the recognition that all created things can only be preserved by the same force that created them, the body of a people can likewise only be held together by the same forces that called it into life and, through its organizational abilities, welded it together and solidified it. All who love their nation and wish for its preservation must therefore see to it that that part which was the driver of its political formation and which oversaw the development of it must exercise its political abilities.

Whoever hands the political leadership of the nation over to any force other than the one that, over the span of ages, built the nation, will sooner or later betray it. We, however, cling to our Volk as it is, and love it in its diversity and its visible wealth of cultural life, and we do not want this community to lose its existence in this world only because the wrong part was entrusted with its political leadership!

And indeed, this has happened.

The moment that the bourgeoisie claimed and obtained the political leadership of the nation, the reasonable, organic development of the most important realm of life was broken.

The German bourgeoisie as a social substance was the product of an elite that rested much more on economic than political functions. With the introduction of money and property as the measure of someone's worth, the liberal age bred a social class which in its inner character accorded with the bourgeoisie. That numerous members of this social class still achieve amazing things in non-material realms has nothing to do with the value systems denoted by the term "bourgeoisie," but has much more to do with their endogenous racial core values. These, in themselves, have nothing to do with the concept of the bourgeoisie, for to be counted among this social class it is enough to have a purely happy commercial disposition, or a cultural and intellectual disposition that translates well into economic success. Under no circumstances are valiant or heroic characteristics necessary to be reckoned with this class. Indeed, the opposite is true: because commercial life mostly has more unheroic than heroic traits, the German bourgeoisie was much less "heroic" than "commercial." The bourgeois parties were the mirror image of this interior spiritual constitution — mere associations of hucksters and self-seekers, without any capacity for the true leadership of our Volk.

And the Volk felt this acutely.

This, then, is the remarkable thing. As a people formed from different racial cores, each part gradually learned to tolerate the other, but under the condition that the part stayed in its allotted domain. That is, the Volk only tolerates music when it is done ably — that is, practiced by the part that is born to it. It only tolerates those mechanics that know their own business and, thanks and praise be to God, only those politicians whose calling is written on their brow.

Our entire life proceeds between leadership and discipleship. The higher the development of a people climbs, the more complicated life gets. The individual person is no longer master of himself anywhere. His entire existence is always determined by the consideration of others. Everywhere he is led, and constantly he must obey. An alien will dictates the time of his sleep as well as his work. When he starts his morning's work, it proceeds on a track that others laid down and that others oversee. The only choice he has is in his youth to choose what train he will get on. As soon as he but takes his seat, he has entrusted his life to the direction of others. It is only natural that he himself does not help any the less in this mutilation of freedom. And yet this all is willingly and patiently endured. In every realm of work, someone's right to lead is automatically recognized when it is apparent that he was born to it. The one who is led does not see this in achievements, but sniffs it out in the demeanor. The boy in school instinctively feels the vocation of his teacher. This one he obeys, and he wages open rebellion against the other. In all areas of life, the Volk tests its leadership through resistance, particularly in the realm of politics. For it is clear: the maintenance of a national community of different racial components only makes sense when it is led and answered for by the part that itself undertook and completed the formation of the nation. Just as every company feels abandoned, deeply unfortunate, and sad when its beloved commander falls, so also every nation falls apart when its leadership fails. People rightfully feel betrayed because, over the course of centuries in a community, they were lifted to a height that now suddenly cannot be maintained when the part of the community responsible for this suddenly drops out. When the bourgeoisie claimed the political leadership of the nation, a part of society imagined itself as the leadership of the people that was never born to it.

And the Volk recognized this and instinctively rejected it. Thus, it was conceivable that a foreign race could, with a primitive slogan, dare to open an old scar within the Volk in an attempt to organize those in the proletariat who, due to the lack of natural leadership, were once again leaderless.

Only because of this was it understandable that a bourgeoisie not in the least suited to political leadership tried to transfer the methods and customs of commercial life into the realm of politics. The anonymous share then corresponds to the anonymous ballot, and the majority share-holder corresponds to the parliamentary coalition! It soon became clear that in the long run you cannot logically, or even ethically or morally, jus-tify private property with either of these. Eventually the time revealed its own inner contradictions, and the easier it then was for a logically-proceeding foreign race to totally rattle the Volk's already instinctively roused mistrust in its political leadership. When the bourgeoisie built it-self upon the wholly apolitical notion of individual ownership, then natu-rally the opposition that existed in the Volk was built around that part that was in itself not functional and is not functional today, either. For this reason, this part suddenly rediscovered in communism its most prim-itive expression of life, dredged up from its murky, ancient past. It is no coincidence then that, hand in hand with this, retrogression in all areas of culture was methodically promoted and executed through communism and its leadership!

Likewise, it is also natural that this bourgeoisie, as a totally inorganic political leadership without any inherent disposition or capability, had to fall apart against the attack of Marxism. For the same reason, every thought on the floor of the bourgeoisie and its political organizations to change the situation was worthless. Every attempt to secure a new lead-ership for the German Volk out of the bourgeois world failed because of the lack of a suitable substance. The question that arose with the collapse in 1918 was first of all whether we still had a large enough core of the ra-cial component that first brought about the creation of our Volk (and therefore is the only part capable of preserving it), and second of all, if we could succeed in finding this part and entrusting it with our political leadership.

And this much was clear: after our new social order developed out of economic functions, an individual German's capability for political leadership could not at all be assumed by his social standing. That is to say: people from economically and therefore socially marginal classes could be just as capable of political leadership, and conversely, many members of higher, commercially or financially preoccupied social circles had to be rejected. The only deciding factor should be the inner disposition needed for this purpose. The task before us was to find these people in all their various positions, careers, and classes.

In truth, this was a socialist action: in striving in every function of life to find the one out of my Volk born to that task and handing him the responsibility without regard for his economic or social origin up to that point, I am acting in the interest of all. If the word socialism is to have any meaning at all, then it can only mean to assign to everyone — with iron fairness and deepest insight — that part of the preservation of the whole that accords to his inborn disposition and consequently his worth. This principle comes from the highest justice because it is logical and reasonable. It is applicable to all functions of life, and with that also to the entire realm of political leadership of a people. It was then only a question of which method we would use to find these people who would be the preservers of our Volk and the successors of its creators. There was only one possibility for this: one could not conclude their ability from their race, but one had to conclude their racial suitability based on their ability. But the ability could be determined by individuals' reactions to a newly proclaimed idea. This is the unfailing method for finding the people you want to find, for everyone responds only to that call which resonates with his innermost being.

If you promote profit seeking as the content of your movement, all the egoists will attach themselves. If you preach cowardly subservience, what is subservient will come. If you elevate theft, looting, and pillaging as ideals, the underworld will organize into criminal gangs. One only thinks of property, speaks only of business, and can unite one's followers only in economic parties. But if you demand sacrifice, courage, bravery, loyalty, faith, and heroism, the part of the Volk that considers these virtues to be their own will report for duty.

But these were the factors that have made history in all times. The content of what we mean by the term history is the formation of nations and states, as well as their preservation.

Thus, in the year 1919, I established a program and laid down a trend that deliberately struck the pacifistic-democratic world in its face. If people of this sort still existed in our Volk, then victory would be inevitable, for then this fanaticism of determination and deed would draw its people to it. Wherever there were those with these characteristics, one day they would have to hear their own blood's voice and, like it or not, follow the movement that is the expression of their innermost being. This could have taken five, or ten, or twenty years, but gradually within the state of democracy arose the state of authority; in the empire of opportunism there formed a core of fanatical devotion and reckless determination.

There could only be one danger to this development: if the opponent recognized the principle, gained clarity on this idea, and avoided all resistance, or if on the first day they annihilated the first germ of this assemblage with the utmost brutality.

Neither was done. This age was no longer capable of the decisiveness necessary to carry out annihilation, nor did it have the nerve, nor even the understanding, for a wholly fitting and sufficient posture. When instead our opponents began to tyrannize the young movement in their bourgeois scope, they supported the natural laws of selection in the most fortunate way. It was then just a matter of time before the leadership of the nation would fall to this hardened human material. And thus, I could wait fourteen years, always more strengthened by the recognition that our hour would have to come. For in these years our movement drew to it the state-building, and therefore state-preserving, power in the German Volk out of all states of life, careers, and social classes, like a magnet attracts steel filings. It proved once again that one can often run a big business very well and yet not lead a group of eight men. And conversely, it showed that born leaders often spring out of farmhouses and laborer's shacks. This was the wonderful thing about this period of the propagation of our idea, as its wave rolled across the whole land and suddenly pulled so many men and women into its orbit. While the bourgeois politicians asked about our program, they had no idea that hundreds of thousands gave themselves to this movement, simply because their inner receptor was tuned to the wavelength of this idea. Thus the artisan suddenly shuttered the workshop, gripped by the feeling that "that's where you belong"; the farmhand walked away from his plow determined to enroll, the worker one day gave his notice, the student threw down his manuscripts and felt the violence of a compulsion that led him into this effervescing force of his Volk.

And herein lies the powerful class-reconciling mission of this movement. There is a new valuation of people, one not gauged by liberal thought, but according to the given standards of nature.

And the more the opponent believes he can hamper development through a terror doled out according to the measure of his character, the more he furthers it. Nietzsche's expression that a blow that does not kill a strong man only makes him stronger finds a thousand confirmations. Every blow heightens our defiance; persecution increases our tough determination, and what does fall brings the movement a great blessing by its falling away. The nation gradually feels the emergence of a new leadership, to which it increasingly gives itself, because it instinctively senses in it something of the power to which it once owed its own emergence.

The same Volk that lives in constant discord with its leadership in this liberal epoch is more and more standing as one man behind its new leadership. The miracle that our opponents never wanted to believe in has become reality.

In this fourteen-year fight, a new arrangement has emerged in our Volk through the adoption of prudent and crucial perspectives. Out of forty-five million adults, three million fighters have organized themselves as carriers of the political leadership of the nation. But today the overwhelming majority of all Germans adhere to their way of thinking. The Volk has placed its destiny in these hands.

With this, the organization has taken on a solemn duty.

It must take care that this kernel, which is destined to ensure the stability of the political leadership of Germany, will always be preserved. The movement must ensure, through some genius method of selection, that any growth that takes place will never change the innermost character of this pillar of our nation. It must watch that the quantity of this core will not be seen as crucial, but rather its inner worthiness and therefore its inner homogeneity. It must know that in the future, selection will have to follow the same hard principles that it imposed upon our destiny in the past. What earlier was provided in part by the oppression by our opponents, we will in future have to replace with our own hardness. We must therefore never shy away from removing from this community any who do not belong to it by virtue of their inner character. Hence, in the course of time, we must tighten the requirements for membership, and not reduce or relax them. But this core can never forget that it must search for its successors amongst the entire Volk. It must, through constant work, lead the whole nation toward its principles, that it may realize them. Only through this uninterrupted work with, and for, and around the Volk will a true bond form, as well as the ability to recognize those in the Volk who belong to this elite. For such a political elite must anxiously watch that no real genius exists in the Volk without being seen by it and incorporated into it. If a nation's political leadership class overlooks its own rightful members in the Volk or even disregards them, then this class bears the responsibility for when the naturally talented finally create their own opportunity for action, even if it is just to organize the slaves as a Spartacus. The born genius will never in the long run let itself be forced, through the respect demanded by a leadership that has become unworthy because incapable, to submit and forsake the almighty command of its own "I." The Volk indeed has the right to demand that in politics, as with all other realms of life, its most capable sons are considered.

Only when such a firm leadership hierarchy develops will it, as a constant pole, succeed in wielding the political leadership in the long run with superiority and determination.

You, my Gauleiters[3] and SA leaders, together with me and numerous other functionaries, leaders, and office-holders of the movement, are responsible for ensuring that these insights are borne in mind and realized. For our lives are perishable. Our immortality in this world lies only in the correctness of the principles that we entrust to the lives of the Volk. The present cannot give us more in terms of the love and trust of the people than it has already given us. The future will one day weigh us in the same measure as we thought of it. Therefore, may our God guard us against making those mistakes that, founded in human self-interest, favor taking successes in the present without regard for their effects on the future. While we devote ourselves to the tending of our own fated blood, it would be best for us to also help protect other nations from sicknesses that cross from race to race, from one people to another. If just one people in West or Central Europe falls to Bolshevism, this poison will eat away further and leave the oldest and most beautiful cultural artifact of earth desolate and ruined.

In taking on this fight, Germany is merely fulfilling a truly European mission, as it has often done in its history.

---

[3] Party district leaders.

THE FÜHRER'S SPEECHES AT THE 1935 PARTY CONGRESS OF FREEDOM

THE COURSE OF THE NSDAP'S
SEVENTH PARTY CONGRESS

An introduction

September 10th through 16th, 1935

On Tuesday September 10th, 1935, at 4:20 in the afternoon, the Führer's aircraft landed at the Nuremberg airport. Shortly thereafter, Adolf Hitler drove into the city of the Reich Party Congresses through a single cheering mass of people thronging the streets. From 5:30 until 6 o'clock the ceremonious tolling of all of Nuremberg's church bells announced the start of the seventh Reich Party Congress of the NSDAP, the Reich Party Congress of Freedom.

At the same hour in the Rathaus hall, the heads of party and state awaited the Führer for a ceremonious welcome. In the name of the City of Nuremberg, the city's chief mayor, party comrade Liebel, after the old custom, gave the Führer the guest gift: a precious facsimile of the old German imperial sword.

In the evening, a festive rendition of *Die Meistersinger von Nürnberg* was performed at the newly built opera house under the baton of Wilhelm Furtwängler, with the participation of outstanding singers.

On Wednesday, the solemn opening of the Party Congress in the Luitpold hall was begun with a speech by the Führer's deputy Rudolf Hess, as is customary. To honor the movement's fallen, the SA's chief of staff, Viktor Lutze, read out the names of those who fell in the freedom fight for a National Socialist Germany. After some welcoming remarks by the Franconian leader, Gauleiter Party Comrade Julius Streicher, Gauleiter Party Comrade Adolf Wagner read out the proclamation of the Führer.

In the afternoon the Führer completed the groundbreaking ceremony for the Congress Hall. That evening was the great cultural conference in the opera house, led by Reichsleiter Alfred Rosenberg, where he announced the NSDAP Prize for Art and Science, founded by the Führer. In a wide-ranging speech, the Führer spoke on the new German art.

Thursday was the Day of Honor for the Reich Labor Service. In the early afternoon fifty-four thousand workmen marched to the Führer on the Zeppelin Field. The Führer gave a speech before his workmen that was received with the greatest cheers.

Following that, at 6 o'clock the Party Congress resumed in the Luitpold Hall. Reichsleiter Alfred Rosenberg, Hauptamtsleiter Dr. Wagner, and Reichsleiter R. Walther Darré spoke.

With the evening came the traditional torch procession of the political leaders through the streets of Nuremberg, which reached its highpoint in the march past the Führer at the plaza in front of the main train station. Every district was represented in this torch procession by three hundred political leaders and their flag delegations.

Friday was largely taken up with special conferences of individual party branches in various halls throughout the city. The conference of the Foreign Organization took place first. Rudolf Hess spoke here, and the Führer himself appeared here and took the floor.

The Party Congress was continued at 10 o'clock the following morning in the Congress Hall. Reichsleiter Dr. Goebbels, Reichorganisationsleiter Dr. Ley, and Hauptamtsleiter Hilgenfeldt spoke.

Following the afternoon conferences, a hundred thousand political leaders with twenty thousand flags marched before the Führer in the Zeppelin field. The Führer spoke to them about the tasks of the movement.

The conference of the National Socialist Women's League was at 8 o'clock that night in the Congress Hall, where the Reich Women's League leader Scholtz-Klink spoke. Here, too, the Führer made his appearance and his remarks.

Midmorning on Saturday, fifty thousand Hitler Youth marched on the main arena of the stadium, where the Führer spoke to them.

Following that was the third annual conference of the German Labor Front in the Congress Hall, where the Reich Labor and Economic Council was instituted.

At the subsequent Party Congress, Reichsleiter Amann, Dr. Frank, and

Hauptamtsleiter Dr. Todt gave their remarks.

Already in the afternoon the big Volks Fest began on the premises of the Zeppelin Field and the stadium, which was run by the organization Kraft Durch Freude. The Volks Fest culminated in a uniquely beautiful fireworks show.

Early on Sunday morning began the immense march onto the Luitpold Field of the 116,000 men of the SA, SS, NSKK, and the Air Corps. With this, the Reich Party Congress reached its apex. The honoring of the dead and the Führer's address, in which he gave the SA the watchword for the new year, were again unforgettable experiences.

Around noon began the five-hour long parade of the columns past the Führer on the festively decorated Adolf-Hitler-Plaza.

On Sunday evening, Hauptdienstleiter Reinhardt, Reich Press Chief Dietrich, and Reich Work Leader Ludovici spoke.

On Monday the great bivouac of all units of the Wehrmacht on the Zeppelin Field finally ended, and the Grand Tattoo was performed before the Führer.

Midday on Tuesday, September 17th, the Führer left the city of Nuremberg. Thus the seventh Reich Party Congress of the NSDAP reached its conclusion.

— Dr. Walther Schmitt

RECEPTION OF THE FÜHRER IN
THE CITY OF NUREMBERG

September 10th, 1935

The answer of the Führer to Chief Mayor Liebel's welcome remarks

Herr Oberbürgermeister:

I thank you and the city of Nuremberg for your heartfelt welcome today. For the fifth time we celebrate the greatest festival of our movement here. Again, countless people from every German district came to this city, which is so dear and precious to us all, filled with the power of the National Socialist idea. Even more so than in years past, Nuremberg's unique character will impress itself upon our party comrades. The city of Germany's glorious old culture is increasingly also becoming the city of the new German rising.

The constructions and facilities that are to serve these celebrations are tremendous. With this year's essentially completed expansion of the Luitpoldhain, the first of the National Socialist Reich Party Congress' exceptional venues is complete. The Luitpoldhain has grown especially dear to us because, even during the time of our struggle, one of the first flag consecrations took place in Nuremberg on it. The temporary suspension of the renovation of the Zeppelin Field gives the movement's political organization and especially the Wehrmacht a place to assemble until the grand new March Field is completed.

It is a great joy for us all to be able to consecrate this new facility in such a grand fashion with the people's army of the German nation. Now, after the rebuilding of the Reich's might and strength, we are especially happy to celebrate the Reich Party Congress in this not only beautiful, but once so strongly fortified city. The symbolic sign of German imperial power that you have presented to me here as a gift will always remind me anew of this memorable Party Congress of the third year of the National Socialist revolution and the first year of the new German freedom.[4] I thank you once again, Chief Mayor Liebel, for this reception and this wonderful present, and I ask you all to hail the old city of the Reich Party Congresses with our German greeting: Nuremberg Heil!

---

[4] Here Hitler refers to the reintroduction of conscription, a symbol of Germany's liberation from the strictures of the Treaty of Versailles. Hence the 1935 Congress was the Congress of Freedom.

THE PROCLAMATION OF THE FÜHRER AT THE OPENING OF THE 1935 PARTY CONGRESS

September 11th, 1935

Party comrades! National Socialists!

For the seventh time the National Socialist movement celebrates its Reich Party Congress: in the sixteenth year of the movement's founding, in the twelfth year after its first Party Congress and its first revolutionary uprising, in the eleventh year of its refoundation, and in the third year after its victory.

What a tremendous experience these sixteen years encompass!

At the beginning of our fight, Germany was in the midst of a chaotic decline, and the steerers of German destiny were of a mind to throw away our national honor along with our strength and freedom. A nation so militarily brave, sold and betrayed by its own leadership.

And today, sixteen years later?

When in 1933 we rightly designated our Party Congress as that of victory, and two years ago we felt the solidification of National Socialist power as the defining characteristic of that time, then we can mark these days' rally as the Reich Party Congress of Freedom with proudest satisfaction.

We all may be biased by the tempo of these events taking place to think that their present and lasting implications have made themselves clear enough in everyone's minds. Only history will one day show that in barely three years since we took power, a transformation took place in Germany that was truly not anticipated by our opponents, and is today still not understood by individual and indifferent bourgeois elements, but which was always believed in by National Socialists with fanatical fervor. It is a transformation that represents a historic repudiation of the collapse of 1918.

Germany's hardest fall is answered by its greatest resurrection!

And we always sense that the most crucial thing for this is the inner renewal of our Volk as well as the restoration of the political honor, and with it the human honor, of the nation. For all that we have accomplished these past three years in various other areas of life, such accomplishments pale in comparison to this. Indeed, the individual primarily perceives that worry that oppresses him personally as the worst. The collective drive for self-preservation unfortunately also includes the egoism of millions of individuals. And they are hit with the hardships of everyday life.

And so the farmer looks to the payoff of his work, the worker to the wages of his time, the craftsman to the status of his business, the home-owner to the income of his rents, the entrepreneur to the profitability of his factory, just as the unemployed looks to the possibility of finding work or to the amount of his benefits. Everyone feels his hardship, sees it as the most crucial, feels its strain to be the most sensitive. Those are bad times, in which perspective is lost; times in which the great laws that, in determining the path of the collective, also shape the lives of individuals, are ignored and misunderstood.

On this, our third Party Congress since we took over power, we Na-tional Socialists can point with pride at all that has been accomplished in general and in the thousand divided individual realms (seen from a pure-ly material perspective). When we see the Volk as a great organism and we grasp that every accomplishment, no matter where and in what spe-cial form it occurs, is in the end for the good of the whole body, then we can begin to measure how great the gift to our Volk is of having reduced our unemployment from six million to one and three quarters of a mil-lion. We have unlocked an advantage for our nation that can hardly be comprehended by the individual. The approximately five million people that we have added to our national workforce since our coming to power means on average thirty to forty million work hours every workday that we have given to and rescued for the German Volk. No matter what this manpower is used for in each case, altogether we have given the nation the results of nine billion work hours in a year. This gigantic achievement, which is also shared across our whole nation, is not for the benefit of a few millionaires, but directly or indirectly helps the collective betterment of life and consequently the existence of our Volk. And while a fifteen-year decline may not be overcome in three years, the continuation of these efforts in so many areas of life will, in the course of time, necessarily visibly and noticeably raise the living standard and cultural well-being not just of the German Volk, but of individual German people as well. What the nation has accomplished in the diverse areas of its common economic life in these three years under National Socialist leadership will be shown in detail at the special presentations later this week. As great as this achievement is, it pales compared to the work that we have taken on with our program for the restoration of the nation's honor and freedom. Without these, all other measures would be in vain. And this especially in a world and an age that is uneasy like never before, and that is further from the reign of a higher law being asserted than ever!

My party comrades! You will understand my thoughts if I ask you, in this solemn hour, to turn your gaze out of this hall and beyond the German Volk out into the wider world. Unrest and uncertainty are the primary impressions of such a sight. The law is weak, and pretense rules the world. But woe to him who is himself weak! In the end, his wealth provides the moral justification for the right of the strong to subjugate him. In freeing slaves, slaves are made; in destroying classes, classes are born. The Marxist theorists espousing "a world without war" are constructing the greatest instrument of war; the apostles of international reconciliation fill the world with the most intolerant hatred and the most infamous sedition; the alliances of peace study the potential for and methods of the coming war: in short, a man would not feel very well to be forced to walk through such a pit of snakes without defenses. For fifteen years our Volk has tasted what it is like to be at the mercy of those who may just as well be of good or of ill will. We have had the opportunity to test out the practical side of those sympathies that are bestowed upon those who fall and are forced to place their hope in the law or even in understanding. Where are Wilson's Fourteen Points, and where is the world today?

But now we Germans can observe this view with innermost peace, because the Reich is no longer a plaything, is no object for the wantonness of others, but is secured. And it is not secured through contracts, pacts, treaties, and agreements, but through the determined will of the leadership and the real strength of the nation. It is not necessary for Germany to prove this security to the rest of the world by some demonstration. It is enough that we know it ourselves.

Besides, we can feel this security all the more because the German Volk and its government have no other intention than to live in peace and friendship with our neighbors. We know those agitators too well, whose only desire is the transformation of Europe into a battlefield, to not understand the reasons and goals for their yearning. But the more international Jewish communism thinks it can use a general European chaos to raise its flag of upheaval and forcibly establish a Bolshevist state at the cost of freedom and living standards, all the more we National Socialists — whose honor it is to be the most fanatical adversary of this international plunder — will have a real opportunity to measure and prove the restoration of our military strength.

We see our army as the shield that protects our ability to carry out peaceful work.

And if we have to make sacrifices, heavy sacrifices, then we would rather make them for our freedom and our work than for further contributions to the debt imposed upon us at Versailles.

This is the army of the National Socialist state. It is our most precious and our proudest possession. It is not a new army; it is that same renowned German army that can claim to be the keeper and preserver of an incomparable tradition. All of us who once were part of this army see it as the greatest reward for our fifteen-year labor that Providence put the German Volk's most hallowed treasure back in trusty hands.

The nation can once again rest easy knowing that the strongest shield of peace will be held over its freedom and its work for the future.

That the Reich now possesses a strong safeguard and protection thanks to its new armed forces is also in no small part because the National Socialist Party survived the turmoil of political confusion and tension.

Its idea forged the movement that pulled Germany back from chaos, decline, and destruction.

The nation also has the movement to thank for all that happened this year. It laid the spiritual groundwork for one of the greatest upheavals and uprisings in world history.

There is no greater justification than the simple comparison of its three years of activity with the doings of the prior fifteen years. To quickly summarize, history will judge the accomplishments of those fifteen years as purely detrimental to the German nation's life and future, and will mark the three years of the National Socialist Party's regime as the most positive development for new life and new progress.

The premise of this success was that National Socialism attempted reshaping the nation from the inside instead of from the outside, which attitude has come into special contrast this past year with that of the rest of the world. The movement's ideological educational mission has never stepped into greater focus than in this past year. There is a reason this mission is the focal point for the hate of all the nation's enemies, internal as well as external. We feel it is an honor to have been the main subject of a weeklong congress in Moscow that, as a graphic illustration of the concept of "non-interference," dealt with the revolutionizing of the European and non-European nations, which is to say Bolshevik subjugation of these nations under a small Jewish-Bolshevik literary and intellectual clique. Quite rightly we are seen as the main obstacle to the global spread and enactment of these Bolshevik schemes. National Socialism harbors no aggressive intentions against any European nation. On the contrary, we are convinced that if the immortal culture of Europe should not collapse as a whole, then the European nations must live their own lives as defined and regulated by traditions and historical and economic necessities. In upholding this understanding for the German Volk, we believe we will also be doing a good deed for the other European states.

In its fifteen-year fight, the National Socialist Party defeated communism in Germany so thoroughly that — excepting the Jewish wire-pullers — it only haunts the minds of a few unteachable fools and daydreamers. With this, we do not mean to refer to those international criminals found in all nations, amongst all peoples, who, as longtime residents of the prisons, sense a chance for freedom and a new profitable enterprise in the Bolshevik revolutions.

We are under no illusion that this danger is not real, and we know it will remain so for the time being. Therefore, we are armed for every action at any hour. The party is also an agonistic one, and so far, it has thrown all its opponents to the ground. In the future, it will shy away even less from battles with such entities, because it has already proved its strength against these opponents in the past.

When our well-meaning advisors naively ask why we even fight these entities that we ourselves, after all, deem as so infinitesimally small, and why we do not instead magnanimously let them be, then I would like to once and for all give all of you, my party comrades and all fellow Germans, this definitive explanation:

Our opponents had fifteen years' time and before that even more than fifty years to prove their abilities. They let Germany deteriorate morally, politically, and economically. We no longer have any reason to talk to them. Power is in our hands and we will keep it, and we will have no patience for anyone organizing against this power, but we will meet every emergence the moment it rears its head. It would suit our enemies to again commercialize our honor, freedom, and substance now, after we have stood Germany upright again and built it up with unspeakable effort!

No! You must not get us wrong.

Because we know how laughably small the number of our opponents is, we—as the only ones charged with the German Volk—will beat them back anywhere that they appear. The high protection they get from their friends throughout the rest of the world does not lessen our resolve, but indeed only strengthens it.

Right now, it is strikingly obvious what the German nation could expect from these elements. It can be seen in the trembling hopes with which all international powers hostile to Germany are observing, welcoming, and promoting them. Our most bitter enemies send them their best regards. It is the sign of a complete misjudgment of the German nation's mentality that it is believed on both sides that such an alliance could rattle a state whose leadership has from the outset deliberately placed the national honor at the forefront of all its decisions. For it is the National Socialist movement's greatest commendation that it does not possess this international protection.

I turn my attention to these phenomena today in order to give you, my party comrades, and with you the nation, an analysis of these forces' motivations and methods.

In our fifteen-year struggle for power over Germany, we got to know three adversaries as the main proponents of the decline. They are interdependent and are each equally culpable for Germany's collapse: 1) Jewish Marxism and, related to it, parliamentary democracy; 2) The politically and morally pestilent Centrists; and 3) Certain elements of an unteachable, stupidly reactionary citizenry.

For fifteen years we had to slog it out with these entities. Because of this, we had the opportunity to get to know them through and through. In the end, National Socialism bested these three political entities, despite them holding power and despite them applying that power without scruples; despite an unmitigated terror that murdered hundreds of people and injured the lives and limbs of thousands; despite a barbaric campaign against the wives and children of our compatriots, whose families were so often delivered into starvation through the deliberate impoverishment of their fathers! It does not surprise us National Socialists that today Moscow is still making entreaties to the clerisy of the Centrists. In our time fighting them, we never knew them to be anything other than connected to each other. Arm in arm they tried preventing the uplift of the German nation by any means. They cannot blur this memory by their own refusal to remember it or by indignantly denying such facts.

In March 1933, during the National Socialist revolution, when we probed this structure, our enemies thought the best thing to do was to play dead. They no longer possessed any power, but the nation still had the memories of their criminal mismanagement and betrayal fresh in their minds, and so it was best for them to disappear from public life. But at that time, they lived in a tremendous delusion. Their hubris never let them consider that they should delve more deeply into National Socialist thought—even as an opponent thereof. Thus, they thought that the year 1933 meant nothing more than a change of government, as if there was a new helmsman and a new crew on the German ship of state. Then they believed they could wait it out until the new crew got tired or worn out and one day would dissolve itself. And of course, they would think that the new men would be just like the old and do their business until they returned home satiated. And so, it was understandable that they went along with our consolidation of power with bittersweet politeness and stood by like tame spectators, waiting for the end of their race with strong inner hopes. What they missed back then was the fact that it was not so much that the ship got a new crew, but more like the ship completely changed its direction. Germany righted its course. Three years later they stand there with their silent hopes and realize with a shock that the ship is passing beyond the limits of their horizons. Indeed, now our consolidation leaves them behind. Their distress and disappointment could not even be hidden by bark tanners. The most foolish among them, perhaps because they are the youngest and most inexperienced, believe that through lots of kicking and screaming they can stop the ship and catch up. They will take a tumble trying this. To Marxism and especially to its Jewish wire-pullers we have this to say:

We gave you the chance—perhaps with too great magnanimity—to be forgotten in the course of time if you showed enough restraint. We feel that this leniency was misunderstood. The consequences had to come, and did come. The National Socialist state will march forward in overcoming this danger. I want to make clear that the fight against the internal enemies of the nation will never stop due to the inadequacy of some formal bureaucracy. The German nation will deploy its living organization to help the things necessary for its life break though when the normal bureaucracy of the state is unsuited to solving a problem. It is a gross delusion to think that the nation exists for some official entity, and that it must capitulate when such an entity is not able to solve a challenge. On the contrary: what the state can solve, the state *will* solve. But what the state cannot solve despite its best effort will be solved by the movement. For the state is only one organizational form of the nation's life, but it is driven and ruled by the immediate expression of the nation's life, of the party, and of the National Socialist movement. Looking backward and considering past experiences, people in some circles are of the opinion that, just as earlier states and their normal apparatuses could not prevail against Jewish Marxism and its kindred phenomena, the current state will also have to capitulate to them, and that at most, it can convince the world that only certain problems lie within its competence. Here one falls into the worst delusion. Party, state, army, economy, administration: all are just means to an end. The end is the preservation of the nation. This is a fundamental principle of the National Socialist point of view. What is obviously detrimental to the preservation of the nation must be removed. When one institution is not suited to take on a task, then another must take it on and complete it. We all—and particularly those of you who stand in leadership positions in the state and in the movement—will one day be judged not on our official conduct, but on the successful realization of a program, namely the securing of our national life. And one principle in particular has to be fought through with fanatical tenacity: an enemy of the National Socialist state, whether internal or external, should find no sympathy or aid in Germany.

We now live in the midst of a turbulent world. Only iron principles and uncompromising adherence will make us strong in order to prevent Germany from sinking into Bolshevik chaos, and we recognize the threats and warnings in other places. It is understandable that our opponents do not love these principles. It need not unsettle us that these principles are not yet recognized (indeed recognized as the only correct and necessary ones) everywhere outside of Germany. Because perhaps in a short time the world will not be deciding whether these principles are agreeable or not, but the choice will be to either fall into the human catastrophe of Bolshevism or to save itself with the same or similar principles.

This determination to suffocate certain dangers under all circumstances — if necessary, even in embryo — will also not shy away from using legislation to put better suited institutions in charge of functions that the state appears unsuited for because it may be foreign to the state's very being! This will be decided by the will of the leadership, not by the will of the individual. Our strength lies in our discipline.

If, in relation to this, I bring up the dangers of the politicizing religious confessions, it is only because we see in them those long-known entities that are siblings of Marxism.

I would like to express several principles regarding this:

The party does not have, and has never had any intention of waging some battle against Christianity. Quite the opposite; it has tried to create an evangelical Reich Church through the consolidation of impossibly many Protestant regional churches without in the slightest getting involved with any question of faith. Further, it has tried, through the completion of the *Reichskonkordat*, to forge a mutually beneficial and enduring relationship with the Catholic Church. Finally, it has worked to remove the organizations of the atheist movement in Germany, and in this way, it has sanitized our whole life of these phenomena, which the Christian denominations should also consider it their mission to fight. But the National Socialist will have no patience for the politicization of the confessions through some roundabout method. And here one must not doubt the resolve of the movement and the state! We have already fought the political clergy once before and threw them out of the parliaments, and this after a long fight during which we held no political power and they held all of it. But today we have this power and we will weather the battle over these principles more easily. We will never fight this battle as a battle against Christianity or even against either one of the two confessions. But we will then fight for keeping our public life clean of those priests who failed their vocation, who should have been politicians and not caretakers of souls. We will fight for the unmasking of those who claim the creed is in danger while they themselves are unfortunately all too free of their creed when the opportunity arises. I do not have to remind you that we National Socialists do not really want this fight. For we see the Jewish Bolshevik danger that is now looming over the world all too clearly to not want to devote every ounce of our strength to fighting it. A communist victory would just as much be a problem for the twenty-six state-level churches as for the Catholic Centrists. In any case, wherever Bolshevism has come to power, the "churches militant" put up a much less honorable fight than the "militant" National Socialist movement in Germany, which, with its countless martyrs, rounded up the communist murderers and arsonists.

The third group of our adversaries can only be judged pathological. It is those people who have finally recognized that, in its posture toward its tasks and in the tempo and magnitude of their fulfillment, today's state and nation have left them behind, and their popularity has waned. Instead of then realizing what is superfluous in their existence, they pray to their old god that he turns the future into the past. As far as they indulge in such longings quietly, we have no reason to disturb their reminiscing. But we will swiftly and completely repudiate any attempts to turn tradition-bound communities into loudspeakers for their secret wishes. The German Volk does not want to hear such music. Yes, it once honored the composers, but it has no respect for the poor epigones and small conductors who today haunt about like the last ghosts of a bourgeois heritage.

That world is dead, and the dead should finally stay still.

But if one takes a good look at these entities that believe they could never reconcile with the new Germany, then one will immediately notice the following:

First, all these entities are only unified in the negative sense—that is, they see the current state as their common enemy. But they do not share even the smallest idea in common.

Second, what is more, what would Germany come to if this hodgepodge ever regained influence and relevance? Through centuries, our Volk was scattered by countless opinions and understandings: first tribal, then dynastic, then religious, and finally it was split politically and ideologically.

As National Socialism fought for power, there were thirty-seven parties, two confessions, countless associations, and so on, vying for Germany. After an unprecedented information war and after countless sacrifices, we were able to bring nine-tenths of our Volk to an understanding and to subordinate them to one will. The remainder of the thirty-seven parties, of the confessions, and the former associations make up the last tenth — in short, that mess that has been dragging Germany from one disaster to another for centuries. And so, when we peacefully look at the successes the last few years have given us, we can recognize it as proof of the following:

The most valuable thing is and remains the movement, which has unified the nation and has let its many desires emerge as a single will.

What remarkable security and peace Germany possesses today. Everywhere we look around us, we see the ferment of decomposition, the elements of dissolution. Endless strikes, lockouts, street fights, destruction, hatred, and civil war. Rootless, international, wandering Jewish scholars go around the nations, counter to any healthy reason, and whip people up against each other. Under the screen of representing class interests, they mobilize civil war, which only ensures their own interests are satisfactorily served.

We see the consequences.

In a world where we should really be living in abundance, scarcity reigns. Countries that are occupied by hardly fifteen people per square kilometer suffer from hunger. States that are blessed with all imaginable raw materials cannot seem to reduce their armies of unemployed men.

It is a triumph of its effectiveness that in a country where 137 people live per square kilometer, which has no colonies, which is missing most raw materials, which has been squeezed dry for fifteen years, which has lost all foreign capital, which had to pay fifty billion in reparations, which stood at the total ruin of its economy, the National Socialist regime managed, with the greatest care, to preserve this country's chance to exist and to reduce its unemployment, so that today we are in a better position than the richest nations of the earth.

The individual presentations will give you, my party comrades, a picture of the exertions that were necessary for this goal. You will then see how great an accomplishment it was to solve the problems that pressed us from all sides.

When we took over the regime, Germany found itself in a condition of total decay. Our opponents prophesied that we would be done for in a few weeks. And since then, they have been prophesying the same unperturbed — if only in ever greater timeframes. The opposite has happened. Sure, we are a poor nation, but not because National Socialism has ruled for two years, but because the criminal regiment of our parties threw

Germany into not only a revolution, but into an internal chaos, and because for fifteen years this state was the defenseless object of every manner of international extortion. And for this reason, it is also our greatest accomplishment that in the midst of this heroic fight for self-assertion we also effected the restoration of the German armed forces in order to assure that we will never again have to endure the fate we just escaped.

If in today's events I give you, my party comrades, and with you the German Volk, a brief overview of the past year, it is in order to show you the logical fulfillment of the duties we have taken over, and to derive out of this the tasks of the future.

1. The National Socialist Party

The last Party Congress was still under the influence of the victory over an internal crisis within the movement. Dishonorable lunatics had attempted to fashion the party into an instrument of their own personal interests. Since then even the dregs of this attempt have been liquidated. This year the party has solidified itself a great deal. Its internal organization has been further enlarged. Many state positions were filled with reliable party comrades. Unfortunately, fate took one of our very best fighters, Party Comrade Schemm, from our midst too early. With him we lost an apostle of the National Socialist rising.

The most pressing internal party matter, made necessary due to the successful revolution, was the staking out of the new domains of work. At the forefront stood the deepened recognition that with the restoration of the army, the National Socialist state gained a new pillar with its own special and exclusive purpose. This not only led to an overhaul of assignments within the movement, but also the liquidation of those institutions that in the course of this development would have challenged order in the future.

This year the party, the SA, and the SS were simplified in their administrations, but their memberships were subjected to sharper trials and discernment. The result was a quantitative decrease, but a qualitative improvement.

The feeling of togetherness experienced by the old party comrades not only did not slacken, but—quite the opposite—it deepened greatly. Even this year the Party Congress itself counts as a joyous reunion celebration for the old fighters. The young new guard that has joined the movement will not change the character of this pugnacious political elite of the German nation, but will solidify it.

2. The State

The fight that the movement has written on its flag since the day of its refoundation has been waged with historically unprecedented success. The Reich reached to a greater and greater extent into the hands of National Socialism. But the effect of this fight was never more palpable than in the past twelve months. Germany became free. With March 16th, the National Socialist administration gave the German nation equality through its own strength. The repair of our army gives Germany its necessary protection by land. The establishment of our air force secures our German homeland against flame and gas. Delineated in its size due to the London naval agreement, our new war fleet protects German trade and the German coastline.

This year of 1934–1935 is a year of great internal reformatory work in almost all areas of our legislation and administration. Compulsory labor service was instituted!

3. The German Economy

We can talk about it now: 1934 unfortunately brought us a very poor harvest. We are still burdened by it. But still, we were able to care for the German people by securing them the nourishment necessary for life. That this was accomplished despite many constraints is a feat that the great mass of our people may not be fully conscious of.

The hardships stemming from this harvest did sometimes lead to a temporary shortage of this or that foodstuff. Only we were determined not to capitulate under any circumstances, despite what was longingly hoped for by the international press. And we got through the crisis successfully. Several times we were forced to prevent the price increases that were sometimes understandable given the bad harvest, and other times unjustified.

National Socialist economic policy proceeded from one principle: under no circumstances can we allow the increase of wages or salaries and under no circumstances can we allow the rise of prices, because an instance of either automatically necessitates the other.

This year and every year we had the unbudging will to not let the German Volk stumble into another inflation. Every wage increase as well as every price increase leads to that. If every conscienceless egoist or thoughtless idiot tries to derive the right to price gouge from some shortage, which will always come and go, then if the government were to relent, we would restart the spiral of the year 1921 and earn the German Volk a second inflation. Therefore, from now on, we will attack such elements with brutal abandon, and if it does not go amicably, we will not recoil from making them conform to the common national interest through the concentration camp.

Certainly, the government could have at least temporarily saved itself some trouble if it had been willing to devalue the Reichsmark, as other states have done with their currencies. We refrained. Firstly, because while we may have saved ourselves some trouble, sooner or later it would have thrown millions of our fellow countrymen into greater troubles, namely those who through their trust in the state would have seen their few saved pennies devalued again. And secondly, we do not at all believe that the global crisis will be lifted through this method; in fact, we are firm as a rock in our conviction that lifting this global economic crisis requires the establishment of a system of stable currency. This will also soon transform the currently almost prehistoric state of trade back into a free and modern exchange. Further, the National Socialist administration was determined not to fall into the old economy of debt under any circumstances, but instead to, on principle, only buy as much as we then wanted to sell ourselves. If the odd person finds it lamentable that this or that luxury article — or as far as I'm concerned, even a necessary household item — is unavailable in Germany because we do not import it, then let us make this worthy comrade aware of the following: we have enough to worry about with feeding the German Volk. As long as we have not secured an adequate life for every single comrade, we do not care whether this or that luxury article can be brought to Germany. He who believes he cannot abide without adorning his existence in this way, let him turn his back on God's poor Germany and let him go where they have more sympathy for such needs and richer opportunities for their satisfaction — perhaps, if it pleases him, to Soviet Russia.

We, however, intend to not make any new debts, and we have actually significantly reduced our international debts.

By doing this, we have been able to partly reduce the interest rates of our foreign debts, as well as our domestic interest rate.

In order to buy the foodstuffs and raw materials that we lack, the administration has tried to maintain our exports. And indeed, Germany's participation in international trade did not decrease any more than other countries', despite a global Jewish boycott.

Insofar as exports are unable to make the purchase of necessary foodstuffs and raw materials available, we are determined to make Germany independent of imports by the production of our own materials.

And here I do not mean "ersatz goods," but the same goods, or totally equal or new goods.

That means, for example: the creation of gasoline from coal was introduced to the greatest extent and, in the coming years, through the starting up of new factories, it will cover a large percentage of German fuel use.

The development and manufacture of German pulp was taken on with great resolve.

Now that the creation of artificial rubber can be considered completely solved, the construction of the first facilities was begun immediately.

Similar things were accomplished in many other areas, like with the development of our own oil wells and of our own old and new ore deposits, and so on.

A generous reordering of our industry took place parallel to this. With all this, the German people must keep in mind that we had not only to care for private economic needs, but also the restoration of the German armed forces.

At the same time, the administration turned its eye toward the development of transportation. All ongoing projects were continued and great new tasks were added. The motorization of German transportation is proceeding apace of the construction of the tremendous new streets meant for it. The most obvious proof of the energy and competence of our economic administration is seen in the fact that this year we reached the number of five million people who have found work and bread again since we took power.

But insofar as all our efforts were not able to provide sufficient employment for individual people or they remained in distress due to low wages, the great organization of our social services tries to spring to their aid. Certainly, even this will not fulfill every hope, but when in history has such a tremendous accomplishment been achieved? When Soviet Russia, with barely fifteen people per square kilometer, has millions on the brink of starvation and countless who have already died of hunger, then the fact that we, by only our own power, were able to feed 137 per square kilometer is something marvelous. By the way, we are never satisfied with our accomplishments. Our goal is to always, always exert ourselves anew for the well-being of the German Volk. What we accomplish with this will make us happy, and what we fail at will never shake us. We will perpetually try new things to reach our goal in the end. And I want to say to all those who lurk greedily awaiting every failure: he who shoots often will eventually hit near his target. Only someone who has never taken a shot can swear that they've never had a miss. Thanks to the inimitable sloppiness of our predecessors, the problems that we found are so enormous that we unfortunately did not have any models for how it could be done. It is well, then, that today we have become the model for others in numerous measures. Almost every step we took was a step into the unknown. But we had no other choice! Or should we have waited until the other states reduced their unemployment and seen how they did it? Or should we sit and watch how Russia will manage to feed its fifteen people per square kilometer?

No! We dared it, and I can declare here with pride, my party comrades, that we have won. This Party Congress will give you a much more detailed and comprehensive picture of National Socialist achievements of the past year. But it is certain that greater efforts have never been made to pull a people back from the precipice of its economic, political, and moral dissolution. This also sets us our tasks for the coming year.

We will aggressively attack the level of unemployment again.

We will work hard to maintain the relationship between work and wage, and we will not recoil from anything in subduing the elements of disruption, no matter where they show themselves or who they are. We will continue the tremendous socialist work of our Labor Front. We will strengthen the German Volk through its army in order to make it a safe stronghold of European peace and European culture. We will continue all the work we have taken on and add to it with new efforts to keep Germany economically viable and raise its living standards.

Above all, as it is the fount of our strength, we will internally solidify and strengthen the movement, and we will proceed in its spirit in forming the German man into a true community.

We are convinced that this last task is our hardest. For this last task we have to overcome the most prejudice; it is the most hindered by the results and bad traditions of a long past, and it is the most doubted by the small of heart.

Our confidence that this task will one day be conclusively solved is justified only by the successes we have already had in this area. Indeed, a thing that can only be preserved inertly will never be good. We do not want to fall into the misconception of thinking that because one becomes a National Socialist once he then remains one forever. Only he who feels an unswerving duty toward the idea, and who serves it and promotes it, is a National Socialist. What we experienced together in our long fight, we also have to constantly teach anew to the coming generation, so that they do not quickly forget the experiences of the past. And so, my party comrades, on this seventh Party Congress of the movement, we want to focus more sharply than ever on the fact that the National Socialist Party must fulfill an eternal and uninterrupted mission of educating our Volk and continuing its existence. Whatever we achieve, the person who experiences it remains the priority. No matter what we intend, in the end it is only that person that can determine it to be a success and give the final blessing to our actions. The National Socialist understanding is, therefore, not a matter of the party book, but rather the party book can only be an outward confirmation of this inner understanding. But this understanding obliges us to a continued self-improvement and likewise a constant promotion and proselytization.

The 1935 Party Congress takes place in an agitated time. But in this internationally agitated time, the National Socialist must always return to his great mission and renew his confidence in the movement, just as he did earlier during the struggle for power whenever heavy storm clouds loomed. And so, just as then we always renewed our trust in the movement and maintained our faith, so we cannot now lose it when we return to the same source from which we drew strength during our monumental fifteen-year fight. Because the Bolshevik Jew in Moscow is declaring war against the world and preaching its destruction, we National Socialists want to grip our glorious banner all the more tightly and carry it before us with the holy determination to fight against the old enemy without concern for our lives, so that Germany maintains its honor, and freedom, and the principles of the life of the future.

Long live the German Reich!
Long live the National Socialist movement!

THE FÜHRER'S SPEECH AT
THE GROUNDBREAKING OF
THE CONGRESS HALL

September 11th, 1935

National Socialists! Party comrades!

Sixteen years ago, the spiritual groundbreaking of one of the most important occurrences of Germany's life took place. It was one of the boldest decisions in world history when we few men decided to free Germany of the shackles of its internal despoilers and of its international servitude. After sixteen hard years, this plan resulted in a decisive historic success. A world of internal adversaries and obstacles was overcome, and a new world is ready to emerge. Today, we place for the German Volk the cornerstone of this new world's first great memorial. A hall will arise here that is to see the elite of the National Socialist Reich gather every year for centuries. If this movement should ever fall silent, then this will stand here for millennia and speak for it.

In the midst of a holy grove of ancient oaks, people will admire this first giant of the Third Reich's architecture with reverent awe.

With this vision, I lay the cornerstone of the Congress Hall of the Reich Party Congresses in Nuremberg in the year 1935, the year of the German nation's freedom, hard-won by the National Socialist movement.

THE FÜHRER'S SPEECH AT
THE CULTURAL CONFERENCE

September 11th, 1935

When the fire from the dome of the Reichstag began to redden the sky on February 27th, 1933, it was as if fate had made the communist arsonists illuminate the magnitude of this historic turning point for the nation. The shadow of a new Bolshevik revolt loomed threateningly over the Reich. One of the greatest social and economic catastrophes threatened to destroy Germany. All the foundations of our common life were exhausted. This age had already demanded courage from many of us in the Great War, and later during the long fight for the movement and against the nation's enemies. But what was this life-or-death courage compared to the courage that was demanded of us in that moment when we had to answer the question: would we take over the leadership of the Reich, and with it the responsibility over our Volk's existence or non-existence? How hard it was in those months to enact those measures that might help avert the catastrophe, while at the same time defending against and beating the last attack of the destroyers of our nation and Reich. It was truly a wild struggle against all the elements and manifestations of Germany's decline within, and then against the eager enemies without.

It will one day be remarked with astonishment that in this same time when National Socialism and its leadership were heroically engaged in a struggle over existence or non-existence, life and death, German art gave signs of the first impulses of a new life and resurrection. While the parties were vanquished, regional resistance was broken, and the sole and exclusive sovereignty of the Reich was solidified. While the Centrists and Marxism were beaten and pursued, the unions snuffed out, and National Socialist thought and ideas were continually called into reality, there was still time to lay the foundations for a new temple to the goddess of art. A revolution blew over the state and at the same time planted the germ for a new high culture. And truly not in a negative sense! Whatever scores we had to settle with our cultural criminals, we really did not spend too much time holding these corrupters of art accountable. Since then, we decided: we will not engage in endless debates with people who — judging by their own works — must be either fools or traitors. Yes, we only ever considered most of the leaders of these cultural Herostratuses to be criminals.[5] Every personal interaction with them should land them either in prison or the insane asylum, depending on whether they regard the miscarriages of their depraved fantasies as genuine inner experiences or if these products were made in obeisance to an equally sad trend.

Not to mention the Jewish Bolshevik literati who recognize and utilize such "cultural pursuits" as a means of sowing internal instability and disorientation. We were all the more determined in our new state to deal with and promote the arts in a positive way. And likewise, we were resolved to not, under any circumstances, let the Dadaistic-Cubistic, and futuristic experience, and "objectivity" babblers have a part in this rebirth of culture. This will be the most meaningful consequence of the recognition of the type of cultural rot that lies behind us, and this decision must be all the firmer because not only are we correcting the decay behind us, but we are also setting a cultural precedent for the coming centuries for the first German national state that is pure in essence.

It is not surprising that in such an age two objections are made against such an effort, objections that, by the way, have always accompanied all cultural achievements in the past. I will not concern myself with those hypocrites who, recognizing the meaning and implications of our intentions, cannot resist throwing all kinds of objections, opinions, and complaints against us to hem us in, thanks to their unconquerable hatred for the German Volk and its future. Really, their rejection of us is our greatest commendation. I will only address those objections that easily issue from the mouths of small-spirited but trusting people:

---

[5] A reference to Herostratus of Ephesus, who burned down the Temple of Artemis. His name is a byword for those who seek notoriety at any price.

The first: considering the tremendous political and economic tasks before us, is now really the time to busy yourself with artistic and cultural problems, which may have been important under other circumstances or in other centuries, but are not necessary or urgent today? Is practical work not more important right now than art, theater, music, and so on — things that might be beautiful, but not necessary for life? Is it right to construct monuments instead of limiting ourselves to the more material tasks in sober objectivity?

And the second objection: can we allow ourselves to sacrifice for the arts in a time when we are surrounded by so much poverty, need, misery, and sorrow? Is art not ultimately a luxury compared to the universal necessity of bread?

I think it necessary to briefly examine and answer these objections.

Art is not a phenomenon of human life that can be called up at will and then let go or put into retirement. Indeed, a people's cultural ability is either fundamentally present or fundamentally not present. It belongs to the whole complex of the racial values and constitution of a people. The functional effects of these abilities on creative and enduring achievements proceed according to the same laws of constant evolution and increase as other human capacities do. Just as one cannot suspend a people's engagement with mathematics and physics without significantly setting back the rest of the world's progress in this area, so you cannot suspend cultural activity without necessarily causing a general cultural setback and then decline. For example, it is impossible to temporarily shut down the by far most intrinsic art form since antiquity — opera — and then to open it up again in its full splendor. It is not just that the required personnel will not be available to put on the work, but no, the capacity to attract the public requires continual nurture and schooling for the public just as well as for the artists. This is true for all art in general.

No age can exempt itself from the duty to cultivate art. Otherwise, they would lose not only the ability to create art, but also the ability to understand or experience art. For both skills are inseparably tied together. Through his work, the creative artist increases and ennobles his nation's fortune, just as conversely the general sense of art that he helped develop and maintain becomes fertile ground for the birth, growth, and embrace of new creative powers.

If cultural activity as such cannot bear such a suspension for a short or a long period, then it should not be allowed to endure very much damage, and in an age whose political and economic problems urgently demand the strengthening of a nation's internal state, exactly then such a forbearance of culture is to be avoided. This is important to understand. In all ages, the great cultural achievements of humanity were the highest achievements of communal life. Whether literally or purely spiritually, a people's deepest strength of being manifests itself in them. It is never more necessary to lead a people to this infinite strength of its eternal inner being than in times when political or economic worries make it all too easy for their faith in its higher values and in its mission to falter. When the small human spirit, hounded by sorrow and worry, fails in its faith in the greatness and future of his people, then it is time to set it aright again by showing it the evidence of the people's inner, immortal, and highest values, which cannot be denied or ignored due to political or economic need. And the more the natural vital needs of a nation are ignored or suppressed, or even just disputed, then it is all the more important to give these natural aspirations the character of a higher law through the visible demonstration of a people's higher values, which history shows are the eternal witnesses of not just the greatness, but also the moral right to life of a people.

Yes, if a people were so unfortunate as to have these living witnesses shut their mouths, then the stones will cry out. History hardly knows any positively notable nation that did not, through its cultural values, create its own memorial. But the destroyers see these traces of accomplishment and only lament it.

What would the Egyptians be without their pyramids and temples, without the adornments of their earthly life, or the Greeks without Athens and the Acropolis, or Rome without its architecture? What would our German kind be without the cathedrals and palaces, and the Middle Ages without town halls, guild halls, and so forth, or even religion without churches and cathedrals? We would not even know that there once was a people called the Maya if it were not for the tremendous ruins of their cities that shock and intrigue the present and continually inspire and capture our interest and research into these legendary people. No: no nation lives longer than the artifacts of its culture!

When art and its works have such a tremendous and enduring effect, unrivaled by human activity, then the preoccupation with art is all the more necessary the more despicably the general political and economic affairs of an age oppress and confuse us. Nothing will better make a people conscious that the human and political worries of the moment are temporary compared to the immortal creative power and the greatness of a nation. Art can give a people the most beautiful consolation by raising it above the smallness of the moment, as well as the smallness of its tormentors. And even if conquered, through its undying achievements, such a people will retrospectively be elevated to true victory above its opponents in history.

The objection that only the small portion of a people that understands and experiences art is interested in it is wrong. By the same right one could portray any other function of national life as unimportant because the whole community does not appear to have a direct stake in it.

Or would someone like to claim that the mass of a nation has a direct stake in the peak advances of chemistry, physics, and all the other highest manifestations of life or the humanities? I, in contrast, am convinced that art actually has by far the greatest influence on the mass of peoples, because it is the most unspoiled and immediate rendering of a people's spiritual life, but only as long as it gives a true picture of the spiritual life and the capacities of a people, and not the distortion of the same.

This gives a very sure indication of the worth or worthlessness of art. Perhaps the most damning condemnation of the whole Dadaistic art industry of the last decades is that the great mass of the Volk turned away from this Jewish Bolshevik parody of culture and in the end showed no interest at all anymore.

In the end, the only more or less faithful admirers of this nonsense were its own creators. Under such circumstances, the circle of those interested in art is quite small, encompassing the half-wits, degenerates, and the powers interested in the nation's destruction, all of which — thanks be to God — are still in the minority. Putting *this* aside — which cannot really be called art, but cultural nonsense — as art elevates itself above the level of self-interest and to the heights of the Volk's common good, it will have a plethora of positive effects on the good of the nation. And it is no different with art than it is with all other peak human activities. We will forever find another step up in its practice and in its understanding. Happy is that nation whose art is so high that not a single person can reach its summit. Out of the number of productive artists, few ever reach the summit of human achievement; likewise, understanding cannot be shared equally by all. But every person can find inner satisfaction on the path toward this height, no matter on what step their understanding finds its limit.

If it really ascribes revolutionary meaning to itself, the National Socialist Party has to use all means available to turn this presumption into a justified claim. It has to convince the Volk of its general and its special mission through demonstrations of the highest cultural faculty and its visible effects. The party will only make its own work and struggle easier if it increases the Volk's understanding for the greatness of the party's intentions through the profound effects that have, in all ages, emanated from the great cultural works, and in particular from architecture.

If you want to build up a peoples' pride, you must give them a visible reason to be proud. The work and sacrifice to build the Parthenon were paid once, but the Greek world's pride endures, and the admiration of the world around and after them is inextinguishable. We have but one great wish to hope for: that Providence will give us the great masters who can make our soul sound in music and immortalize it in stone. We know that here, more than anywhere else, that bitter sentence applies: "Many think themselves called, but few are chosen."

But insofar as we believe we have brought true expression to the character and will of our Volk, so we also believe in our ability to recognize and find the corresponding cultural expression. We will discover those artists who can give the state of the German Volk the cultural stamp of the Germanic race, thereby proving it to be a valid one.

The second objection is that in times of material hardship, we should forgo artistic activity because it is ultimately a luxury that is well and good when humanity is doing well in all other areas, but must be thrown out as long as there are material needs that are not completely satisfied. This objection has accompanied art just as long as hardship itself. Who believes that in some age of the highest human cultural development there was no hardship? Does anyone believe that when the Egyptians were building their temple cities and pyramids, or the Babylonians their splendid buildings, that the people in their ranks experienced no hardship? Has this objection not been levied against every great work and every shaper of culture? But the simplest rebuke of this objection is contained in another question: does anyone believe that there would have been no hardship if the Greeks had not built the Acropolis? Or does anyone believe that there would have been no human poverty if the Middle Ages had forgone the construction of their cathedrals? Or, to take an even closer example: as Ludwig I elevated Munich to a city of art, the very same arguments were made against his efforts! So, did poor and needy people exist in Bavaria only after Ludwig I began his great projects? And to bring us back to the present, now even more easily understood: National Socialism will beautify Germany through art in all areas. Should we abstain because there will be the needy among us, too? When these things were not being accomplished, was there not hardship among us?

The opposite!

If humanity had not ennobled its existence through the great works of culture, it would have not found the ladder that leads from material hardship of the most primitive existence to a higher humanity. In the end this leads to a societal order that, to the extent it sees and acknowledges the great eternal values of a people, feels a clear drive toward the cultivation of communal life, as well as the necessary regard for the life of the individual.

Therefore, the poorer the cultivation of culture in a people, the lower the general living standard, and the greater the hardship of its citizens.

The whole of human progress came from and comes from the progressive conservation of labor from the production of things formerly perceived as necessary for life, transferring it instead to newly unlocked endeavors that are always only open to a small number of materially and spiritually qualified people.

Art, too, goes along this path, as a beautification of life. But it is not in the slightest an expression of a "capitalist" tendency! On the contrary: all of humanity's great cultural works grew as creative efforts for the communal feeling and are, in their origin and in their form, the expression of the communal spirit and ideal.

It is no coincidence, then, that all of humanity's great ideological communal phenomena are immortalized through great cultural works. Yes, those ages of religious internalization that were most disconnected from materialism had the greatest cultural works to show for themselves. Conversely, thoroughly capitalistically-infested Jewry has never and will never possess its own art.

Although this very people has often commanded immeasurable individual fortunes over long spans of time, it has never brought itself to develop its own architectural style or its own music. Even the last iteration of the construction of its temple in Jerusalem was done with the help of foreign architects, just as still today the construction of most synagogues is entrusted to German, French, or Italian architects!

Therefore, I am convinced that a few years of National Socialist leadership among the Volk and in the state will give the German people more and greater things in the realm of cultural achievement than the past several decades of the Jewish regime altogether. And it should fill us with joyful pride that through a peculiar providence, Germany's greatest architect since Schinkel could erect his first, and unfortunately his last monumental stonework in the new Reich and for the movement, as landmarks of a truly German tectonics.

If one wanted to refute the second objection even more, one could point out that the great human cultural works give out again just as much money in wages during their creation as the portions of the earnings that they claimed from the other areas of human activity. In the end, these cultural works pay for themselves in a purely materialistic sense, and help raise the standard of living for all, quite apart from whether it helps the general ennoblement of humanity.

Through it, general self-assurance is raised, and with this the productivity of all. However, this has a prerequisite: to reach such a goal, art must really be a proclamation of the noble and beautiful, a pillar of what is natural and healthy.

If art is this, then no sacrifice is too great for it. And if it is not this, then it is a shame for every Mark that was given for it. Because then it is not an element of health and of construction and the continuation of life, but a sign of degeneration and decline. What goes around under the title of "the cult of the primitive" is not the expression of a naive, unspoiled soul, but of a thoroughly corrupt and sick degeneracy.

To allude to a particularly crass example: he who excuses the paintings and sculptures of our Dadaistic, Cubistic, and futuristic or smug impressionists by calling it a primitive mode of expression, he just has no idea that it is not the task of art to remind man of his symptoms of degeneration, but rather to confront those symptoms of degeneration by pointing toward the eternally healthy and beautiful. If these art subverters presume to give expression to the "primitive" within our Volk's sensibility, then our Volk has certainly outgrown the primitivity of such art-barbarians millennia ago. It does not only reject such mischief, but holds its perpetrators to be either swindlers or lunatics!

But we in the Third Reich have no intention of letting either of these loose on our Volk! The post hoc excuse that at a certain time you had to take part in this fashion in a spectacular way to even get noticed is, in our eyes, an excuse for the downright spineless behavior of such personalities. And moreover, they give these excuses at the wrong time and to the wrong people. Today, when some composer remembers his horrible error with the excuse that he would have not been noticed without such caterwauling, then we have to answer this sad, sorrowful explanation with a correspondingly clear response: politically, we all faced off against the same entity. It was the same music and the same insanity.

In order to enter the public consciousness more lightly and easily, we too could have made the same sacrifice for this opportunity, but that would have meant becoming more Bolshevist than the Bolsheviks. Back then we decided to take up arms against the general political depravity as lonesome fighters, and after fifteen years of this insanity, we slowly became the masters. Our sympathy and regard belong only to those men who in the other fields had the courage to not bow to the riffraff or give reverence to Bolshevik insanity, but who fought openly and honorably with a brave heart for a mission they believed in.

They also want to get us with the objection that art has the mission to serve reality, and therefore has in its purview not just the pleasant, but also the unpleasant; not only beauty, but also ugliness. True, art has always dealt with the tragic problems of life and the tension between good and evil, between the useful and the harmful, and used this for its creations. However, it examined this tension never in order to give a triumph to the harmful, but that it might point to the useful as necessary. It is not art's mission to wallow in the mire for the mire's sake, painting man only in a state of decay, drawing cretins as symbols of motherhood and crooked idiots as representatives of manly strength.

If a so-called "artist" feels called to give such a representation of man always from the perspective of the worthless and sick, then he has to do it in an age when the general opinion appreciates it. Today, this age is over, and so it is also over for this sort of art ape.

And we are confident that we are not making a mistake if we become ever harder and sharper in this rejection. For he who is chosen by Providence to give an outward, living, and visible expression to the eternal healthy character of a people will never find his way to such errors.

We are not talking here about an "endangered creative freedom." Just as we deny the murderer the right to strike down the body of his fellow man and do not call this an infringement on his freedom, so we also cannot accord anyone the right to murder the soul of a people lest we infringe on his perverse fantasy and licentiousness.

At the same time, we are aware that the cultural works of the present, especially in architecture, should be regarded as beautiful in their proportions and relations forever, just as they are materially useful and serve a purpose in the present.

There is hardly any word that has been used for more nonsense in this realm than the word "objective."[6] All really great architects have built objectively — that is, in their constructions they fulfilled the objective requirements and expectations of their age.

These objective but often all-too-human tasks were in any case not seen with the same importance in all ages, and so were dealt with differently. It is a capital error to think that a Schinkel would have been incapable of building lavatory facilities objectively and according to purpose. Firstly, the conditions of hygiene were different than today, and secondly, at that time they did not yet attach much importance to such things. It is, however, an even greater error to think that it is impossible for a modern, aesthetically pleasing construction to masterfully solve these issues that are today seen as necessities.

It is not the special gift of an artist, but an obvious bare minimum that a building can satisfy the general primitive necessities required for it to fulfill its purpose. The crucial thing is that the work as a whole has a form that corresponds to and expresses its purposes.

I keep bringing the problems of architecture to the foreground of these cultural observations because they seem to us especially urgent and, generally, they lie close to our heart. If fate wants to withhold from us a great composer, painter, or sculptor, then through nurturing what we have available we could get by, even if we could not totally make up for the shortfall. The nation has such an immeasurable treasure of immortal works in these realms that we could get along quite well for a time with the careful nurturing of these. But there are great architectural tasks that urgently need to be undertaken and cannot be delayed. This urgency is because we need them to fulfill their purposes now, and also because the

---

[6] Here, Hitler refers to the Weimar-era art movement known as the New Objectivity. The movement's architectural output was minimal; its theoretical underpinnings, which included an insistence on geometrical design, minimalism, and flat planes of color, will be familiar to contemporary readers through the influence the movement exerted on the longer lasting Bauhaus and De Stijl styles, as well as the Memphis style of interior design commonly derided as "globohomo."

required craftsmanship is slowly dying out.

However, in a people that has been a playground for cunning swindlers or sick lunatics for decades, it will be hard to find the right attitude toward the great architectonic tasks of the present without falling into either the soulless imitation of the old or unbridled confusion.

It seems to me that the most important thing is to separate the creation of public monuments from private construction. A construction has to be a worthy representation of its commissioner (that is, the public), and a striking fulfillment of its tasks. The worthy solution to this task has just as little to do with ostentatious intrusiveness as it does with false "modesty." Today, the inability to find an artistically impressive and valid solution is too often motivated by the total absence of modesty when it comes to the designer's "sentiments."

This "modesty," which usually just means the architect's artistic narrowness, should under no circumstances be equated with objectivity, as so often happens. Objectivity means nothing other than to build a building for the purpose it is meant for. Modesty then would mean that in doing so, you achieve a maximum of function using a minimum of means. Too often this minimum of means is replaced with the minimum of talent, which then is supposed to be made up for with a maximum of more or less enlightening explanations. Buildings must speak for themselves. You do not build to create an opportunity for a literary treatise, just as such far-reaching loquaciousness cannot transform a bad construction into a good one.

The true architect, internalizing the purpose of the task set to him, will find the solution that gives the most striking outward expression for it — that is, he will get it done without attaching a philosophical explanation for how it fits the purpose. For example, out of the purpose and cultural historical conditions he is given, he will create a theater that appears unambiguously as a theater.

In doing so, he will take into account the sum of cultural historical impressions, and he will take care to fulfill the tasks that the present assigns. This means that he will not evoke the impression of a Greek temple, nor of a romantic castle or a grain silo. Likewise, he will not abstain from artistically using modern construction materials, just as he will not be afraid to reach back to the past to form elements stemming from similar racial dispositions that can either be further developed or refined or that can be seen as essential syllables in the language of architecture.

A truly gifted artist is marked by the ability to express new thoughts even with words that have already been coined. Still, there is a surfeit of modern tasks left for which the past has delivered neither example nor model. But exactly *these* present the opportunity for a truly gifted genius to expand the vocabulary of forms. Combining task and purpose with the materials of modernity, he will seek that synthesis that, being a clear fulfillment and pushing mathematical understanding forward, represents a true institution and can be called *art*.

The measure for judging beauty will always lie in clear purposiveness; the artist's task is to find this. To perceive, understand, and value it is the task of those who are responsible for creating and awarding the public commissions.

Fundamentally, we should really keep an eye on the men who set and the men who complete all truly monumental tasks, to ensure that the commission is one that may originate in its time, but that through the greatest execution becomes a timeless one.

It is necessary for this purpose that the really great tasks are also assigned with importance — that is, if they are to be worthy of eternity, public commissions must be brought into a certain relation with the magnitudes of everyday life.

It is impossible to give a people strong internal stability if the large communal buildings do not rise markedly above those buildings who owe their existence mostly to the capitalistic interests of the few.

It is impossible to bring the state's monument-building up to a magnitude that is equivalent to the last two or three centuries while bourgeois construction in the private or capitalist realm has increased exponentially in size and number. What gave ancient and medieval cities their characteristic and admirable traits was not the size of their bourgeois private buildings, but much more the elevated artifacts of their communal life. These did not have to be tediously searched for; rather the private buildings of the bourgeois stood deep in their shadow. So long as the defining traits of our modern chief cities are stunning views of warehouses, bazaars, hotels, office buildings in the form of skyscrapers, and so on, then we cannot speak of art or of any real culture. Here it would be better to stick to simple modesty. Unfortunately, in the bourgeois age, the elaboration of public life was hampered in favor of the objectives of private capitalist commercial life. The great cultural mission of National Socialism is to leave this tendency behind.

Not artistic considerations alone, but also political ones must prompt us, with a view to the examples of the past, to give the new Reich a worthy cultural embodiment.

Nothing is better suited for shutting up the little nagger than the eternal speech of great art. Millennia bow in reverent silence before its utterances. May God grant that we set our tasks in such a way that they will be equal to the greatness of our nation. This is indeed a difficult undertaking.

The great heroic things our Volk has done in two thousand years of history belong together with the tremendous experiences of humanity. There were centuries in which the works of art in Germany — as in the rest of Europe — matched humanity's greatness of soul. The lonesome majesty of our cathedrals gives the unmatchable measure for the truly monumental cultural disposition of these ages. Beyond admiring the works themselves, they force us to stand in awe of those generations who were capable of the planning and execution of such grand thoughts.

Since then, our Volk has risen and fallen in the tides of fortune. We ourselves have been witnesses to our own world-defying heroism, deepest disappointment, and harrowing bewilderment. Through us and in us the nation has lifted itself again. When today we call German art to new tasks, then we want to ask not just for the satisfaction of our wishes and hopes in the present, but we want to think in terms of a thousand-year legacy.

In revering this eternal national genius, we are calling the great creative spirit of the past into the present. People will grow into such higher tasks, and we have no right to doubt that if the Almighty gives us the courage to demand the immortal, He will give us the strength to achieve the immortal. Our cathedrals are witnesses to the greatness of the past! The greatness of the present will one day be measured by the eternal works that it leaves behind. Only then will Germany experience a new flowering of its art; only then will our Volk attain the consciousness of a higher purpose.

THE FÜHRER TO THE WORKMEN

September 12th, 1935

My workers!

One of the National Socialist movement's boldest agenda items is this: to heal the rift in this nation that has hitherto been split into classes and meld it into one coherent body.

Only one sentence, but an immense attempt!

Today we see that this attempt is more and more becoming a reality. I wish that all the Reich's Germans could see you, my German comrades, in this moment. They would come away convinced that the unification of the German Volk into one body is no phantasm, no fantastical talking point, but reality, and as reality, a mighty factor for the future and the life of the German Volk!

We never despaired that such a bold program would not be completed in weeks or months. We knew that the road from vision to reality and consummation would have to be a long one. But we are not only on the road; no, the young up-and-coming German generation is already striving into the goal, into consummation.

One of National Socialism's means of achieving this national community was the idea that all German people had to go through the school of work, so that they would get to know each other, and consequently the prejudices of the bourgeoisie would be rooted out so strongly that they would never return.

Life necessarily divides us into many groups and professions. A task of the political and spiritual education of the nation is to again overcome this division.

This task is envisaged primarily for the Labor Service. Through work, it unites all Germans and makes a community out of them.

For this purpose, it should press the same work tool into everyone's hand, the tool that a people honors the most: the spade.[7]

Thus, you march under the rifle of peace, under the weapon of our new inner self-affirmation! Thus, you march today through the whole German Reich!

The nation's eye rests upon you, its hope!

In you it sees something better than what it itself was in its past. If the whole German Volk saw you here today, I believe that every last doubter would be converted, believing that the establishment of a new nation, a new community of our Volk, is no idle chatter, but a reality!

When you stand before me here today as a community, I know how hard the road was to establish the national mandatory Labor Service as it is today, starting from nothing and at first through the voluntary Labor Service. I know that this is the work of one man, a man who through this work has dug his name into German history as a party comrade and a fellow fighter: your leader of the Reich Labor Service and our party comrade and old National Socialist fellow fighter Hierl.

You stand here today thanks to this man's fanatical tenacity and unshakably tough advocacy for the adoption of mandatory labor service. All of you, in each of your positions, should learn from this man what toughness can accomplish. You should take this as your personal example. Then you will be just as good, and true sons of our Volk.

In a few days you will depart from here back to your camps. The bare spades will then again work the German earth. Only you will never lose the memory of this day, but will take it with you.

And the nation will also preserve the memory of this day, and a year later fifty thousand representatives and witnesses of this host of German workmen will again stand here. This will repeat year after year, decade after decade, and century after century, until finally all our efforts and our unshakable, uninterrupted education of the German Volk makes it into a true German national community, un-tearable and indivisible, one

---

[7] The Labor Service's symbol was the spade.

block, as you now stand here.

My men! One day it will not be understood that the past was any different. But we, we want to be proud to have been the first standard-bearers and pioneers. And you can be proud that you are the first class of the New German Reich Labor Service. That is *your* pride, but for us all it is a great joy and a great assurance.

With one call toward the assembled comrades, the Führer closes: "Heil workmen!" And the response reaches him from fifty-four thousand hot hearts and burning pairs of eyes: "Heil, mein Führer!" The Führer concludes with: "Heil Germany!" The entire field answers him, "Heil Germany!"

Then the Führer leaves the stand after saying goodbye to Hierl and his colleagues. The presentation march heralded the Führer's departure as he drove past the earth-brown columns, who had raised their spades in salute. A ceremony was at an end, which was a singular, mighty, and deeply gripping demonstration of the young Germany – an affirmation for the German youth of work, Führer, and Reich. It was a ceremony that truly became a liturgy for the hundred thousand people that were united on that field, both workers and spectators. It was an hour in which the German man and the German soul shaped for itself new forms of self-representation.

After a recess, the columns of the Reich Labor Service left the Zeppelin Field for their big march through the city.

THE FÜHRER BEFORE THE
GERMAN EXPATRIATES

September 13th, 1935

At the beginning of his speech, the Führer talked about how it is necessary for the Reich-German members of the NSDAP in foreign countries to feel like they are living members in the German Volk community. National Socialism, which was showing itself during these days in Nuremberg as the incarnation of the German character, presents the possibility for this. What they had a chance to see here in Nuremberg is so great and meaningful to Germany's future that every single Reich-German and comrade abroad can feel satisfied knowing that he is a part of such a community.

The Führer then expressed that the German Volk has today become not only a state, but a national body pulsing with a vital and inner life. This is the great thing that National Socialism gives the German people: the German who is now abroad does not have to be a lost member, but can stay a living and active member of the national community. The individual knows then that his life will not be a life lost to the community, but that his life can somehow be useful and serve the community, even if he has to live apart for a while. This is the wonderful thing about the National Socialist organization and leadership of the Volk.

But from this, every individual also receives obligations. It is not enough for him to simply know that he still has German citizenship. He also has the duty to replace the possibility of taking part in the internal political life with his internal participation in our national life, which the National Socialist movement shows us how to do. He has the duty everywhere and at all times to feel himself to be a Volk-comrade.

When he cannot properly take part in the living community, then at least he can take part in the racial community that is everywhere appearing thanks to the foreign branches of the NSDAP. He is a member of the National Socialist movement, the National Socialist Party, and therefore a comrade, who is just as obligated to live according to the principles of the new vision as those in the Fatherland.

He cannot say that he is let loose from the community spirit because he is abroad; quite the opposite: because he has no chance to help shape the fate of the state-community, he must therefore stand with the Volk-community and work for it all the more.

This assumes that he does everything he can that National Socialism might demand of an individual. And he must place the feeling of being a member of the Volk in the foreground before all other tribes or status. It may even be easier for the German living abroad, because the farther he lives from the homeland, the more will divisiveness and its meaningless illusions sink into the background, and the more the old jumble of regional, tribal, and party interests dissolve into the interests of the greater German Reich.

The farther away he is from the homeland, the more he loses the ability to see all the countless subdivisions, and thus it grows into a singular unity all the quicker.

The Führer spoke of the miracle that is the National Socialist movement, which always only wants the German as human – no matter where he is from, what education, what wisdom or fortune he has, but the German man as flesh and blood, not just now, but in the future.

Always again interrupted by thunderous acclaim, the Führer concluded his remarks with a heartfelt appeal to the Germans abroad to join themselves to this German Volk and its duties, no matter where the individual finds himself working.

THE FÜHRER TO THE POLITICAL LEADERS

September 13th, 1935

Party comrades! Once again, we experience this highest celebration of the movement, the Party Congress at Nuremberg. We call ourselves a party, and yet we are Germany! Germany in its unity, Germany in its new will, in its new outlook on life, and also in its new vigor. We call ourselves a party because in this movement, in these people, this Germany finds the center of gravity of its spirit and its will.

It is not possible to bring sixty-eight million together, shoulder to shoulder, and yet despite this here you stand before me, not merely as a hundred fifty thousand or a hundred eighty thousand political leaders of the National Socialist Party, but in you Germany and the German Volk stands before me. For today's German Volk has only your will. Today you are the living leadership of the Volk. Always again on this day it is deeply moving for me to see my old comrades-in-arms from the long years of struggle. It is deeply moving to see around me the men who, with unequaled courage and singular faith, took on a world of ideas, notions, and perceptions to forge a new Germany.

Whoever sees this here for the first time, without knowing the long fight that came before, he has no idea how hard it was to reach all this. But you, you were that old guard who once followed me with a faithful heart. You were my first followers who believed in me. And so, you were the German Volk's most faithful, most loyal, and best sons.

It is not only nice for you to see the entire leadership of the movement before you on this day, and to see the man to whom you entrusted your fate. It is just as nice for me to see you again, my old fighters, and to be able to look you in the eyes. It is also necessary for all of us, no matter what fate plans for us, to never forget the road that we had to walk to get to this place today. It is good and beneficial for us leaders to be able to look into these countless trusty old faces, to whom Germany owes everything, because it was not clever reason that got Germany out of trouble, but your faithfulness. It was *your* heart, *your* feeling, *your* will. You helped us and you achieved it.

It is good that we can see each other like this every year again—you see the Führer and the Führer sees you. Let this be a lesson to those who would want a separation between the Führer and his followers, who do not understand that no separation can exist between us. They like to say: the Führer, yes! But is the party really necessary? I do not ask, *is* this necessary, but *was* this necessary? A general without officers or soldiers, some would quite like that! I will not be a general without soldiers; I will rather always remain your Führer.

For me, you are the political officers of the German nation, bound to me for better or worse, just as I am bound to you for better or worse. Not one person conquered Germany, but all of us together conquered Germany. One person won you over, and you won over the German Volk! One person won through his will, and you won through your will. One person stood at the forefront before the Reich, and you stood each of you at the forefront of the fight before a district, precinct, or regional group, and everywhere that the National Socialist stood at the forefront, he was better than the opponents who stood against him!

The ongoing success of a military is unthinkable if a genius chief of staff possesses an incapable army, and so it is here. A genius military commander can only actualize his thoughts and plans if he possesses an instrument that is thoroughly superior to the enemy's. And that I conquered Germany I owe to this instrument that was forged in the National Socialist movement and its organization. Is this fight now complete? The seizure of power is a never-ending process—which is to say, that the old maxim applies here more than anywhere: in order to preserve that which you have inherited, you must acquire it anew.

No nation in history has had its liberty granted to it as a gift, and none will ever maintain its liberty as a gift! Again and again this precious good must be continually preserved. We National Socialists are determined to do so! We do not believe that our development is at an end; to the contrary, we will keep working, and keep improving, and keep making ourselves ever worthier of wielding exclusive power on behalf of the German Volk.

This is how the fight continues. We are coming to the period of our second great task: the continuing education and guardianship of our Volk. Education for the purpose of introducing ourselves and the German Volk ever more to world of National Socialist ideas, and guardianship in order to be constantly vigilant that there be no backslide or decline. Ours shall not be the fate that the world met in 1918. As we come together year after year for this general assembly, so we continuously hold assemblies across the German nation. And this is necessary. You are very favored by fortune, for your school was the school of struggle.

This school formed you old people, but the German youth has to go to the school of the old. The youth can learn something from this: that one must judge the meaning of man from a higher perspective than origin, career, or status.

Where would Germany be if its resurrection had to wait on those who once believed themselves called to the leadership of the nation? There is only one calling, which is only visible in struggle. Raise the banner of courage, sacrifice, devotion, and see who rallies to this banner. Those who are drawn by this banner are those called to lead a nation, and no one else.

Our party has now existed for sixteen years. Surely this is an unbearably long time for our opponents, but for us it is barely a beginning, because if our opponents believe that they might wait it out for the end of this movement and survive it, they have not even experienced the start!

When we began this struggle, we laid down hard maxims and certain principles for ourselves. In staying true and championing them year after year we became great and strong. Often the sky hung dark above us while our opponents made merry. But it was exactly times like these that proved the old maxim: only what withstands the storm winds is truly strong! What can be broken is no good! We put iron principles that were hard and heavy upon ourselves back then and followed them without compromise, and we do not dare think to deviate even a centimeter from these principles in the future. We determine our path, we determine our pace on this path, but none of us any longer can determine the goal, for it is fixed!

There might be a few individuals in Germany who either see our movement as an unfathomable phenomenon or cannot understand the reason why it could come to be, and even less the reasons for why it indeed had to exist and why it will never fall. They have not felt even a whiff of the spirit that rules this movement; they have never perceived the power of these ideals. They stayed cold, believing that a people and a state is nothing more than a dead machine that can only be operated from a rationally cognizable stance. They have not understood that these sixty-eight million people could never be governed by command like they can be through the appeal to their deep instinct and to their conscience. Where would we be, had we not found the way to the soul of our Volk?

What has led us here, why do we stand here, why will we again next year, why will the German youth stand here now and in the future? Because it was commanded? No: because their hearts command them! An inner voice commands them! Because they believe in the movement and its leadership! The power of idealism alone has brought about these world-shaking deeds. If the power of idealism needed an even greater proof, then this movement is it. Its inception was in idealism, not analytical contemplation!

What can one man, who sets out to take on the world alone, what can he expect? I dared it because I believed I knew the heartbeat of my Volk, and I do not think I was mistaken.

And you all have felt this, because each one of you came to the day of decision. It was not sophistical rationality, but an inner voice that commanded you. Reason would have advised you against joining me. Faith alone gave you the command. What idealism, what power idealism has!

We, who this year got to experience as our proudest joy the restoration of our peerless army, we all know that its last and greatest strength is found in the Volk that supports it. No one needs idealism more than the soldier. When that hour comes, that hard, decisive, austere hour, what else can sustain him? Only the words *faith, idealism.* Do not be fooled! All other half measures are miniscule compared to the force of this calling, this inner voice.

So today we are especially happy that we have in our midst, for the first time, the representatives of our new national German army, the army from whence we all came, almost without exception, and to which the German Volk in the future will give its sons, entrusting them to loyal hands to make them into brave, decent, reliable, and secure men.

We know that our army will not indoctrinate them into belligerent militarism, as little as we have ever done that. It will just make them into reliable, decent comrades who feel duty-bound to their nation in a time of need and danger, and who will bravely and properly defend the liberty of their Volk if fate ever subjects them to the hardest trial. That is the reason for the restoration of our army. It was not formed to lead wars of aggression, but only to protect and defend our Volk, so that it will not have to be subjected to such a sad lot as it has recently had to suffer for fifteen years. It is not here to take away the freedom of others, but to protect German freedom. But this army will be able to carry out its difficult duty more easily the healthier are the young German men we send to it.

And that is our task, to politically raise that German man clean and pure, so that he will really be a vigorous member of our national community, and so that he will also take in for himself some of this pure and great idealism, which ruled the age of the struggle for German freedom.

For as long as this idealism exists in Germany, Germany will never vanish!

AT THE CELEBRATION
OF THE HITLER YOUTH

September 14th, 1935

Youth of Germany! You are mustered here for the third time, fifty thousand representatives of a group that grows every year. The mass of those that appear here has always gotten heavier. Not just numerically, no; we see it: heavier in terms of value. When I remember back to the first assembly and then the second, and compare these to today's, then I see the same development that we see in the rest of German life today: our Volk is becoming visibly more disciplined, more firm, more upright, and the youth leads the way. The ideal of a man was not always seen the same in our Volk. There were times, long ago and almost incomprehensible to us, when the ideal of the young German man was the beer-guzzling and hard-drinking lad. Happily, today we no longer see the beer-guzzling lad; he has been replaced with the young man who can withstand storm and stress, the hard young man. What matters is not how many glasses of beer he can drink, but how many hits he can take; not how many nights he can slack around, but how long he can march. Today we see the ideal of the German Volk not in the beer-swilling lad, but in men and women who are healthy to the core, who are firm.

What we want from our German youth is something different than what the past wanted. In our eyes, the German boy of the future must be lithe and lissome, swift as a greyhound, tough as leather, and hard as Krupp steel. We must bring up a new man so that our Volk will not perish from the degenerative effects of time.

We do not talk; rather we act. We have taken on this task, educating this Volk in a new school to give it an education that begins with the youth and that shall never end. In the future, the young man will be lifted from one school to another. It will begin with the child, and it will end with the old fighter of the movement. No one should say that there was a time when he was left on his own. Everyone is obligated to serve his Volk, everyone is obligated to equip himself for this service, to physically steel himself and to spiritually prepare and fortify himself.

The earlier these preparations start, the better. In the future we will not let ten or fifteen years be wasted in German education, only to later have to make good again what was spoiled. Our intention and our unshakable will is that we are already engendering the same spirit in the hearts of the youth that we want to see in greater Germany as the only possible one that can sustain the future. And we not only *want* this, but we will carry it through. You are a slice of this development, much firmer and sturdier than three years ago. And I know it will get better and better in the coming years.

A time is coming when the German Volk will look at its youth with a bright joy, and then we will all go easily and confidently into our old age with the innermost happy conviction, safe in the knowledge that our life struggle was not for nothing. It is already marching close behind us. And this is the spirit of our spirit, this our resolve, our hardness, this the representation of the life of our race.

We will steel ourselves so that every storm finds us strong. We will never forget that the sum of all virtues and strengths will only be effective when they are subject to one will and one command. We stand here now, not by coincidence, not because each person did what he pleased, but because the command of your Reich Youth Leader ordered you here, and because this order was converted into a thousand individual orders. And in obedience to this order, an organization arose out of millions of individual German boys, and out of tens of thousands of comrades living in Germany emerged today's rally, this assembly today. Nothing is possible if a single will does not command, a will which all others obey, beginning at the top and only ending all the way at the bottom. And this is the second great task besides physical education and fitness.

We are a fellowship, but fellowship means following, and it means giving fealty. We must educate our Volk to recognize their duty to follow whenever someone is appointed to command, and to obey him, because in the next hour it might be that it is their turn to command, and they rely on others' obedience. It is the expression of an authoritarian state, not a weak pattering democracy, that everyone can be proud to be able to obey, because they know that when I need to command, I will also have to find obedience. Germany is not a chicken coop where everyone clucks and crows and runs into each other; we are a people that learns from a young age to be disciplined.

If others do not understand us, then we do not understand them, either. What most have not understood is that discipline has never been the worst thing in the world; quite the opposite.

We did not lay our hands on our lap and explain "that is not our place; there is nothing to be done." No: something *is* to be done! And we did it! And you, my boys and girls, you are living signs of the success of our work. You are the sign that the idea came to life in the German Reich. And you are the evidence for how this idea experienced its actualization. Believe me, a time will come when the German youth will have a wonderfully healthful and beaming countenance, healthy, open, upright, bold, and peace-loving. We are not ruffians. If the rest of the world misinterprets our discipline, then we cannot help it. Fewer squabbles will come out of this discipline than out of the parliamentary-democratic mess of today. We are going our way, and we do not want to cross anyone else's path. Let the others leave us alone on our path. This is the only caveat we must have for our love of peace. Do harm to none and tolerate harm from none!

If we chart and establish this life-path for the German Volk, then I believe we will also gradually bring other nations around to an understanding for such a decent disposition, and out of such an inner understanding, they may even reach out a brotherly hand toward us. But we should never forget that friendship is only earned by the strong and defended by the strong. And so we want to make ourselves strong; that is our watchword. And you are responsible to me that this wish is fulfilled. You are the future of the nation, the future of the German Reich!

AT THE ROLL CALL
OF THE BROWN ARMY

September 15th, 1935

Men and fellow fighters of the National Socialist Party!

Again we are gathered at a Party Congress in Nuremberg. Again the old SA and SS men, and the men of all the fighting organizations of the movement, came out of all the German districts in order to celebrate this reunion in the city of our Reich Party Congress.

Who would not be moved to see the many loyal faces that we know from the times of struggle. Party comrades! I see SA and SS men who have marched undeterred for ten, and twelve, or more years behind a flag. This time, too, they followed the flag to Nuremberg. This year it is an especially proud feeling to be able to greet you here today. To me, you are the old guard of the National Socialist movement, the National Socialist revolution, and the uprising of the German Volk. When Jewish Bolshevism in Moscow sends us a clear threat these days, here stands Germany's answer!

For the fifth time we celebrate this gathering of the National Socialist fighting force on the occasion of the Reich Party Congress in Nuremberg. For the fifth time in the history of our party and its structure, we are meeting here at this spot. This spot has changed its face. It has become prouder and more beautiful. But it has stayed our trusty old spot. And this feeling grips me when I see you here, my SA and SS men.

You strike a new appearance here today. I see what has been learned again in one year, what has improved in the movement. But if this outward image changes, it is only proof that the spirit of the old, yes, the good old times remains, the times when the SA man and the SS man never asked where they were marching, but simply stood by the flag.

And it is well and good that the changing of these times that we are lucky enough to experience shows itself on you. For in this last year, Germany has again entered a great historical turning. It is you, my men of the SA, who will feel it clearly in but a few months, because many thousands of released soldiers from the first class of our new German army will join your ranks.

As we ourselves once came here, now year after year the German Volk that has been trained for the nation's defense will flock here, and these men will find the best German home within your ranks. What was previously a temporary two-year schooling for the nation and then lost, to the detriment of the party, will now be given over to trusty hands to preserve for the German Volk.

Then we will have closed the circle of our nation's education. The boy will enter into the Jungvolk, and the kids will enter the Hitler Youth; then this youth will join the SA, the SS, and the other groups, and the SA and SS men will one day join the Labor Service, and from there the army, and the soldier of the Volk will return to the organization of the movement, the party, the SA and SS, and never again will our Volk degenerate as it unfortunately once degenerated!

We learned from the worst times of German history; we took those lessons to heart, and we have drawn the consequences out of them. We are determined to raise a new generation, and who can doubt that the fathers of this generation, which will not live only in our fantasy, are standing right in front of us? It is a tough generation that we are choosing; not because we want to pick a fight with others, but because we want to ensure that others will not want to pick a fight with us. And in it, we want to also see the most vibrant community that can exist in a people: the community of mutual sacrifice, of a common upbringing toward achievement and unbreakable camaraderie.

We have come here from all over the whole German Reich. You came from the east, and west, and north, and south, from out of the depravity of Germany's political past, and yet you became one; you banded together through thick and thin, as it should be within a people. In these long years of struggle, you learned that nothing is given, that everything must be earned. What can a disunited and tattered and decayed Volk earn for itself? It earns nothing but the treatment that we experienced. This condition is now over. The German Volk has found the way to unity and prudence within its men and its women, and you are the guarantors that this will never again be otherwise.

And when you return from here to your districts, your cities, your marketplaces, and your little villages, there each one of you must be a standard-bearer for the movement and the National Socialist Party, and you must carry the flag of the National Socialist state.

And today I again consecrate new standards for you. They will join the ranks of the old standards, and you will love and honor them like the dear standards from our movement's long years of struggle for Germany. And you will carry them before you, and next year will place them here again, so that the nation sees them and knows that *these are the standards behind which Germany marches.* And you will do this all the more as this flag, under which Germany fought for its freedom, will receive the highest honor that can be given it.

And so I salute you, my old SA man; I salute you, my old SS man, and salute those of you who have newly joined us, and I ask you to join in our old battle cry of the movement:

Germany—Sieg Heil!

Sieg Heil! Sieg Heil!

THE FÜHRER'S SPEECH AT
THE NOTABLE REICHSTAG
SESSION IN NUREMBERG

September 15th, 1935

Delegates of the German Reichstag! On behalf of the government of the German Reich, I have asked Reich President Göring to call the German Reichstag into session in Nuremberg today.

This place was chosen because it has a deep connection through the National Socialist movement with the laws that are proposed to you today, and this time was chosen because the greatest number of delegates still find themselves in Nuremberg as fellow party members.

I would like to make a few short general comments on the occasion of the laws proposed to you by an initiative motion.

The first part of the Reich Party Congress in Nuremberg is at an end. Tomorrow the day of the armed forces will conclude it. The image that this celebration offers the movement is a summary of this past year in stark relief. The German Volk has found its way to a historically unprecedented unity and discipline. This expression of the firmness of the movement is also an expression of the strength of today's regime.

What the German nation has for centuries longed for in vain it now possesses: the unified Volk of brothers, free of the mutual prejudices and inhibitions of the past. This inner strength will be reflected tomorrow in the image of the armed forces. It should not be a mass demonstration, but merely a statement of the inner value of our new army.

The German Volk can count itself fortunate knowing that it has wrested back this strength that was lying dormant through such long and horrible suffering, and this especially during a time that seems to be set apart for serious crises. Germany is healthy again. Its institutions are in order outside and inside.

In such times, the leadership of the Reich is an even greater responsibility. There can be only one guideline for all our behavior: our great and unshakable love of peace!

Such an announcement seems necessary to me right now, because a certain international press is constantly hard at work trying to draw Germany into the orbit of its machinations.

Soon they'll discuss how Germany will march against France, then they'll report the assumption that we will turn against Austria, then again the fear that we'll attack Russia, I do not know where. These threats will then usually be presented as arguments for the necessity of the various coalitions desired at the moment to oppose us.

And yet this same press generously awards Germany's friendship, treating it like an object that is immediately available to every statesman who wants to but stretch out his hand.

I need not remind you, my delegates, men of the Reichstag, that the German government does not make its decisions out of an attitude against anyone, but purely out of our sense of responsibility toward Germany.

The purpose of our work is not to spend the results of our work in a frivolous and scatterbrained adventure. The purpose of building up the German army was not to threaten or even take the freedom of some other European people, but purely to preserve the freedom of the German Volk.

The foreign policy and diplomatic behavior of the German government is primarily determined by this perspective.

For this reason, we also do not take stances on events that do not affect Germany, and we wish to not get sucked into such events.

Thus, it is with all the greater concern that the German Volk is following current events in Lithuania. During total peace, years after the armistice, Germany was robbed of Memelland.[8] The League of Nations legitimized this theft, and for their protection, they merely gave the Memel Germans a contractually guaranteed autonomy.

For years now, the German element in this territory has been mistreat-

---

[8] Memel Territory, now Klaipeda in Lithuania.

ed and abused, contrary to the law and the contract. A great nation has to constantly watch as members of its blood, who were ambushed and torn away from the Reich during total peace, are treated worse than criminals are in normal countries, illegally and against the terms of the contract.

Their only crime is merely that they are Germans and wish to remain Germans. At least until now, the speeches of the responsible powers in Kaunas remained merely external formulations without any meaning or internal consequences.

The government of the German Reich views these developments with alertness and bitterness. It would be laudable if the League of Nations would enforce its interest in having the autonomy of the Memel Territory respected and making this practically viable, before events here also shape themselves into something that all sides will one day regret. The electoral preparations taking place there now are a mockery of justice and duty!

Germany is not making any unreasonable demands when it asks that Lithuania be held accountable to the signed contracts, by appropriate means.

Ultimately, a nation of sixty million has the right to demand that it at least not be respected less than the caprice of a nation of two million.

Unfortunately, while an understanding between nations is more necessary than ever, we are seeing that the Bolshevik International is carrying out its revolutionary incitement anew from Moscow, according to plan. The spectacle of the Comintern Congress in Moscow very effectively underlines the honesty of that same regime's "policy of noninterference."

Informed by our own experience and, as far as we can determine, by that of other states, we know we should expect nothing from protests and demonstrations in Moscow, and thus we are determined to stand up against Bolshevik revolutionary incitement in Germany with the powerful weapons of the National Socialist enlightenment. This party convention can have left no doubt that National Socialism can readily handle any plans and attempts by Moscow's Bolshevism to find a foothold in Germany or to wage revolution in Germany.

Further, we have to state that it is Jewish elements that here and almost everywhere are the pillars of this incitement and replacement of peoples.

The insult to our German flag — which has been remedied by the American government through an explanation in a most loyal way — is an illustration of the Jewish attitude toward Germany, even in an official capacity, and it is a potent confirmation of the correctness of our National Socialist lawgiving, which from the outset aims to preemptively prevent similar incidents from occurring in our German administration or judiciary.

But should we need another illustration of the correctness of our opinion, then this is generously supplied by the agitation for a renewed boycott against Germany set in motion by Jewish elements.

This international unrest in the world seems to have unfortunately awakened Jews in Germany to the notion that the time has come to openly set Jewish interests against German national interests in the Reich. There are the most frequent complaints from countless localities about the provocative behavior of individual members of this race; the noticeable frequency and uniformity of the reports leads one to conclude that that there is a certain orderliness to these incidents.

This behavior escalated into demonstrations that took place in a Berlin cinema against a harmless foreign film, by which the Jewish circles felt bothered.

To prevent these events from causing unmanageable and very rash acts of resistance among the outraged populace, we are left only with the option of a legislative regulation of these problems. The government of the German Reich is guided in this by the hope of creating, through a one-time secular solution, a level ground on which it is possible for the German Volk to have a tolerable relationship with the Jewish race. If this hope is not fulfilled, and domestic and international Jewish incitement continues, then we will have to reexamine the situation.

I now recommend that the Reichstag adopt the laws that Party Comrade Göring will read out.

The first and second laws remove a debt of gratitude to the movement under whose sign Germany regained its freedom by fulfilling an important point of the National Socialist Party's program.

The third is the attempt at a legal regulation, after repeated failures, of a problem whose final solution should be legally handed over to the National Socialist Party. The National Socialist Party stands behind all three laws, and behind it stands the German nation.

I ask you to adopt these laws!

After the reading and the subsequent unanimous adoption, the Führer ap-proached the railing of the gallery and directed the following concluding remarks to the house:

My dear delegates!

You have now approved a law whose meaning will only be under-stood after many centuries in its fullness. Take care, however, that the nation itself does not leave the path of the law! Take care that our Volk itself walks the path of the law! Take care that this law will be ennobled through the unparalleled discipline of the whole German Volk, for whom you are responsible!

TO THE SOLDIERS OF
THE ARMED FORCES

September 16th, 1935

For the second time, groups from the army and navy muster at this place. For the first time, they do so under the condition of the new freedom of defense. Now you are joined by the new groups of our German armed forces, who can be shown to the German Volk in such a picture.

The German was always a good soldier. Armed service was never a compulsory service for our Volk, but was in all times of our history the highest service of honor. Thus, it was all the more painful and oppressive for the honor-loving and decent German man to not be allowed to be a soldier, and under the most degrading and demoralizing conditions at that. The extent to which we have overcome this condition is shown to you, my soldiers, and today to the whole German people by this image of the combination of the German man as soldier with modern technological weaponry.

Now every young German man, as long as he is deemed worthy by his nation, will once again join your ranks. And you will once again do service with the weapons that are common to the world today.

This service demands sacrifice from every single one of you. Every one of you must bring a sacrifice of personal freedom; you must bring obedience, subordination, but also hardness, endurance, and above all, a sense of duty.

Those people who believe that this sacrifice must be pressed out of the German people are mistaken. In all centuries, German men have rendered this willingly, and have been proud of this service. It is not just during peace that the German as soldier has joyfully brought this sacrifice to the nation, but not the least during times when the Reich's distress called him to the defense of Volk and Fatherland. The German was not only a good peacetime soldier, but always also a brave fighter.

But what do all the sacrifices that are demanded of you and of us today mean in comparison to the sacrifices that were demanded twenty years ago of millions of us and our comrades? May each of you, if ever you find a soldier's service too hard, remember that eight days of drumfire demanded more sacrifice from the battalions and regiments of our old army than a whole year of peacetime service.

The German people at arms did not break from this. It only broke because it lost its inner unity, its inner faith in its own right. But this faith has returned today, and not only hundreds of thousands of you have this faith, my soldiers, but millions of our countrymen envelop you with this hot faith, with this hot confidence, and with this warm love.

And when you have to make personal sacrifices of obedience, duty, subordination, hardness, endurance, and efficiency, do not forget, my soldiers, that the German people are also making great sacrifices for you. It is hard for the German people to build up what is standing here today and in countless other places throughout Germany. The German Volk makes hard sacrifices and makes them gladly. In the first place, it does not want to have its sons poorly equipped, and secondly, it does not want Germany to be defenseless. And so, we will continue to make these sacrifices together, the Volk for you, and you for the Volk! For Germany, our Volk, and our dear German Reich!

And besides, we make these sacrifices convinced that we do not need a war to reap their rewards.

Germany once had a proud and brave army; it had heroic fighters. That is the natural thing for German soldiers. But it was not only the nation's defense in war, but during peace it was also the Volk's glorious school. It made us all into men; to look upon it always bolstered our faith in the future of our Volk. This glorious army is not dead; it only rested, and it now revives in you!

In the tip of your weapons and on your helmets you, my comrades, carry an unsurpassed noble legacy. You are not something artificial, something without tradition, something without history. Whatever else there is in Germany, it falls behind the tradition that you embody and can embody! You do not need to go and win renown for the German army — it already has this; you only have to preserve it!

And if you stand here today equipped with steel and bronze, it is not because we think this is necessary to repair the German people's honor. As long as this honor has been carried by soldiers, no one in the world has been able to take it!

Germany has not lost its military honor, and least of all in the last war. Therefore, we do not need to retrieve this honor. But we will ensure that in the future, so much honor, so much valor, and so much sacrifice will not be for nothing, as it once was.

This old army, for which you are the continuation, and for which you have to be the representative and carrier of tradition, brought to the altar of its Fatherland the greatest sacrifices that any military has ever given to its nation.

Show yourselves worthy of these sacrifices! Take care that the nation can rely on you as much as it could once rely on our great old army! Take care that the nation's trust can be yours, as it once belonged to the army whose helmet you wear from those famed times. Then the Volk will love you; it will see the best of itself in you, as it will send its best sons to your peerless organization year after year. Then the German Volk will believe in its army and will gladly and joyfully make every sacrifice with the conviction that this will preserve the peace of the nation and guarantee the education of the German Volk.

For you became men, and we want the whole German youth to go through this ultimate school and become men like you are. We want to raise a hard generation that is strong, reliable, loyal, obedient, and decent, so that we do not need to be ashamed of our Volk before history.

This is the plea of the nation, its hope and demand for you! And I know you will fulfill this demand, and this hope, and this plea, because you are the New German Reich's new soldiers!

THE FÜHRER'S CONCLUDING REMARKS
AT THE 1935 PARTY CONGRESS

September 16th, 1935

Party comrades! National Socialists!

What time but the week of the Reich Party Congress could oblige us more to look past the events and appearances of a limited present into the past and future? For all that these days contain in intoxicating impressions, for us the most gripping is always the appearance of our Volk, which we can never and nowhere see more clearly and joyfully than here. Who is not moved by the feeling that the hundreds of thousands marching past our eyes in these hours are not individuals belonging to the present, but the timeless expression of the life force of our Volk, emerging from the past and pointing toward the future? They are the messengers of the German nation's historical existence!

In its radiant youth we see the guarantor of the unspoiled life force of our race. In these hundreds of thousands of men we feel the signs of an abounding will to life. Our Volk walked its path like this through millennia, and if we close our eyes for a moment, we believe we hear the march-step of all those who belonged to our blood since grayest prehistory, and we believe that we still hear its reverberations in the most distant future.

This sublime demonstration of our Volk's eternal life is well-suited for us to busy ourselves with the tasks that arise from this day and this time, and that have an eternal significance.

How is it possible that this Volk, whose march-step seems so self-assured and unshakeable, could lose its way so often in history? Are the bitter events in the life of the German nation the result of an inability to master the problems of life, or does its cause lie in a deficit of courage, in an unwillingness to sacrifice, or in the inability to make great decisions?

No!

There is indeed no other nation that has had to muster more courage for the preservation of its existence than the German. Fate has certainly not demanded greater and more painful sacrifices from any other nation than ours. Decisions were born from out of its ranks that belong to the boldest that human daring has ever attempted. We ourselves are the people that fate has left as witnesses to a truly tragic sacrifice of blood, the unshakeable bravery of the living, the proud self-sacrifice of those chosen to die, and the boundless boldness and decisiveness of great military commanders.

No! No nation has laid greater sacrifices on the altar of the God who judges nations than the German nation!

And yet we ourselves had to experience what a meager historical valuation it ended up with. Measured against the successes of other nations, the results of Germany's struggle are deeply lamentable.

In recognizing this fact without any self-deception, a concern for the future obliges us to investigate its causes.

Such a recognition cannot be explained by pointing at a few failed great men, just as the continued success of a nation cannot be the result of a continuous string of geniuses. No! The deepest reason for this historical failure is the unfortunately all too common weakness of internal cohesion and stability of the nation, as well as the often coincidentally and necessarily flawed constitution of our state. The examination of our historical course of development shows us a row of bitter insights.

In the age when the Germans first stepped into historical view for us their descendants, they were a large family according to blood, but they were not one Volk in their understanding and feeling. In their historical heritage, in their customs of life, and in their language, the German tribes of prehistory were so varied from each other that only a few very gifted heroes could dream of the goal of unifying these tribes in just a political unit.

When we ourselves still had to struggle against tribal and regional constitutions, and heritages and traditions in 1933, should it be surprising that a Cheruscan chief could unify the German tribes only as long as all of them were under a common threat?[9]

This common bond of blood between these German tribes was sometimes the dominant principle of a few of them while danger loomed, but it failed to be recognized as natural and necessary by the whole. Neither a spiritual nor an organizational-political unity formed that was stronger than the feelings of tribal bonds. That the first attempt at unification failed already during the life of the audacious hero is well known, but few are conscious of the fact that during the turbulence of the Völkerwanderung, barely three hundred years later, the individual tribes that made up this first German unification were already lost to history.

We can deduce from this fact that the merging of the German tribes into a nation was not a conscious or even desired process of nation-building, but a process of state formation that was reached due to different intentions. This means then that German people could only be unified through the oppression of the separate cultural lives of the individual German tribes. At the same time, an antagonism emerged between the state organization and the individual folkdoms, as Germans did not become conscious members of a nation instead of conscious members of their tribes. This was a difficult and for many centuries a painful process. Countless individual features and symbols fell victim to this process. We may be sorry to lose a few individual characteristics, but we should not dam up history just because the path that leads dozens of German tribes to a single German nation suppresses ten thousand often valuable victims and traditions — it has to.

It is also wrong to lament that this path of building the German Volk demanded the sacrifice of political and religious sovereignty. The things that fell in this century had to fall. It is also not right to analyze the inner motives of those we know as the framers of the first great German super-state. Providence wanted the German tribes to form into a German Volk and worked to make this nation formation happen. Who wants to reveal or analyze the inner soul, the thoughts, and the motivating forces of those great Germanic kaisers, who strived by a hard sword for a greater German unification beyond the individual fates of various tribes! And it is another stroke of Providence that two aids were available to them, with-

---

[9] A reference to Arminius.

out which there could have been no Germanic state formation, and then no premise for the formation of the German Volk, or at least not in this relatively short time. For nations step into our historical view when they are already an organizational unit and ready to reach the zenith of their strength, their vitality, and their influence. The length of their preceding development remains hidden from us. Without a view of the states of antiquity, and without the philosophical help of Christianity, German state-formation would have been unthinkable in any age. The fate of Europe and the rest of the world, as far as the White race is concerned, would then also be unimaginable, and in any case would be inconceivable today.

Christianity offered the first consciously felt and expressed unity against the entirely divergent tendencies of the individual tribes. It delivered a religious-ideological basis for the formation of a state organization that was not and could not be characteristic of individual tribes. This path was historically necessary if a German Volk was to ever form out of the countless German tribes. It was on this initially religious and political platform that exclusive tribal characteristics could be eliminated and overcome over the course of many centuries in favor of ones that were new, and yet still based in blood and a common heritage; with this an inner cohesion could form. But just as every birth is tied to pain, so the birth of a people is also not painless. Who can complain that history took a path that Providence could not have chosen any better to reach the end, which even the complainers desired? During this period of the German Volk's formation there was a necessary opposition between the state-idea and state-goal against folkdom; this opposition was regrettable but needed, as long as the folkdom did not grow beyond the unconscious limitations of the tribes and into the gradually perceptible stage of a nation, now recognized as necessary and natural. The men who were the drivers behind this process were on a mission from Providence, which wanted us Germans to become one Volk.

Two phenomena arise from this to the height of irrefutable facts:

First, Christianity gave this first Germanic state-formation, this first unification of all German tribes, a higher unity through an intellectually rich religious paradigm and a common morality. What had to fall fell when our Volk wanted to climb up out of the confusion of small little states toward one great political and cultural unity.

Second, the monarchy that was inspired by the ancient concept of the state and that dissolved the earlier dukedom led to a serviceable organization and, importantly, it preserved what was already accomplished.

The unification of the German tribes into a state—that is, an organizational unity—took place over many centuries. The sacrifices this required are countless, and the fates of the many who fell during this process are tragic. No matter how great the confusion and mistakes of this time may have been, in these ups and downs, and pendulum swings of the centuries, and through many painful hardships, the German nation was born. As the religious crisis swept over the German Volk and Christianity began to split into different confessions, the first basis for Germanic state-formation gradually receded in favor of the second one. As the ideological foundation became more uncertain, the organizational form of the state became ever more prominent, and eventually found its final (albeit temporary) expression in the state of absolute monarchy. For as religious schism shattered the religious platform, so the monarchical platform was shattered by the intellectual thrust of the French Revolution.

The ferment of decomposition, as Mommsen calls the Jews, began to appropriate the ideas of a social consciousness intrinsic to our Volk in order to invert it into an opposite that is as irrational as it is dangerous, and then to let this loose upon humanity as Marxist socialism. Through the detour of parliamentary democracy, the monarchy was dissolved, and with it the purely organizational state.

By their participation in parliamentary democracy and sinking down into this anarchical fight, the Christian denominations did not prevent this dissolution, but it did do incalculable damage to Christianity. Whoever pursues his political goals under this premise becomes—willingly or unwillingly—an ally of international Marxism, and aids the destruction of this political entity that was founded on and grew out of totally different premises. All participation on this level means recognition of the principles under which this dissolution happened; it means an agreement with the guises, activities, and methods that can only harm the German state and nation through their internal untruth and illogic, as seen from a German standpoint. The parliamentary democratic constitutional monarchy or the parliamentary democratic republic were always impossible for Germany, and were fated to fail sooner or later.

It simply does not work to build up a community upon two or three contradictory principles. It is not possible to make the principle of individual diversity of values into a basis for economic life!

It is not possible to build up the administration and the army upon the principles of personal responsibility, while building the general political leadership of the state on the ideas of parliamentary democracy and personal irresponsibility. It was impossible to deny individual diversity of achievement and influence in politics, and yet to recognize its effects in private property.

This disjointedness of the parliamentary democratic Reich's fundamental principles also explains the insecurity and indecisive halfheartedness of its stance against the dangers that threatened it. The deliberate Marxist method of dismissing certain crucial and important principles and the bedrocks of cultural and political morality and replacing them with more practical notions was crucial here. In this way, the criminal against human society was spared from isolation and was elevated to membership in a new society.

As long as treason is praised as a virtue, the traitor escaped condemnation. As long as cowardice before the enemy enjoys public glorification, the coward is transformed into a hero. When theft is seen as a correction of unequal distribution, the thief is elevated to be the architect of a new social order. When the murderer is described as the result of an unfortunate sociological condition, he will be pitied by the community in the end as an unfortunate victim. In this manner, every virtue becomes a vice and every vice a new ideal.

In its insecurity, the democratic state had to succumb to this storm of Jewish Bolshevism almost automatically and without defenses. The monarchy likewise rolled over just as the Christian denominations did. They were all ineffective in their resistance against this new kind of method of attack; the fact that many other states have not yet succumbed to this does not indicate that they are effectively resisting; it only shows that historical processes take a long time. Only in those places where a new concept and form of resistance emerged out of the depths of their racial life force was there any real rescue.

This resistance cannot be successful if it is limited to purely passive combat. It can only hope to master this Bolshevik destruction if it achieves a positive composition of racial existence, as well as a political form built on an unassailable ideological foundation.

To have an accurate judgment of all of the racial problems, it is necessary to have a starting point from a solid footing; just as when you form a view of the world, the vantage point of the observer is crucial.

The starting point of National Socialist teaching is not in the state, but in the Volk. This means that in order to examine, judge, and right the correctness and consequently the purposiveness of the external organizational forms of the Volk, it is necessary to look beyond these things as means and understand their purpose. That is why the focal point of every National Socialist observation is the living substance that, according to its historical development, we call the "German Volk."

Two thousand years ago this Volk did not exist as a real entity. Consequently, the subsequently developing Germanic state formations based their existence on other foundations. But today this Volk has become a historical reality. It lives, and for the first time it gives us the possibility to clearly discern means from purpose. Now that we recognize that which subsists and that which persists in the Volk, we see in it our only purpose. Its preservation is necessary first, and then we have the basis for the existence and efficacy of ideas. Conversely, its destruction would leave all ideas worthless and meaningless.

Religions also only have a meaning if they serve the preservation of humanity's living substance. Because if the peoples of the word pass away as such, then neither states nor religions remain as eternal fixtures. When it dies, every people takes its dominant political and religious entities and ideas with it. So often in human life, the means gradually begin to be viewed as the purpose. For example, how the Aztec priests always believed and claimed that these ancient Mexicans were created for them and their doctrine. But when these races fell, nothing remained of their doctrines and their priests. If today Bolshevism gets its way and exterminates certain races, then their political and religious beliefs or doctrines and whatever other organizational entities they have will also fade away. When Providence created man, the purpose of human activity was also contained in him and in his preservation.

Therefore, the goal of every idea and of every institution can originally and naturally only be to preserve the God-created Volk as a physically and spiritually healthy substance, decent and pure.

Adopting this as a foundation reveals the measure by which to judge all new things, and to see if they are correct in the abstract. That means, are they correct in the sense of whether they are useful or detrimental to the preservation of a people, or do they even threaten the destruction of a people?

If this explains and acknowledges the meaning of the struggles and battles of life, then our task is simply to find and secure the necessities for the fulfillment of this purpose. If the National Socialist Party wants to serve its purpose as a means, then it must first secure the same selection for its political leadership that takes place in almost all realms of life, and so is available for leadership as well.

Unwillingly and unconsciously, all human vocations ultimately develop according to predispositions. Career choice is nothing other than the choice employed by vocations to pull the people toward it that are best suited for it.

The most solid German institution of the past was the one that maintained the starkest and most intense choice for joining it: the army. Just as the army consciously built itself up based on a screening that selected for the people that felt the most drawn to weaponcraft, so it must be the party's task to gather and foster within its organization the elements of our nation capable of political leadership. This skill, however, has nothing to do with capital, education, birth, and so on, just as the ability to be a soldier is not dependent on miscellaneous bourgeois characteristics.

The only crucial thing is the inner disposition, and thus aptitude. This is vocation. The army gives a constant home to this conscious vocation and thus the basis for the continuation and the results of this capability; in its organization, the party must similarly give the external and visible expression of the political vocation and the basis and possibility for nurturing and improving it.

The party and the army can only be socialist institutions in the highest sense, insofar as they do not look through capitalist perspectives in their development, but look instead exclusively at the element of the Volk's suitability. Consequently, they have to deepen the recognition that as an organization they are extremely dependent on properly prioritizing highest ability; this is their highest law. Thus, they are at the same time really the result of a better, because real, democracy — a democracy that does not burden the whole by elevating the inadequate to have a decisive influence through the anonymity of parliamentary voting and decision, but rather one that serves the whole because in all realms of life and in the struggle for life it first gives the greatest responsibility to the most skilled in its organization.

While the army is an exclusive institution, its mission is not just to preserve itself as the military leadership of the Volk, but also to educate, raise, and form the Volk in the spirit of its military mission. Similarly, the political party's mission is not just to live on as the main organization of the political leadership, but to continue to educate, raise, and improve the Volk in its understanding of self-preservation, and in so doing, to take on into its organization those recognized as skilled, our countrymen who have apparently been called by Providence itself to leadership.

The idea of self-defense and consequently of the military draft has its organizational home and expression in the army. The National Socialist idea has its organizational home in the party. The party represents political understanding, political consciousness, and political will.

Its first task is to ensure that the Volk's leadership in all areas of life accords to its worldview, and second, to enshrine this political understanding in the enduring order of a solid system, thus securing and stabilizing it for all time. It has to fulfill the historic task of examining and getting to know the racial substance of our Volk in all its strengths and weaknesses, and to derive practical inferences from these insights.

1. From these insights, it must decide on and set the major goals for all areas of our whole national life.
2. It has to bring public life into accordance with the duties that follow from the requirements of our Volk's inner character.
3. It has to complete these tasks confidently and self-assuredly, without in the least being fooled into doubting that such an undertaking is justified.

The duty for this undertaking lies in its historically undeniable existence, and its justification will be determined after the fact in the success of its work. Experience has shown that history only withholds this justification from those who were either too weak to survive, or too incapable and therefore too unsuited. In the long run, God's grace only stays with those who earn it. Whoever acts in the name of a God-created Volk, will only act in this capacity so long as he does not sin against the existence or future of this thing that was placed into his hands by the Creator. Thus it is good that seizure of power is always tied to hard struggle. What was hard-won is usually also bravely defended! But the more stable states are, the greater their benefit to their people!

If it is the party's task to form an organization in which the nation's political selection process will find its continual and eternal completion, then it is its duty to ensure that the leadership of the state will have an ideologically stable character. It must then obey the historical command to establish the premise in its organization for stabilizing the leadership of the state through its selection, training, and placement. It must represent the principle that all Germans are to be ideologically educated to be National Socialists, that the best National Socialists become party comrades, and finally that the best party comrades take over the leadership of the state!

For the future of the German state, the National Socialist Party organization has to provide the highest leadership and has to lead generally, and secondly, in its teaching capacity in the National Socialist state, it must educate the National Socialist Volk that upholds it.

From this we see the delineation of the realms of responsibility of party and state.

The state's responsibility is the continuation of the historically contingent and developed administration of the state organization within the framework and by means of the law.

The party's responsibility is:

1. Building up its organization to create a stable, self-perpetuating eternal nucleus of National Socialist doctrine.
2. Educating the entire Volk according to the thoughts of this great idea.
3. Placing the educated in the state: in its leadership and its administration. Furthermore, the principle of mutual respect and support should rule between the two.

This is the goal.

Right now we still find ourselves in the middle of the culmination of a revolution—that is, the National Socialist revolution; this means the seizure of power must gradually find its completion in taking over leadership. This requires a long transitional phase. As the ferments of the old state (that is, of the old partisan world) could not be immediately totally eliminated, there are many areas that require vigilance over their development, which has not yet been totally secured as National Socialist. Thus it can be that the party might be forced to step in and admonish or correct where it is evident that governance is running afoul of National Socialist principles. But these corrections can only succeed more due to the National Socialist government institutions and positions that are already occupied and that are concerned with this issue.

However, the final goal must be that all national and state structures are only made available to National Socialists, which we can accomplish by winning over all Germans into the party and its orbit by means of National Socialist enlightenment and doctrine.

This National Socialism is the ideological foundation for the existence and organization of the German Reich as a National Socialist state. As a worldview, it is forced – if it does not want to betray itself – to be intolerant; this means advocating and following through on the correctness of its views and also its decisions under all circumstances.

Whoever undertakes such a historic mission must subject himself to hard principles. Only the hardest rules and an iron resolve make it possible to unite an already fraught nation, not quite cohesive in its internal composition, into a resilient body, and to successfully lead it politically.

Just as the sickly pacifist could not understand the hardness and exclusivity of Prussian-style upbringing in the army, so also some people today do not want to understand the necessity for National Socialist intolerance, though in reality this should be called its confident sense of responsibility. The reproach that this is foreign to the German character is nonsense. Here it is not up for discussion what is foreign or not foreign to the German Volk, but what is useful to our Volk. Perhaps it also feels foreign to the new recruit in the army to have to blindly follow orders. But it is useful to the whole and thus, in the end, also to himself.

Once an organization has united in itself the elite of those who are suited to the tasks of the organization, then it gains the right to determine the basic requirements for meeting its chosen mission.

In any case, it is more appropriate, beneficial, and worthy of the German character to be unified and led to success by a hard political movement than, by indulging in the temperament and dispositions of the individual, to fall into a thousand pieces and end up as the plaything of superior (because more unified) peoples and their foreign governments.

Let every German consider this. The National Socialist has done tremendous things. It was not our scientists, not our professors and intelligentsia, not soldiers, not artists, not philosophers, thinkers, or poets who pulled our Volk back from the brink; it was only the political soldiership of our party. We are only beginning to feel its effects, and its enduring meaning will only be measured by posterity.

Let everything else fall away, just not it. The German Volk achieved something wonderful in winning the terrific power of authority that lies in the existence and solidity of such a movement. How many insightful men of other nations would be happy if their nations could command such a solidly founded and authoritative organization as Germany possesses today, and few other states besides.

As the circumstances of our times threaten to become more and more insecure and confused, the greater is the value of an institution that gives our Volk clear and definitive principles again, and that has the courage to attack and answer the toughest problems of the present, which in their novelty no other entity has dealt with or solved.

Today the German Volk has already gained the unity of a strong ideological foundation for thought and action in millions of its countrymen. Thus, it has found and decided on a stance that will be decisive for centuries. The practicability of this foundation will be the basis for all future interpretations of this worldview, and a safe harbor for its continual expansion and completion. But because this worldview is still coming into being and developing, it is all the more necessary to recognize the party's authority as the guiding and deciding entity and the final judge. Whoever does not understand this is incapable of thinking historically, creatively, and constructively.

It may aid understanding if we keep taking the army as a comparison. The wish and will for self-assertions, and hence the defense of one's own life, must live in the innermost being and feelings of all men. Yet it is in the living organization of the army that this instinct for self-preservation receives the disciplined guidance that it needs to be fully and practically realized. It alone prevents everyone's self-preservation instinct and everyone's different perceptions, judgments, and opinions from descending into a wild war of all against all. It bridles the wild will of the individual in order to attain an unbridled will of all!

When opinions change and differ on the necessity of a fight, the potential success of a campaign, the nature of a war, or the appropriate strategy—when this confusion threatens, it is especially important that hard, solid leadership gives a coherent line and direction in the army.

Likewise, when the National Socialist worldviews of individuals— many of whom may be in the beginning stages of seeking, seeing, and understanding—are diverse and insecure, and the more everything is still in development, the more important it is that this diversity of views and conclusions bends to the strong and—if necessary—harsh direction of the party through the blind preservation of its authority. This is the highest national interest, and so also the chief duty of every person who cares for and struggles for his Volk.

Here it is not a matter of fallibility or infallibility. As inappropriate as it would be for an army leader, commander, or even the individual soldier to apply his own imagination and opinion as a rubric to judge the correctness of a command given to him, so it would also be inappropriate in political goal-setting and leadership for the wild lone wolf to excuse his actions by asserting the correctness of his opinion or the error of the party's stated opinions, decrees, or commands.

When the party as such demands that its views are accepted as the only valid views on all political-ideological things, then it is first necessary that this principle is followed in its ranks with fanatical conscientiousness; namely, as the party demands the Volk's subordination under the will of the party, so it must also be that within the party the leadership is subordinated to an unalterable law.

There is no release from obedience to this principle. Whosoever injures it in any way injures a principle that until then was a protection to himself, and that then leaves him. Whoever is untrue to this principle, no matter his position, should not expect that those party comrades under him will then treat this principle with any more worth and validity in regards to him. This is the deepest meaning of the ancient Germanic saying, that *infidelity slays its own master.*

Above all, it is impossible to demand the whole nation pay more respect and obedience to the party's decrees than the individual party member is ready to pay to his superior.

In connection to this I must here take a stance against the oft repeated phrase, especially uttered by the bourgeois side: "The Führer yes, but the party, that is a different matter!"

No, sirs!

The Führer is the party, and the party is the Führer. Such as I only feel myself as a part of the party, the party only feels itself as a part of me. When I will close my eyes for the final time, I do not know. But that this party will live on, *this* I know, and that it will successfully shape the future of the German nation beyond all persons, beyond all weakness and strength, *this* I believe, and *this* I know!

It guarantees the stability of the leadership of the Volk and the Reich, and in its own stability, it guarantees the leadership its necessary authority.

The constitution of the New German Reich will grow out of this solid ground. The Führer has to give the nation and the Reich a party that is the ideological framer and political steerer of German destiny. The more naturally and undisputedly this foundation is set up, the stronger Germany will be. As the representative and organizer of the military might of the Volk, the army must preserve the organized military strength of the Reich and put it at the disposal of the Führer chosen by the movement, for after a new Führer is proclaimed by the movement, he is the master of the party, the head of the Reich, and the commander-in-chief of the armed forces.

If these principles become the unshakeable foundation of the German Volk and its state structures, then Germany will stand up against all the storms that await it.

The two backbone entities of the new Reich should be aware, though, that only together will they be up to their tasks. The party gives the army the Volk, and the Volk gives the army soldiers, but both together thus provide the German Reich the security of inner peace and strength needed for its self-assertion.

Today, as Führer of the Reich and nation, I can personally still help and advise. Only our principles can lead from the personal to the eternal. Leaders will come and leaders will die, but Germany must live. This assertion alone will lead Germany to its life.

But we all will one day be judged against the type and the historical durability of what we build today!

My party comrades, co-leaders of the Volk and the army: we were chosen by destiny to make history in the highest sense of the word. What was denied to millions of people, Providence has given to us. We will still be remembered by the most distant posterity for our works. They should note as the most remarkable and noblest thing that, in an age of faithlessness and general treachery, a fellowship of the greatest mutual fealty was able to form in Germany during our time like never before. We at least know this one thing then: a page of world history will be dedicated to us, the men who together built and secured the New German Reich through the National Socialist Party and the German army.

Then one day we will forever stand beside each other in the pantheon of history, forever bonded in indissoluble loyalty, as we were in the time of our great struggle and its great consummation.

My party comrades!

The seventh Reich Party Congress is fast rushing to a close. Deeply moved, the hundreds of thousands of our fighters return to their lives —

that is, back to their fight. This fight will find them equipped with new courage, new tenacity, and filled with a new strength of purpose. Swelling with emotion, they will remember these historic days and hours, and will yearn for and look forward to the week when the next Reich assembly will bring the old fellow fighters and the new guard together again.

With this joyful assurance we greet the German Volk and our single National Socialist movement.

National Socialist Party, our German Volk and Reich, and its army — Sieg Heil!

THE FÜHRER'S SPEECHES
AT THE 1936 PARTY
CONGRESS OF HONOR

THE COURSE OF THE NSDAP'S EIGHTH PARTY CONGRESS

An introduction

The 1936 Reich Party Congress symbolically began with the Führer's arrival at the Nuremberg Main Train Station at 3:30 that afternoon. Nuremberg greeted the Führer with a festive mood and a forest of National Socialist flags and symbols. All the churches of the old free imperial city ceremoniously rang out from 5:30 to 6 o'clock that evening.

Party Comrade Dr. Dietrich, Press Chief of the NSDAP, held a press reception in the early afternoon at the Kulturvereinshaus, at which not only the German, but also the international press was well represented.

At 4 o'clock on the dot, the Infantry Instruction Battalion picked up the 110 flags of the old army and navy at the division headquarters and brought them to the army's camp, where they were set up in the flag tent.

At 6 o'clock that evening, the Führer was festively received by Chief Mayor Liebel in the presence of the leading men of the party in the large hall of the Rathaus. As a gift of honor from the city, the chief mayor gave the Führer a valuable archival document from the year 1542 related to the fortification of the old imperial city of Nuremberg. In his thank-you speech, the Führer announced that once the Reich Party Congress grounds are complete, they will be the largest facility that will have ever been built.

The festive overture of this first day sounded its last note with the performance of *Die Meistersinger von Nürnberg* in the opera house, with the Führer and his guest of honor in attendance.

In the early morning, 1,600 Hitler Youths marched past the Führer at the Deutscher Hof. Most of them had been on their Adolf-Hitler-March for weeks, and had brought their Hitler Youth banners to Nuremberg by foot.

At 11 o'clock, the Party Congress was formally opened by the Führer's deputy. Thereupon, Gauleiter Adolf Wagner read the Führer's great proclamation.

In the afternoon, Party Comrade Hess opened the great literary exhibition, "The Political Germany." Multiple work conferences began at this same hour, such as the conference of the chief bureau of the NSBO,[10] and of the chief bureau of Handwerk und Handel in the large hall of the Rathaus, and the conference of the Hitler Youth leaders in the conference hall of the Rathaus.

In the evening the great cultural conference of the NSDAP was in the opera house. Here, after Reichsleiter Rosenberg awarded Heinrich Anacker and Professor Lenard the NSDAP's prizes for art and science, the Führer took the stand to deliver a foundational speech about German culture.

The third day of the Party Congress of Honor began with the parade and assembly of the Reich Labor Service on the Zeppelin Field. Forty-five thousand workmen marched past Adolf Hitler for two hours, who then spoke to them after the announcement by Reich Labor Leader Hierl.

The assembly on the newly designed Zeppelin Field turned into the great march of the Reich Labor Service through the streets of the festive city, which were thronging with thousands of people.

At 6 o'clock that evening, the Party Congress continued. Reichsleiter Rosenberg spoke about "The Decisive World Conflict" and Reich Propaganda Leader Goebbels about "Bolshevism in Theory and Practice."

The third day came to an end with the torch procession and the march of thirty thousand political leaders past the Führer at the Deutscher Hof.

The fourth day brought a full slate of special conferences in the morning as well as in the afternoon. The Foreign Organization had its solemn hour in Hercules Hall, the highpoint of which was the consecration of the flags by the Führer's deputy Rudolf Hess.

At 10:30 the following morning, the Party Congress continued.

---

[10] Nationalsozialistische Betriebszellenorganissation (also NSBZO): The National Socialist Factory Cell Organization.

Hauptamtsleiter Reischle and Hilgenfeldt Reich Doctors' Leader Wagner rounded out the picture of the contrast between Bolshevik dissolution and National Socialist work for uplift through speeches about the destruction and liberation of the peasantry, the destruction and securing of families, and about the demographic and racial-political problems.

In the afternoon, the women gathered in the Congress Hall under the leadership of Reich Women's Leader Scholtz-Klink and Hauptamtsleiter Hilgenfeldt to hear the words of the Führer. This day found its highlight along with its uplifting conclusion in the incomparable solemn hour of the political leaders on the Zeppelin Field, where twenty-five thousand flags marched before the Führer. Here the Führer also spoke his words after the honoring of the dead. The nighttime assembly was a powerful confirmation of the allegiance of the corps of political leaders to Adolf Hitler.

On the fifth day of the Reich Party Congress, at 10 o'clock, in the main arena of the stadium and bathed in radiant sunlight, the Führer spoke to the Hitler Youth mustered there.

At 11:30 the same morning, the fourth annual conference of the German Labor Front began in the Congress Hall. The Führer spoke here as well. Furthermore, the president of the Reich Chamber of Commerce, Party Comrade Hecker, Reich Minister Seldte, and Reich Organization Leader Ley all spoke here, as well.

While the Main Organization Bureau had already gathered for their conference in the Katharinenbau at 8 o'clock that morning, the National Socialist People's Welfare gathered at noon in Hercules Hall.

The Party Congress resumed at 3 o'clock that afternoon. The first speaker, Reichsleiter Frank, spoke about National Socialist legal policy; Reichsleiter Dietrich spoke about the problems of the press. The third speaker was Reichsleiter Amann, who spoke about the restructuring of the German press. Party Comrade Reinhardt, the state secretary in the Reich Finance Ministry, had the final word, and was able to illustrate National Socialism's constructive work with impressive data.

At 3 o'clock, the gates of the stadium facility, which was set up with particular richness this year, opened for the Volksfest of half a million. Germany's best athletes met there and gave demonstrations of their Olympic skill for the thrilled mass of people.

The traditional giant fireworks closed the day.

The great roll call of the SA, SS, and NSKK was on Sunday in the Luitpold Arena, in front of the Führer. Here the Führer spoke to his Brown Army. Then followed the great march of the brown formations through the city of Nuremberg, past the Führer at Adolf-Hitler Plaza.

The Party Congress resumed at 6:30 in the evening. There were three speakers: Reich Organization Leader Ley on "The Worker in the New Germany and in the Soviet State," Reich Inspector for German Road Engineering Todt on "German Road Construction," and Reich Labor Leader Hierl on "The Task and Performance of the Reich Labor Service."

As it was in the past year, the last day of the 1936 Reich Party Congress belonged to the young German armed forces. At daybreak, the SA commenced its pack march to Feucht. While the whole afternoon was filled with special meetings of individual offices and commissions, the squadrons of our air force roared over the roof of the old imperial city, and the formations of our army and navy troops mustered on the Zeppelin Field for their first demonstrations.

At 11 in the morning, the victory towers of the SA in Camp Langwasser were dedicated.

The demonstrations of the armed forces had everyone enthralled, and lasted throughout the day. They reached their apex in the afternoon with the great parade before the Führer. The commander-in-chief spoke at the end of this march to the nation's men-at-arms.

The Party Congress resumed in the evening in order to hear the Führer's great concluding remarks. After this, the Führer's deputy closed the Congress.

All the military bands that attended the Reich Party Congress performed the grand tattoo at midnight in front of the Führer at the Deutscher Hof. This marked the end of the Reich Party Congress of Honor.

— Dr. Walther Schmitt

RECEPTION OF THE FÜHRER IN
THE CITY OF NUREMBERG

September 8th, 1936

The Führer's answer to the welcoming address of Chief Mayor Liebel

Herr Oberbürgermeister! Please accept my thanks once again for the heartfelt welcome that you and the city of Nuremberg have prepared for me. It is the sixth time that we meet in the city of the Reich Party Congress, and the National Socialist movement, its fighters and followers, and moreover the whole German Volk will leave Nuremberg's walls newly strengthened and fortified.

I have often had occasion in the past months to follow the progress of the great constructions and improvements that are planned in this city to serve the great festival of our Volk. Whereas last year we experienced the completion of Luitpold Arena, this year the facilities of the Zeppelin Field give us a premonition of the completion of the whole Reich Party Congress Grounds. Thus, the completion of one rally ground will follow the next. A new stadium of the greatest proportions is to be built. The Congress Hall will grow out of the ground, until in six years the entire colossal work can be celebrated as the largest facility that will have ever been built in the world.

Once again, we sense the wonderful contrast between the old and the new beauty of this city. Yet we know that in a few decades the two will meld together into a whole that we call Nuremberg. I am especially pleased that you, Herr Oberbürgermeister, in the name of the city of Nuremberg, give me the old plans and drawings of these beloved old fortifications, towers, defensive corridors, and moats as a present. This will not only be a beloved reminder of the city of the Reich Party Congress, but also a reminder of the hardest year of my own historic work, in which — by the grace of God—I was able to strengthen our Reich's defense and heighten its security.

And so, I thank you again, Herr Oberbürgermeister, for this reception, for this dear present, and I only ask you to pass on this thanks to the whole city, for what would our Party Congresses in Nuremberg be without the Nurembergers themselves? I ask you again, now as always, to greet the old city of our Reich Party Congresses with our German salute: Nuremberg Heil!

THE PROCLAMATION OF THE FÜHRER AT THE OPENING OF THE 1936 PARTY CONGRESS

September 9th, 1936

Party comrades! National Socialists!

National Socialist Germany has once again gathered for the great demonstration. The political fighters and soldiers meet for the eighth Reich Party Congress on this Nuremberg ground that is so hallowed for us National Socialists. While in the past the conferences of the parties were once filled with struggles between different interest groups and power cliques, these conferences of our National Socialist movement are weeks of an intense vow to our idea and to our movement and — for the past four years — to our Volk in the National Socialist Third Reich.

At these greatest demonstrations of our movement, the strongest support for the correctness of our doctrine and principles has always been from visible and repeated success.

And thus, measured against what has already been reached, the tasks that these conferences set for the future have always seemed reachable, even self-evident. But when do we have a better opportunity to look back in satisfaction on what we have accomplished so far than at this fourth Reich Party Congress since we took power?

As in this hour we open the Congress of Honor, we are filled with two sentiments:

First, how can we not look back with immense pride at the past four years, and especially this last one?

Second, what vindication we feel for our efforts, especially as we look around the tattered and floundering rest of the world today!

How many years — even decades — go by in the life of a people without it earning any special mark and any future recognition! How often the inertia of historical processes erases the lives of whole generations from the memory of posterity. Eventless decades flow as a quiet river without achieving the greatness required for historical mention, even though concerned and hustling people lived in them, too. And when posterity remembers three or four years of a nation's history as especially remarkable, it is usually those years of collapse that earn such notoriety, and seldom the years of an actual national rebirth. The breakdown of an empire, the collapse of an economy, the revolutionary destruction of a state structure, the destruction of an authority — all take a shorter time than their construction.

In contrast to this, we National Socialists can proudly make the claim that even Germany's collapse in November 1918 happened at a slower pace than the national resurgence of the past four years.

How thick and viscous the flow of time during the regime before the National Socialist revolution now seems. Indeed, it went increasingly downhill from year to year, but so little sticks in our memory, without any events to fill it and without the involved people possessing any greatness. Each year was like the next. Governments came and governments went. People were replaced and then appeared again. And yet, the more the personnel changed, the less meaningful events were objectively. The question always remained: why all this coming and going, when the results were always the same? And the decline always stayed the same.

In the year 1933, after its fourteen-year struggle for the German man, National Socialism was entrusted with the leadership of the Reich.

And what a miracle has occurred in these barely four years! On this fourth Reich Party Congress since our seizure of power, we National Socialists can stand before the eyes of our followers and enter under the judgment of the nation with unqualified pride.

Now, was this a true revolution, or was it not? Is this upheaval justified to our Volk today by its fruits, or is it not? And above all: who besides us could have brought about this miracle?

National Socialists!

If every Reich Party Congress so far has been a day of vindication for our fight and struggle, then this has never been more the case than for today's. No other could fill us with more gratification than this one! For we have entered an immeasurable ascent in all areas of national life in the last four years.

The tempo and scale of this political ascent is unparalleled; above all, the internal consolidation of the German nation is historically unparalleled. But the most tremendous, crowning achievement of this German ascent was experienced in the twelve months that have elapsed since the seventh Reich Party Congress.

On January 30th, 1933, in a short proclamation, I announced the agenda of our fight to the German people. At that point, I asked for four years' time. After their elapse, I wanted the German people to have judgment over the fulfillment or non-fulfillment of this promise.

Our opponents were convinced that we would never have a chance to ask the nation to pronounce this judgment, because they reckoned the longest our regime could possibly last was six or twelve weeks.

But what has National Socialism made out of Germany in these four years? Which of these opponents could have the gall to step up as our detractors today?

What back then seemed to them to be fantastical and unreachable in my proclamation now seems to us like the humblest description of the achievements that tower above it.

Back then these opponents claimed it was impossible to fulfill the program for the year 1933, which now seems so small. What would they have said if I had shown them the program that the National Socialist administration indeed did complete in four short years?

How they would have mocked us, if I had explained to them on January 30th, 1933, that in four years Germany would have reduced its unemployment by five million down to one million; that the forcible dispossession of German farmers would be ended; that German agriculture would have higher revenues than in any previous year in peacetime; that the gross national product would increase from $\mathcal{RM}$ 41 billion to $\mathcal{RM}$ 56 billion; that German small businesses and the German trades would experience a new bloom; that international trade would recover again; that German port cities would no longer resemble dead ship graveyards, and that in 1936 alone, over 640,000 tons of ships would be under construction in German shipyards; that countless factories would not merely double, but triple and quadruple their workforce, and that countless others would be newly built in barely four years; that a Krupp factory would again quake with the hum and hammering of the machines of the German resurgence, and that all these companies would now recognize as their highest law service to the nation, and no longer unscrupulous individual gain; that the still automobile factories would not only be resuscitated, but would have unprecedented growth, and that the production of motor vehicles would increase from forty-five thousand in the year 1932 to almost a quarter of a million; that in four years the deficits of our states and cities would be eliminated; that the Reich would receive a tax surplus of nearly five billion; that the German Reich Railway would be rehabilitated, and that its trains would run as the fastest in the world; that the German Reich would build roads that, ever since there has been human culture, have not been built with such size and beauty, and that of their projected seven thousand kilometers, after only four years, over one thousand kilometers would have been completed and over four thousand kilometers under construction; that tremendous new settlements with hundreds of thousands of houses would emerge, while new constructions would rise up in old cities that are in a league with the largest in the world; that hundreds of gigantic bridges would span chasms and valleys, and that German culture would prove its immortal value in these and other achievements; that German theater would undergo a resurrection, just as German music would; that through all this, the German Volk would take a lively part in this sweeping spiritual renewal, and that all this would happen without a single Jew appearing in its spiritual leadership anymore!

If I had prophesied then that in four years the whole German press would be filled with a new ethos and only serve German interests, that a new law of professional honor would be proclaimed for the German economy, yes, that the German man would indeed experience a renewal of his character and his conduct; had I predicted then, that after these four years there would be only one Volk, that there would be no social democracy, no communism, no Centrism, but also no bourgeois party that could sin against German life; that there would be no more unions to incite against the employer, and no monopoly to deprive the employee; that after these four years there would no longer be state governments, that there would be no state legislatures anymore, that sixteen flags and sixteen traditions would cease to be and be outrun, and that starting from the worker to the soldier, the whole nation would only anymore march behind one creed and under one flag — what would they even have said if I had prophesied, that in these four years Germany would have freed itself of the slave-chains of Versailles, that the Reich would again have a military draft, that every German would serve two years for the freedom of his country as in peace, that we would be constructing a new fleet to protect our coasts and our commerce, and a new air force would guarantee the safety of our cities, factories, and industrial plants, that the Rhineland would be brought under the control of the German nation and so the Reich would again exercise sovereignty over its entire territory; what would they have said, had I prophesied that this then-so-torn Volk would, before even four years passed, march to the polls with 99 percent turnout, and 99 percent would give their *yes* to the National Socialist politics of restoration, of honor, and of freedom?

Had I prophesied this and all the many other things we have since accomplished four years ago, then they would have branded me as a lunatic, to the laughter of the whole world. But now this has all become reality. This is the feat of barely four years. Who can begrudge it if we all, who were active in this feat, look back on this achievement with satisfaction? Germany's National Socialist political leadership has completed this miracle in this short time, and the National Socialist army that has joined it has fortified this miracle.

Today the Reich is more fortified in its political leadership and its military security than ever before.

But the second great marvel must fill us with bitter satisfaction, and that is the realization that we were unfortunately all too right in our other prophecies.

Unrest, hate, and mistrust fill the rest of the world.

With the exception of one great power and a few other countries, we see the spasms of Bolshevik insurrection and revolution almost everywhere in Europe.

National Socialists!

Is it not almost something symbolic, that while hate rules and ruins are made in other countries, an Olympic celebration of the noblest humanity could take place in Berlin, surrounded by the cheers of a gladdened Volk? No, despite all their best efforts, even the Jewish correspondents can no longer spin this truth and invert into its opposite what millions were able and are able to feel for themselves and see with their own eyes! And this tremendous celebration also gave another answer to the agitations of this damnable clique of international disturbers of the peace.

All these countless people who have now had the chance to see the new Germany for themselves, they cannot deny that, no matter how immense and amazing Germany's rise was, it was not won at the expense of another nation. For who have we harmed in these four years? From whom have we taken anything? Who has lost anything from our rise? If only our critics in other nations had everywhere completed the same inner work as us, instead of believing the wicked international agitators, there could have been, especially in Europe, a firmer community of nations today, which could then more easily master our common needs through communal efforts.

In any case, this amazing and historically unprecedented rise did not fall into our lap as unearned luck; it was the result of unheard-of efforts and nerve-racking worry. What a dumb and thoughtlessly fault-finding world thought, with blatant Schadenfreude, was an ingenious criticism, was simply true. In these four years, the government of the German Volk has had more worries than all other governments may have had in half a century!

But these worries do not weigh on the German government morally, but always mentally and unfortunately also physically; because we were not responsible for the causes of these worries, but rather a fateful past was, as well as unfortunately our own Volk's often too great lack of understanding, and others' inability and unwillingness to understand.

How often did the shameless enemy campaign of lies almost lustfully pounce on the news of a shortage of fat in Germany, the shortage of butter, the shortage of eggs, the shortage of meat?

What a bedlam in the heads of these literary gentlemen. Indeed, it was easier for these critics to record the consequences of an insane human folly than it was difficult for us to overcome these consequences.

While these Judeo-Bolshevik agitators talk of world revolution, and would love to turn human culture into ashes and dust, National Socialist Germany worked with immense effort and difficulty to the limits of its ability to alleviate hardship within the borders of its Reich and to secure the life of the nation into the future.

In those countries whose critics attack us with as much hate as they do superficiality, how easy would it be for their statesmen to solve their economic problems, compared to the difficulty that Germany faced? What do others have to say about hardship when, for example, they possess fifteen or twenty times as much land and soil per capita as Germany? What can they say about difficulties when, in the realm of their monetary sovereignty, they command all the raw materials of the earth?

The challenges of our national economic condition are unendingly difficult.

The 136 people per square kilometer in Germany could never — even with the greatest effort and most ingenious use of all available living space — secure their total self-sufficiency in food. What the German farmer has achieved in these past years is something singular and unprecedented. What the National Socialist state accomplished in cultivating every last heath and every last moor in Germany is not to be surpassed.

Still, there will always be a shortage in several areas of our nourishment despite this. To make up for this shortage through imports is all the more difficult, because we unfortunately do not possess any important raw materials in Germany.

Thus, the German economy is forced to make up for this lack of foodstuffs and raw materials through an industrial export that has to happen under all circumstances, because foodstuffs are an unavoidably necessary import.

It is regrettable that the rest of the world has no sympathy for the character and magnitude of these tasks, thanks to a treatment of these problems that is as frivolous as it is vapid — yes, even unnecessarily hateful. For Germany to buy a unit of value of fat, a greater value of another good has to be exported. Being a requirement for this import, we have to export at all costs, because with food we are talking about something necessary for *life*, not — as some foreign statesmen unfortunately seem to think — evil intentions.

It is then only due to a very regrettable stupidity that some reproach us for having cheap exports, when we are forced to export at all costs to bring home necessary foodstuffs, due to our economic area that is incapable of self-sufficiency.

Then, when an English politician explains that Germany does not need any colonies because it can just buy its raw materials anyway, this statement is about as thoughtful as that well-known Bourbon princess who, when, hearing the revolutionary rabble screaming for bread, puzzled why, if they have no bread, they do not simply eat cake! If the German Volk and the German Reich had not been pressed dry for fifteen years and made to spend all its international savings, if it had not lost all its foreign capital, and above all, if it still possessed its own colonies, then this task would be easier to master.

The argument that colonies would not help us much anyway is unjustified. An administration that can bring about these now undeniable economic feats, under the conditions imposed by Germany's position, would certainly know how to make colonies economically useful. For example, it was harder in our overpopulated country for our governmental and economic leaders to reduce our number of unemployed from 6.5 million to 1 million and at the same time secure everyone's daily bread than it was for other countries, which seem to still be unable to address this question.

Under these circumstances, it required truly monstrous efforts to reduce the number of unemployed and provide them with their daily bread.

Building up a purely domestic economy in Germany is unfortunately only possible on a limited scale, since we lack foodstuffs and raw materials in our current economic territory.

Despite this, we have tried to cultivate all that can be cultivated out of our soil. Obviously, to do so, we had to put an end to the extravagance of free market economics in favor of planned leadership and a planned execution. In doing so, the National Socialist leadership has avoided exerting any more influence on the economy than was absolutely necessary. It also had to put one principle at the forefront of all its considerations and activities.

Neither the economy nor capital are sovereign entities and are thus subject to the law; rather it is the Volk that is sovereign—and thus it alone is the lawgiver.

The Volk does not exist for the economy; rather the economy is the servant of the Volk. And the Volk and the economy are not slaves of capital, but capital is merely an economic tool, and is thus also subordinated to the larger necessities of the preservation of the Volk.

Where would Germany be if we had not gradually enforced these principles in our economic life and let them have their effect? Compared to other peoples, today Germany's largest fortunes are very small. But our average living standard is a relatively high one. The goal of the German economic policy is to raise this living standard among the common people. But as things stand now, this raising can unfortunately not proceed in all directions, but only certain ones.

This is another principle of our National Socialist economic policy: that wages and salaries are not the crucial factor, but production, and with it, that share that goes to each contracting party in the economic process.

National Socialist economic policy has maybe had to forgo certain popular slogans and actions, but by doing so it has spared the German people disappointment.

Our leadership could have very easily raised wages 20, 40, or 50 percent. But a wage increase without an increase in production is a self-deception that the German people have already been through once. According to National Socialist economic understanding, it is insanity to raise wages and then, if possible, to also reduce hours; that would cut productivity. The total earnings of the nation are distributed against the total production that can be consumed. Thus, if the total earnings rise by 15 percent but total production decreases by 15 percent, then this increase in earnings was not just fruitless, but by lowering production, it leads to an outright devaluing of the money supply.

We see an increasing incongruity between total earnings that are rising and total production that is sinking as the last cause of the development of inflation. Thus, it was the National Socialist leadership's iron principle to allow no increase in hourly wages, but to raise living standards through an increase of performance (that is, an increase of production). If today Germany's national economy pays about fifteen billion more in wages and salaries than in 1933, it is only because the total production rose correspondingly. This guarantees that, with increasing wages, the prices stay the same, and thus it is a better result, because it is not a higher reward for the work in and of itself, but for the results of that work.

It is clear that this increase in German production can only occur in those sectors that have enough required materials that we possess in Germany; that is to say, even if we raise the income of our people through the greatest economic efforts and bring every man into employment, all this will still not increase Germany's arable land. In other words, the German grocery market will not be substantially improved with the given limitations of our ground. This is the toughest problem that we face. Since 1933, we have added over five million additional people into our productive economy; this means that we raised their former average income as unemployed by 100 or sometimes 200 percent.

This is certainly the case for most of the many who come into employment. It is understandable that those of our countrymen who are finally at least earning a little, many of whom were undernourished for years, would first storm the grocery markets. But this means that the grocery markets are now overburdened with these five million formerly un-employed people who now have greater buying power. To this we can ascribe the always recurring and seasonal shortages of butter, eggs, fat, and sometimes meat. The argument of our foreign know-it-all advisors that, instead of buying raw materials, our government should buy grocer-ies is as childish as it is willfully dishonest. These raw materials are the prerequisites for having any kind of export, which then enables our mod-est food purchases. If we were to give up this import of raw materials, the consequence would be an immediate increase in joblessness. As the Na-tional Socialist leadership we have an obvious position, though perhaps incomprehensible to foreigners: we are not so much bothered by whether sometimes there is more or less butter, or whether eggs are a little scarcer, but our primary duty is to ensure that we can secure work and a liveli-hood for the broad mass of our Volk, and preserve our people from sink-ing again into the gruesome hardship of unemployment.

We are less interested in ensuring that the upper classes get butter all year round than we are in making sure that the broad masses, if possible, have access to cheap fat, but above all that we do not let them become jobless. Of course, the bourgeois governments of the rest of the world will see this as incomprehensible, but Germany has no bourgeois government, but a National Socialist one. It is, therefore, also a great task of our na-tional economy to steer the consumer power of our people in a direction that we can satisfy with the possibilities of our own national production. As an increase of agricultural production can only occur to a very limited extent, our production must increase in other areas. We have to lead and educate the Volk to consider the national interest in these areas and point their wants and desires in these directions. When foreign critics blame German armament for the German butter shortage, assuring us of arming ourselves instead of buying butter, I would advise the esteemed macroe-conomist to consider: what would happen if the millions of German workers that are currently engaged in domestic German production, in-cluding armament, were to all be employed in factories making articles for export? I'm afraid that these policy geniuses would then really start howling about the unavoidable flooding of the world market with cheap German exports.

The German economy, like any healthy national economy, first has the responsibility to utilize its own potential for the economic support of its Volk as well as possible, and only secondarily to participate with its own healthy economy in the world economy.

Because the National Socialist state does not under any circumstances want to lower our population, but in fact wants to increase the natural fertility of our nation, we are forced to consider the consequences of this development for the future. A substantial increase in territory is not possible, and a substantial increase in exports is hardly foreseeable.

Thus the task of the National Socialist political and economic leadership is to investigate very exactingly which raw materials, fuels, and so forth we can manufacture in Germany on our own.

The money we save in this way should help secure nourishment in the future and any materials that cannot at all be produced by us here. And today I present this as the brand-new four-year program:

In four years, Germany must be totally independent of importing all materials that Germany is in any way capable of producing through our chemistry, engineering, and mining.

The mass of people that will be free after the completion of our rearmament will help the national economy by being employed in the rebuilding of our great German materials industry. With this, we hope to again increase our national production in many areas, and to make this a part of our domestic economic circulation. We would use the revenues from our exports first on purchasing foodstuffs or, as the case may be, the purchase of those still missing raw materials.

I have not mentioned just now the ordinances necessary for the execution of this tremendous German economic plan. The plan will succeed with National Socialist energy and vigor. Independent of that, Germany cannot give up on a solution for its colonial claims. The German Volk's right to life is just as great as the rights of other nations!

My National Socialist comrades, I know that this program presents us with a tremendous task. However, in many areas it is already scientifically solved: new methods of production are being tested, and are already being decided upon and implemented. Thus, it will only be a question of our energy and determination to actualize this program. As National Socialists we have never known the word "impossible," and we do not want to let it degrade our vocabulary in the future.

In four years, we will again deliver vindication to the nation regarding the gigantic work of the securing of its nourishment, and thus its life and its independence.

Now the mouths of Western democrats might spew anew the complaint that we give no freedom for self-interest even in the economy, but instead put the economy in the straitjacket of state planning. But you, my fellow countrymen, will understand that this is not about democracy or freedom, but existence or non-existence. This is not a debate about the freedom or profits of a few industrialists, but about the life and freedom of the German nation. Whoever believes that he cannot exist with this freedom and this life has no right to exist in our community. Posterity will not ask us whether in this critical and dangerous age we upheld democratic freedom — mere licentiousness — but whether we were able to protect a great Volk from political and economic destruction. Besides, we have millions of decent, working people in our cities and in the country. They give us their trust, and they expect us to make decisions that will preserve their life. Compared to this, how laughable and meaningless is the talk of certain democrats and Jewish journalists.

If this task of the economic preservation of our Volk is to succeed, it will require a great constitutional effort and the determined will of our Volk. Without internal social peace, this colossal program cannot be solved.

The National Socialist government is a government so sovereign and so far above all economic obstacles that, in its eyes, the terms "employer" and "employee" are meaningless. Before the interests of the nation, there are no employers and employees; there are only those engaged in work and the whole Volk. Only with social peace can we complete the huge tasks of our national economic condition. Where would we be today if we had the chaos of strikes and lockouts like other countries do? Where would Germany be, if everyone felt he could determine his own wages or salary according to his own whim? The more clearly we see the magnitude of the tasks before us, the more we realize the necessity of totally engaging all working Germans in the completion of these tasks. It also becomes clearer that this engagement cannot be hampered by selfish interests or by insane institutions, wherein one is only capable of babbling when it is time for action.

I would not look to the German future with such confidence, and I would not set these tasks with such trust or believe in their solutions, if I did not know that social freedom is guaranteed within Germany through the National Socialist Party, and that the engagement of German willpower and manpower is founded in the will of our movement. It is the instrument that reaches beyond people and time that is available to the

Volk's and Reich's leadership that is itself founded in it.

In just these days, when everywhere we witness the signs of catastrophe among nations, I can look confidently at the movement that has achieved the miracle of the last four years, and that will continue to lead Germany in the preservation of its existence.

Just as Germany could only solve these past tasks and can only solve our coming tasks under the condition of the internal peace of the nation, so we believe that the European community of nations and states can only look forward to a happy future if it maintains peace between nations. But no matter what, it is our fierce determination that Germany can under no circumstances be left to become the defenseless pawn of some foreign military power.

We have enjoyed enough of the experiences of the past eighteen years. We know the lot of those who believe that they, while powerless, can hope for foreign justice or aid. We see the signs of an evil age rising around us. What we preached for years about the greatest danger of this closing second millennium of our Christian history is becoming a terrible reality. The Bolshevik wire-pullers are beginning their undermining work everywhere. In an age when bourgeois statesmen speak of non-interference, an international headquarters of Jewish revolution is upending the continent from Moscow, through the airwaves and through thousands of financial and activist channels. Do not let anyone tell us that we in Germany will develop a psychosis through the continual evidence of these facts and of these dangers.

We are National Socialists. Therefore, we have never been afraid of Bolshevism. But we also do not belong to that bourgeois guild that, even at the precipice, still dances to the tune of "are you afraid of the big bad wolf," and shuts its eyes and does not want to call white "white" and red "red" until, finally, the brutal facts suddenly force their eyes open, and then they scurry under their beds with chattering teeth.

We National Socialists have never been afraid of communism. We just recognized the destructive Jewish doctrines of worldwide sedition, studied their devilish methods of preparation, and warned of their consequences. By the way, even when I was Führer of the movement, with not even a hundred followers yet, compared to the millions of the communist movement in Germany, I always had the conviction that we would beat it and root it out of Germany. We warned about this movement in Germany for fifteen years, while the bourgeoisie laughed. We destroyed it, while the bourgeoisie trembled pitifully and capitulated to it. Today we do not fear a Bolshevik invasion of Germany, not because we do not believe in it, but because we are determined to make the nation so strong that it can defend against any external attack with the most brutal resolve, just as National Socialism has already dealt with this sedition domestically.

This is the reason for our military measures. These German measures will wax or wane to the degree that the dangers that threaten us increase or decrease. It gives us no pleasure to restrict the strength of our Volk to arms manufacturing and the barracks. However, we are also man enough to stare hard and cold into the eyes of this necessity.

And here in this proclamation I would like to express, to the whole German Volk, that I am convinced that to defend Germany's external peace, just as I secured our internal peace, it is necessary to not shy away from any measures that can not only give the nation a feeling of security, but that above all makes us feel the independence of the Reich is absolutely guaranteed. The Moscow communist agitators Neumann, Béla Kun, and their comrades, who today lay waste to Spain under orders from the Comintern movement, will play no role in Germany, and the incitement of the Moscow stations that are transforming unhappy Spain into a pile of ashes and rubble will not be repeated in Germany. The National Socialist Party and the National Socialist army of the Third Reich will make sure of that. But the German Volk has no other wish than to live in peace and friendship with all those who want peace and who leave us alone in our own land.

Consequently, in consultation with the Reich War Minister, I have decided that the two-year term of service for our army will be enacted forthwith. I know that the young German man will obey this necessity without even a whimper. Germany's current government has a right to demand this of the Germans, because all of us served not just two years during peace, but four years in the greatest war of all time. And we did it for Germany, for our Volk, for the German homeland. And the National Socialist movement wrestled fifteen years and demanded the greatest sacrifices of its followers to save Germany from the internal Bolshevik enemy and adversary.

In this love for our Volk and in our readiness to commit ourselves to the very last for freedom and independence, we feel kinship with all those nations who are moved by the same impulse. But Germany can be happy to know that its internal and external peace is protected and secured through its own strength. The more turbulent the world around us becomes, the deeper the German Volk's loyalty to the National Socialist movement will become—the movement to which it owes its historic resurrection. All the more, it will admire the strong leadership that saved it from its own brokenness and made it into a proud, confident Volk, eliminating the forces of dissolution and pulling the nation together in the very last hour to master its political, cultural, and economic challenges. And the more the sky above our Fatherland reddens from communist upheaval, the more National Socialist Germany will feel love and devotion to its army, to which we owe our greatest and proudest traditions.

She once raised us, too. We came out of her, we who then established the party, the SA, the SS, and the NSKK. It gave us the men with whom we established our first storm troopers, the guard of our movement. And for all time to come, the young sons of our Volk shall again belong to it for two years, so that they gain the strength and skill in the struggle for the Fatherland's independence and freedom to protect the German nation.

On this fourth Reich Party Congress since we took power, I am in position to express this freely. I look back happily on this proudest achievement of our National Socialist government and our National Socialist soldiery.

Now, generation after generation will again make this noblest sacrifice that a man can offer.

In the year 1936, in the fourth year of the National Socialist regime, the German Volk has ended its period of dishonor.

Long live the National Socialist movement, long live our National Socialist army, long live our German Reich!

THE FÜHRER'S SPEECH AT
THE CULTURAL CONFERENCE

September 9th, 1936

Who can doubt that today we no longer live on the eve, but in the midst of one of the greatest controversies that has ever beset humanity? There is an unbearable tension hanging above the nations. And as always, it will not be solved promptly and everywhere at once, but through geographically and temporally disparate actions that are nonetheless internally tied together. The international character of this happening follows from the internationality of its causes and of the forces involved.

Just as all great world struggles find their deepest causes only in the drive of individual nations for preservation and survival, so also the controversy of our day follows from the life goals and objectives of certain races. They are rattling a world order that we took for granted and that seemed unchangeable, both in its structuring of the individual national organisms as well as in the manner of our living together and beside each other. As always, only very few of the people who are involved or who are affected by these occurrences actually become conscious that the seemingly loosely related events, or events that are far apart in time and the course of history, are actually points of a complete narrative, acts of a single drama.

A century and a half ago, the world was surprised and troubled by the terrible forces of the French Revolution. A genius war god emerges out of the chaos, and storms the already weakened European world. The pious prayers and patriotic hymns are drowned out by the furioso of the Marseillaise. Dynasties and states are broken in the storms of this combative period.

A few decades later, the signal fires burn across Europe once again. A new wave of revolutionary convulsions sweeps across the ancient states of the continent from the land of liberty, equality, and fraternity. And in short order, ever more dynasties fall, and more states transform from their traditional authoritarian forms into modern democracies. But the more the holiness of the old principles disappears, the greater grows the unrest that grips Europe. States die and nations are born. Ancient nations become brittle and fragile, and the fundamental racial elements of nations disappear from our eyes behind a socialist veil as all the classes begin struggling against each other, as they did before in the time of their forging.

The dissoluteness in political developments also gets translated into economic life. What was a servant for centuries is now the master. In capitalism, what was formerly a means seeks to become an end in itself. Through this disturbance of a hitherto organic development, it sows the seeds of further destruction. A seemingly impersonal global power thus reaches into the personal fates of people. An aging Moltke had the horrible hunch that a time was nearing when soldiers would have to take up the sword for financial interests. An American investigative committee has lifted the veil of ignorance from the eyes of the people for a part of the events of the World War and has vindicated the great field marshal's predictions. This seemingly meaningless war corrodes the nations of the earth and forges the means for new collapses in the multifaceted realm of man's organizational, economic, and cultural activity.

The hardest social struggles overshadow the lives of nations in recent decades; social revolutions destroy each other. And while we are here gathering the great community of our nation, in another country, the community of their nation is being destroyed and torn apart. The bloody civil war begets new hatred between people and begets further evil that only bodes ill for the rest of the world. We can summarize the past century and a half of human history like this. Whatever events might seem coincidental, unique, or totally independent in these years, will one day be recognized as the more or less necessary consequence of one single political plotline.

Certainly, most of the actors, whether they are acting or acted upon, will not be conscious of this as such a historical process. Who among you can discern the consequences of laws from a motivated cause? How many believe they are able to form history through their own will and strength, and yet are mere stones in a game whose beginning, middle, and end will always be strange and undiscoverable to them!

Today, after two millennia, the fall of the ancient world seems to us like the obvious result of an inevitable series of causes that worked their effects across half a millennium and that include internal as well as external causes. We call these events Christianity and the Barbarian Invasions. A thousand years later, the inevitability of these historical events of this period already became clear to a few genius seers. Cause and effect are no more secret today. But all those who back then thought to determine the tragic course of events in detail had hardly any insight into the higher inevitability of the plotline that they were subject to. So pressure begets pressure, hardship begets hardship, resistance awakens new violence, and new violence leads to new resistance, all without the recipient, who reciprocates the blow he was dealt, ever being in a position to see through or get a wider view of the greater plot, in which destiny has deigned to let him play a modest role.

But that is how it ever was, and how it will ever be. He who stands underneath the trees will not recognize the forest. He who fights for the individual destiny of nations will rarely grasp the common destiny. Insight into centuries will usually be locked to one who devotes all his senses, thoughts, and actions for the sake of decades.

And despite this, every age of human history has had prophets who were able to see beyond their own lifespan and recognize causes and the inevitability of the overall process. Happy are the nations where such prophets are not writers, but statesmen! For the prophet's silent insight counts for little or nothing in the face of the more pressing real events in the life of a people, unless the prophesying finds its forceful substantiation through its own indisputable historical merit.

It was possible for a Frederick the Great or a Kaiser Joseph II to draw practical conclusions from the premonition of the collapse of the existing human social order. Through this, they were able to negate a whole number of precursor causes that seemed to justify the coming revolutionary events; the infectiousness of the idea that drove the French Revolution was thus prevented in Germany!

Such historical exceptions still do not invalidate the rule that, in most cases, contemporaries do not recognize the deeper causes and the inevitability of the course of their own time's history.

So, we cannot shake the feeling that only a fraction of people — and especially unfortunately, only a fraction of their leaders — have the correct recognition of the causes and the context of the historical events of the present.

Mankind's path from individual to family, to clan, to tribe, and to state winds through an immeasurable span of time.

The scope and magnitude of communal capacity grows proportionately to the progress of organizational centralization.

The formation of every society has depended and always will depend upon the overcoming of the unbridled libertinism of the individual in favor of taking on binding duties and burdens for the whole.

As long as men exist, the conflict between seemingly unlimited freedom for the good of the individual and the imposed unfreedom for the good of the community will always remain.

The unlimited freedom of the individual prohibits the formation of a greater community and consequently makes the seemingly free individual into a helpless object of the severity of this world's struggle for survival.

The organization of larger communities requires the sacrifice of unbridled individual freedom, and at the same time it maintains a higher and protected standard of living for the individual through its communal ability and the communal safety it makes possible. This is also the prerequisite for all human culture — indeed, for the elevated place mankind has in this world at all.

Every successful attempt to practically implement the striving for individual freedom leads to anarchy. The organizational centralization of individuals through a limiting of individual freedom for the good of the organization of a greater community eventually leads to the state.

The premise and foundation for the existence of the state is and remains the authority of the will that wants to maintain the state.

The spiritual premise for bringing about anarchy, the spiritual foundation of every anarchy, is democracy. No state has ever formed through today's democracy, but every great empire has found its destruction in this kind of democracy. Yes: this democracy's final excesses necessarily lead to anarchy, while authority (or better yet, the authoritarian principle) just as necessarily leads to the state in its final effects — that is, to a higher social order.

It is clear, however, that every higher social order is only reasonable and tolerable when the authoritative will that governs it arises from the community of blood that is suited to it.

And it is further clear that, just as every other human inheritance has to be earned anew, the inherited human social order must also be fought for and earned anew. As states did not emerge from the democratic principle of unlimited individual freedom, so it can also not be conserved through concessions in this direction. What its creation required in terms of struggle and toughness cannot be maintained through indulgence and weakness.

The organization once lifted itself up at the expense of individual freedom. It is no wonder that in all weak periods, this conquered and bound freedom tries to return to its primordial state. But with democracy, states have opened up the doors and the surest path to the retrogression of their existence. The end of such a path can only be anarchy, the dissolution of human community. The elements opposed to collectivization were not discussed and parlayed with in the age when human society was being built, and so in the age of society's conservation and evolution we also cannot make a pact with anarchy or consider concessions to it.

When the objection is raised that Marxism in no way leads to anarchy, but instead actually tries to build up a new society, then this can only mean to replace one existing human organization with another, which in this case means replacing the existing authoritative will inherent in the nation's community of blood with a different, foreign one. We all know that Bolshevism's goal is to root out the existing organic leadership of a people, replacing it with the Jewish element, foreign to the Aryan peoples. Herein also is founded the internationality of the problem.

Ninety-eight percent of Russia's current leadership in the Soviet republics lies in the hands of Jews, none of whom are either peasants or workers, but merely overbred parasitic global intellectuals who needed a new fertile host. We are seeing the same thing at present as Marxism begins to rage in Spain. The same slaughter and extermination of Spain's autochthonous national and governmental leadership is being perpetrated partly by native and partly by immigrated Jewry.

In the end, the Soviet authoritarian states will sooner or later lead to true anarchy, as the Jewish element possesses a tyrannical capacity, but is never a truly organizational and constructive force. Above all, these elements are driven by an unspeakably cruel will to dominate that has no creative values or skills on its side.

If every higher communal achievement requires a higher community (that is, the state), and if the state itself can only be built upon the overcoming of unlimited permissiveness — that is to say, unbridled individual freedom — then striving for the restoration of this unlimited individual freedom will inevitably not only be connected with the elimination of the state, but of all achievements of the state.

The highest communal achievement of humanity is not at all — as most economists love to think — the so-called economy, but culture. Thus, it is no coincidence that every impulse of anarchy is connected with a wild combat against the noblest communal achievements, namely the cultural ones. In anarchical attempts, the lower individuals bound in the state community have always involuntarily unleashed their anger on those achievements that can be counted as the results of the noblest communal efforts.

We know from Egypt, from the history of the Mesopotamian states, as well as from the more familiar ancient Greco-Roman cultures, that times of anarchical upheaval were always tied to campaigns of destruction against temples, buildings, monuments of art, and so on. There is a straight line that goes from the iconoclasm of the Middle Ages to the *pétroleuses* of the French commune, all the way to the destruction of churches and cultural monuments in Spain.

It is no coincidence that in the moment it believes it can rise up against the state and claim leadership of it, the Jewish element first tries to eliminate the greatest existing communal achievements of the state.

The mockery of given cultural works, the ridicule of honorable historical monuments, the derision of holy cultural inheritances, the cynical parody of immortal masterpieces until all matters of faith are ridiculous, the deliberate inversion of all art-historical concepts into their opposite (making a fool of healthy and natural human sensibilities), the cultivation of everything vile and ugly and markedly sick: all these are just single features of a complete plot of rejecting the highest of humanity's communal works and achievements. And ultimately this is also a rejection of the communal structure as such.

Thus, there is an inseparable connection between the Jews' destructive effects in economic life and their no less destructive effects on all areas of human culture. When these Jews seem to affirm or even further culture, then it is almost always only for the purpose of shrewdly exploiting a noble human work that cannot at that moment be eradicated.

This is a fundamental tenet: no man can have an inner affiliation to a cultural work that is not rooted in the character of his own heritage.

With a generally decent education, it is certainly possible for us to respect and regard the cultural works of other peoples even when they are deeply unintelligible and not very moving to ourselves. But this mindset is totally alien to the Jewish people, which indeed has always been totally unartistic at least in the way of creating, and also has, in its thousand-year history, only ever displayed the ugly trait of negation, and never of affirmation.

From such a view, we can also gain the following: if the blather about the "internationality" of art is as dumb as it is dangerous, then it is no less damaging to believe that politics and culture are two matters that have nothing to do with each other. No, the opposite: if culture is to be regarded as the highest output of a community, and this communal output can only emerge thanks to the existence of a greater communal structure, then it follows that culture is inseparably bound to those eternally creative powers that uphold it and that give wing to its nobler spirit.

Whatever human advancements we can trace are all fleeting and are always displaced by new insights, experiences, and their objective results. We sometimes hear that claim, seemingly so correct and yet so shallow, that the precondition for every art is the economy. No! No! The precondition for the economy and for art is the state, meaning the creative and leadership power that lies within the peoples.

This political creative power finds its more or less happy foundation just as much in the economic and the temporal as in the cultural and eternal. The opinion that the greatest economic wealth of nations is identical to a higher human culture rests on a totally superficial familiarity, if not a blind unfamiliarity, with the history of human development.

What keep the historical image of human states alive for us have always been cultural achievements, not economic ones. There may have been, and certainly there were, people who had a much more blooming economic life than the ancient Greeks. But these live on immortally through history thanks to their cultural achievements, while the others pass into obscurity for the lack of these—and rightly so. For why should humanity be burdened with the knowledge of people whose only purpose in life may have been to fill their bellies, who were also driven by seeking the luxury that lies in fulfilling one's personal needs? That is how it is in individual life. All that wealth that people spend on their basic needs is forgotten, and only the enduring testaments that they build and leave behind will later bear witness for them. The handwritten book of the starving philosopher will live longer in human history than the lucrative enterprise of some vulgarian capitalist.

And do not tell me that this philosopher could not have written his book without the economic process. There have been musicians, immortal to the world, who died of hunger or typhus, while there have been Croesusses who had all their worldly wishes satiated and yet — and thanks be to God that it is so — were forgotten by posterity. The great cultural works are without a doubt the most sublime expression of exaltedness over the other creatures of this world that man has ever found. Yet still they will always be alien to those who neither begin, nor internally take part in this march of humanity, but somehow get stuck in the animalistic. Thus, in all peoples, cultural anarchy lies in wait alongside political anarchy, and cultural irreverence alongside political irreverence.

Thus, cultural and political Bolshevism go hand in hand. But the more homogeneous the mass from which a people forms, the more homogeneous will be their attitude toward the problems of culture, art, and so on. But there will be two eyes that view culture even in the most closed state: the eye of the part that truly forms the state, that factor that truly creates the culture, and the eye of that element that is melded into the community, but always only passive.

But woe if this less valuable element is ever given back all the option of striving for its individual freedom by way of some political loosening or dissolution of this community. This unleashed inferior humanity will then immediately lay the torch to the cultural works of the now-disintegrated community. Germany stood before this fate, too; as communism set fire to the Reichstag, it was supposed to be the start of a program of destruction that would have been no different from the Paris Commune in 1871, or the Bolshevik Revolution, or the attempt, after the arson of the Vienna Palace of Justice, to set the red rooster upon the venerable old cultural metropole on the Danube,[11] or the burning down of Spanish churches and venerable palaces today.

Therefore, human culture is dependent on overcoming this destructive

---

[11] Translator's note: an old German expression meaning to set ablaze.

symptom of human communities, which are themselves dependent on overcoming the Marxist infection, which would ultimately elevate a people whose character is totally culturally uncreative and unartistic to world leadership. The race of state-founders can never outsource or pay for culture, because culture is in all times only conceivable as an expression of the character of the leadership of the peoples.

This is the only way for a cohesive art to form, one that is rooted in the soul of a people and is understood by the character of a people and thus preserved alive. To let a golden temple be built for you by Phoenician architects is no proof of the cultural ability of a people, only of its inherent snobbery. Thus, we can prophesy to today's world that if democratic subversion is not overcome, and with it the danger of an anarchic retrogression of humanity is not avoided, then the world will not experience any growth of culture, only its decline.

The commission, impetus, and completion of humanity's greatest cultural achievements are thanks to the authoritative will that has created and led human communities. The authoritative will has forever been the greatest commissioner of art. It has not only always created the preconditions for cultural achievement, but also determines their form.

The more forcefully the authority of political will appeared in the history of human nations and states, the greater cultural achievements could be. That the highest cultural achievements of all the Western peoples in, for example, the realm of architecture possess such similar traits is only because the force that founded these peoples and states, shaped and formed them, always came from the same root.

This common root also gave us European people the creative capacity for our somehow always similar cultural works, just as our political developments always went according to the same laws, out of the same beginnings, and through the same methods, despite all our familiar quarrels.

When the question of the use of human cultural works is thrown at us—a question that was likewise aimed at Pericles, and we will not be spared it either—it will be answered by the following: the man who thinks exclusively economically can only see his life's purpose in the frame of his economic activity. But he cannot deny that this certainly necessary economic activity was not made possible by chaos, but through order, meaning that before man can have a higher economic activity there must be a form of higher order, a higher organization. It is very bad when the economy presumes to lead states, or even to rescue them. This is a real misfortune, for when humanity starts to think this way, it soon destroys states. The economy did not found the state, but founders of states created the conditions that allow for economic activity.

If the existence of the economy depends on the existence of a higher order, the state, than from a purely economic perspective, everything that primarily promotes, strengthens, and conserves this order is also materially beneficial to the whole. There is nothing that can be a more tremendous testament to the greatness of this order than this order's highest communal achievement. The highest communal achievement is always the cultural, because it represents a general glorification of communal work through its highest achievement, instead of serving merely the satiation of individuals' personal needs and desires.

Hence, cultural activity is an element of the moral justification of human social order.

For this reason, cultural activity is seen as something dangerous, and is attacked, and, when possible, destroyed by everything that seeks to eliminate human order. Conversely, it is logical that its preservation would be significantly in the interest of the preservation of order, but that also means it is in the interest of economic life. Therefore, I can judge the measure of a regime's economic knowledge in any age by the measure of its appreciation of cultural achievements.

Nothing in this world is forever. Everything is and will remain contested. Every concern of the state is nothing other than an attempt to forestall collapse. But there is nothing with which I can forestall the disintegration of the elements of a human society more than with the demonstration of a community's highest, immortal works.

Recognizing and heeding its importance and necessity to life, truly great state and community leaders of all ages have paid particular attention to these demonstrative underpinnings of a community's higher meaning. It is, by the way, a tremendous error to believe that any human society would have been easier if it had forgone certain cultural works. Like everything in this world, poverty and wealth are ultimately only relative terms. He who only thinks in material terms is always to be regarded as the poorest. Whoever is able to steer a people away from a material perception and toward an ideational one will have the least to suffer from ever-present material hardship.

When Marxism mobilizes material instincts, then it is only because it believes this to be the understandable signal for that passive mass within nations that did not form the states but was only formed through state-formation. It is the appeal to those most primitive primal instincts that, once mobilized, can most easily be deployed for the destruction of that community that must take from the individual's freedom for the benefit of the life of a whole, and that can therefore only lead to the material gain of the whole through the idealistic renunciation of the individual.

In erecting temples to the gods, religions lead humanity beyond the temporary fulfillment of individual desires toward the higher experience of a communal ideal. They create a tremendous monument to faith, past which even the most superficial people cannot go without taking notice, without it admonishing and at the same time elevating them!

The usefulness of art should be seen and measured only in this way. It should fill us all with sadness to take the other side of material gain into consideration and, for example, add to our calculations that tourism is a substantial part of our economic life. But tourists only go where either nature or man has created something prodigious or beautiful. Nature's attractions are already established and do not require human correction, while the manmade owe their existence to man's energy and effort, the will, and the willingness to sacrifice. So one builds great structures, one thus increases the attraction of a city or a country, and in the course of a hundred years one would certainly have their investment paid off several times over, in purely material terms. What would Venice be without its palazzi, its churches, or Rome without St. Peter's or its ancient temples, the ruins of its past. I see this kind of justification for cultural achievement as a regrettable concession to political and economic stupidity.

Indeed, the European peoples are so essentially related, that the cultural works of one Volk in most cases are in such agreement with the works of others, that they can be truly and deeply admired by them. Surely this is also useful in the capitalist sense! However, this is not the purpose of constructing great buildings, the efforts of great composers, immortal poets, and deep thinkers. The worth of these works cannot be measured according to superficial purposes, like a sort of international representation or their commercial appraisal. No, it is a demonstration of a people community's justification, existence, and persistence for itself and for others. In bearing witness to a people's standing in this world, such cultural works also secure material gain.

Whatever this gives states or other human communities in terms of the justification of their existence, this also fortifies and helps secure the preconditions for the entire rest of the community's life. And in this sense, the highest ideational value of great art is always also a weighty material value. When the Teutonic Order built its Malbork Castle, this cultural communal work served as the surest objective foundation for this entity, but in a measure that pales in comparison to the true greatness of this event.

May we all learn from this! For National Socialism has the historic mission to establish a new authority in our national body, which was sliding its way toward anarchy by way of democracy. In saving the state from the clutches of a purely economic worldview and recognizing its purpose, we are paving the way for a return of millions of souls into the community of the German Volk.

In an age of destructive subversion and general decline, we are fortifying the community structure of our national life on earth for the purpose of greater achievements, with the result of greater utility for all individuals within our community.

May the tremendous meaning of this slow formation of a new and unshakably confident authority be grasped by all those whose own existence is irrevocably dependent on such an authority. May the pillars of our economy grasp this, may the leaders of our churches grasp this, but above all, let the disciples and proponents, the shapers and creators of our German culture grasp this!

May they all grasp and understand that this work of reestablishing a blind authority that is not subject to subversive criticism in an age where the anarchic tendencies of dissolution are visible everywhere is the most important work that humanity can be tasked with, and that every gnawing and nagging of this authority is a sin against our community, for which every weakening of this authority can only lead toward the crippling of the communal will and the removal of our community structure. May they understand that the reestablishment of such an authority will help us all past all other difficulties, and that conversely the loss of this authority must lead to the greatest catastrophes, some of which we can already see announcing themselves in Europe, and that at the end of this catastrophe, anarchy awaits, or else the establishment of an even more brutal authority.

May the pillars of our Volk's cultural life understand that such an authority can be the truest blessing for our people only if it is rooted in the blood of our Volk. Only then can we forge the preconditions for our Volk's ascent in all domains of human culture!

May they also understand that the National Socialist state, like all other great creations in the world, will require the cultural underpinnings that will allow it to complete its task. Just as human society can only be built on the overcoming of personal freedom — that is, the overcoming of unbridled freedom for the benefit of communal bonds — a similar line must be found in culture, one that lets the creations of individuals be filled with a greater idea that takes their unbridled, capricious, purely private notions, and lends them the lineaments of a common worldview.

But may they also understand that this uniform line will not reveal itself in political, nor in economic, nor in cultural life out of the so-called free play of forces. This free play of forces, introduced by democracy, was ended with National Socialism's victory. The only point of this game could have been to bring the strongest force into view before the eyes of the nation and give it to it as its leadership. This happened! But after the free play of forces, the time comes for communal work and communal reestablishment. Democracy only pulls us down. The principle of the authoritative will, however, wants to end this period of dissolution and inaugurate a new period of ascent, of constructive further development. Thus, the victor of this free play of forces, the National Socialist idea and the movement that carries and promotes it, will take over not only political, but also economic and cultural leadership. It sets the tasks, and it determines the tenor of its fulfillment. No one wields more authority than it, but just as well, no one has higher internal standards.

As politics cannot afford to follow arbitrary notions in a period of construction, as in decent times the individual member of society is not allowed to live out his whims and fancies without regard for others (to sin against his contemporaries), and as such time periods do not allow the economy to operate wantonly according to private interests and personal utility, so also the development of art and culture in such times cannot be at the mercy of individual notions. For such notions do not know the meaning of a communal attitude, and too often they believe they are free of any obligations toward the community and the special tasks it demands. This, however, is a capital error.

A Christian age could only possess a Christian art; a National Socialist age can only possess a National Socialist art.

As the National Socialist state sets the tasks, and indeed has today already set the agenda in the domain of culture, so it will also keep watch over the larger disposition of their completion. And so the period of Bolshevik mockery of art is over in Germany, because this Bolshevik and "modern" art is an anarchical retrogression.

But National Socialist art has to serve our community's development. National Socialist art can no longer tolerate the phenomena of the decadent world that now lies behind us, whose democratic destruction also quite clearly carried over into the cultural domain. We love what is healthy. The best core of our Volk, based on body and soul, shall be the definitive benchmark. We only wish for this core's glorification in our art. The law of our beauty shall always be *health*.

Translated to the architectural, this means clarity, purposiveness, and — arising from both — beauty.

We have nothing to do with those certain elements who know National Socialism only through hearsay and all too easily confuse it with undefinable Nordic phrases, and who now begin their motivational research in some fabulous Atlantic cultural circle. National Socialism strongly rejects this type of Böttcherstraße culture. We see a new generation growing around us. Light, air, and sun present us with a new ideal. In its bodily beauty we experience a rebirth of a truly new art. Its health guarantees its conformity to the rest of our political will and activity.

While we are resolved to make this new man's health and his perception of beauty the benchmark against which we measure all our cultural works, we will also build the path to a truly timeless form that will be founded upon the unchanging character of our Volk. The cultural leadership of our Volk must exert itself in all realms of art. And even today we are happy in the knowledge that this is no mere wish, but we are already experiencing its fruition. As we free our people from the anarchical elements of subversion and thus destruction in the political realm, so we will also remove those in the cultural realm who, either by design or by lack of skill, helped or even still want to help establish the cultural conditions for political collapse.

The National Socialist state will draw its practical applications from these recognitions. We know that the coherent education of a people is not secured in all places at the same time through some announcement, but that the new insight is revealed at a specific time in a specific place.

Thus, we will begin our cultural work with a number of tremendous documentary works, convinced that the undying example of the past will remain the best teacher in all ages. For within this example lies the power to reach that which is unreachable for anarchists, namely *form*, and consequently the ability to create a style.

It is our will that we again find the way through the scatteredness of our individual cultural works to a great style of both fulfilling and increasingly communal work.

This is the purpose of the enormous building projects that we have pursued and will shortly pursue in several places in the Reich.

The new Nuremberg of our Reich Party Congresses emerges out of such intentions. Here we must create to the greatest degree possible a style-setting testament that will be a monument of both pride and belonging to this community for millions of Germans. Out of this same spirit and with the same agenda, the transformation of the capital city of our movement is taking place, and soon also the transformation of Berlin as the capital city of the German Reich. But the great works taking shape here will not only bless our Volk in the present, but will also fill it with pride in the future. The only truly immortal investment of human effort is art!

THE FÜHRER TO THE WORKMEN

September 10th, 1936

As we declared the law of National Socialism in Germany, it was clear to us that we would not be able to abolish the given conditions and create a new condition by way of paper proclamation and decrees. We knew that a true socialism could not form by way of a changing of the company nameplate, a name change for the form of government or social order, but that it is man who gives such forms their inner content and shapes their character. We did not want to overcome one class just to replace it with another, but we as National Socialists wanted to raise our Volk into a new social conception. This task has been the goal of all the measures that we have since enacted, and that—who could argue against this?—are not only changing the outward face, but also the inner character of our Volk.

What we see only a small slice of here, and that fills our hearts to the brim, is the fanfare of a new Germany announcing itself! A new Volk is being born!

When we seized power in Germany and for the first time announced our intention of founding the Reich Labor Service, many of our movement's superficial critics claimed that we pursued this goal only to take our jobless countrymen and our unemployed fledgling youth off the highways and to stick them in "forced labor camps." We know that it is better if the youth does some fruitful work for the community rather than milling about without reason or purpose. But this means more than merely employing the unemployed. We wanted to found a new academy of National Socialist education!

We know that a true national community cannot develop unless certain prejudices are slowly but surely removed. This transformation came without us hardly noticing! What countless of our so-called sophisticated class thought would only pay off far in the future, has paid off today. The spade became the symbol of a new community! As generation after generation is forced to carry this spade, as every German is obligated to take it upon his shoulder without regard for his person or his heritage, the generations will gradually come to bow to the spade. They will recognize the great value that lies in this communal education through communal work, and in the course of time all of them will be deeply moved as they remember the days when as young men they did the same service for our Volk, wore one uniform, and called one weapon of work their own. They will also reminisce about the great camaraderie that grows out of this. The irrelevant small things as well as the difficult things will vanish from their memory, but what will stay is the memory of a grand time of proud service for our national community.

When I see you like this, it becomes hard for me to speak. All of our hearts spill over with joy because of you. You have no idea how much the German Volk has grown to love you! Within just a few years you have become such a part of our national life that we can no longer imagine it without you. Over and above the Hitler Youth, over and above the work of the party organization, over and above the SA, SS, and so on, *you* are another component of the great educational work of our Volk and *you* are the bridge to the graduation of the young man's education in the army. You yourselves will find that what we have created in Germany is much better than what is going on in those countries that still criticize us.

Here with us there is upbuilding! Here there is camaraderie! And here, above all, there is faith in a better humanity and, with it, a better future! What a contrast to those countries where Marxism is trying to wrest power! Cities are burning there; villages are sinking into ashes and ruin; no one knows one another anymore there. Class fights against class, estate against estate, and brother destroys brother. We have chosen the other way: instead of tearing you apart, I have forged you together!

Thus you stand before us today, carrying not only your own faith for the future of our Volk, but also carrying our faith.

We believe in you! In you, we believe in our male and female German youth! Through you we truly regain our faith in our Volk. You make up the most beautiful component of our Volk!

THE FÜHRER SPEAKS TO
THE NATIONAL SOCIALIST
WOMEN'S LEAGUE

September 11th, 1936

In his introduction, the Führer spoke of National Socialism's great educational mission, the results of which are becoming more visible year after year. Once again, the Führer found words about the task and the life of the German woman that went straight to the heart. Out of the fullness of these thoughts, here we give the following:

How our whole Volk is beaming with optimism today. What a gloriously radiant youth we have once again in Germany! Everything is so full of the joys of life, so confident! Believe me: this is the most necessary thing that humans need to live.

Whoever can no longer open their eyes joyfully can also no longer perceive any joy. One needs this optimism in order to live. It begins in the child. What optimism one needs in the first place to gift a child its life! How can it grow? How will it grow? Every mother is convinced that her child is *the* child. This is the healthiest optimism, and when the child is born, the mother embraces it with shining eyes. For her, this little being is an idol, something glorious!

And the child itself begins this path with immeasurable optimism. It wants to live, and it goes into this life with the all-encompassing confidence that such a small creature has. It has this optimism that we seek after throughout our lives, and ultimately even beyond our life. For, when the time comes when this life seems to lean toward its end, then human optimism rises to the utmost extreme. This optimism overcomes the terrible recognition of the end of its life with the radiant optimism for its continuation. Woe to the person or the nation who loses this ability!

Every year we can sense that the inner confidence of the German man has grown again, and that he again gains a sense of his own worth, of his solid footing in this world, and with this, trust in himself and in his community. To win people who follow faithfully and confidently is a precondition for the success of every political leadership. Do I myself not have to be the greatest optimist among you?

Other countries say, "Yes, the men! But the women, they cannot be optimistic among you, they are oppressed, and gagged, and enslaved. You do not want to give them any freedom, any equal rights." So we answer them: "What some see as a yoke, others see as a blessing; what some see as the kingdom of heaven is hell for others, and vice-versa." So long as we have a healthy male sex — and we National Socialists will make sure of that — there will be no female grenade-thrower in Germany, and no female sharpshooter corps. Because this is not *equal* rights, but *inferior* rights for women.

There is an immeasurable breadth of employment opportunities for women. For us, woman has always been the trustiest work and life partner for man. I am often told: "You want to drive women out of the professions." No, I just want to ensure to the greatest extent that a woman has the possibility of co-founding her own family and having children, because this is the very best way she can serve our Volk!

If today there is a female lawyer who accomplishes so much, and her neighbor is a mother with five, six, seven children, all of whom are brought up good and healthy, then I would say: "From the standpoint of the eternal value of our Volk, the woman who had and raised children and thus gave our Volk life in the future, she accomplished more; she did more!"

A real government has the duty to try to make it possible or at least easier for every woman's and every man's heart to choose. We are trying to solve this challenge by raising both sexes healthily by way of our legislation. Beyond this purely legislative work, we have given the German woman something else: for the German woman, for the German girl, we are raising the male youth, the coming men!

I believe that we are on the right path to raising a healthy generation. I have this to say to all the lettered know-it-alls and equal-rights-philosophers: do not be mistaken! There are two worlds in the life of a people: the world of women and the world of men. Nature arranged things right in placing the man at the head of the family and also giving him an additional duty: the protection of the Volk, of the whole. The woman's world, when she is happy, consists of her family, her husband, her children, her home. After this, her view can then venture into the greater whole. Both worlds together form a community in which the Volk live and endure. We want to build up this mutual world of both sexes, where each one recognizes the work that only it alone can do and which only it is allowed to do and must do.

In these eighteen years of my struggle, I have walked a path that insight and a sense of duty have compelled me to walk. I have never looked back. But this path only has meaning if our Volk lives on, if a healthy generation grows into it.

When I drive through Germany, I see in the millions of children the thing that gives this whole effort any meaning at all. I see in them the children that belong to their mothers just as in the same moment they belong to me.

When I see this growing radiant youth, my work always becomes so easy; there is no weakness for me then. I know then what all my work and effort is for, that it is not for the building up of some dismal business that will fade away again, but that it is all done for the building up of something eternal and enduring. I see the German girl, the German woman, the German mother as inseparably connected to this future, and so we also acknowledge the girl, the woman, the mother.

I do not measure the success of our work by the growth of our streets. I do not measure it by our new factories, by the new bridges we are building, by the divisions that we are forming. Rather, at the peak of the evaluation of our work's success, there is the German child, the German youth. If it grows, then I know our Volk will not perish and our work will have not been for nothing.

I am convinced that no one understands the movement more than the German woman. When our opponents claim that we are setting up a tyrannical regime over our women, I can only let them in on this one thing: without women's reliability and really loving devotion to the movement, I could have never led the party to victory. And I know that even in bad times, when the wiseacres and the know-it-alls become unsure, the women will stand with the movement securely out of the confidence of their hearts and will forever link themselves to me.

THE FÜHRER TO THE
POLITICAL LEADERS

September 11th, 1936

My party comrades! Men of the National Socialist movement!

We meet here for the fourth time. How this field has changed in that time! Just like our Reich! And — we can say with much greater pride — just like our Volk!

In these four years, we have seen the miracle of reestablishment, the rise of a beaten down, demoralized, and downtrodden Volk. Today this Volk stands before us straightened out in form and in heart.

When we meet here each year, we can look back on a year of work, but also a year of success. Three years ago this took place amidst a tumultuous world. There were still many who thought they could turn back the wheel of history. A year later, two years ago, there were internal controversies raging amongst us, which were necessary to harden our movement. Last year the cloud of enemy malevolence, foreign rejection, and dangerous misunderstanding still hung over Germany. Now we are on this field again, and all of us — you, me, and the nation — know: the times of internal tensions are behind us, just as the times of foreign threat are behind us.

The German Volk is consolidated just as we here are brought together. Just as you, my flag bearers, marched here in columns, so the German Volk is organized under your flags and marches in a column behind your flags! In this year's proclamation to the German Volk, I was able to remind them of all the wonderful things that have been accomplished this year. This celebration reminds us of what has become of the German Volk. What a spirit has taken hold of our people! How it has become proud and manly again, how it has overcome all the powers of subversion, decay, and unworthiness and found its way back to honor! How proud we can be again of our Volk! My fellow fighters, this miracle of renewal in our Volk is not a gift from heaven for the unworthy.

Never has the resurrection of a people been wrestled for with greater fanaticism, greater devotion, greater self-sacrifice than by our movement in these past eighteen years!

We have wrestled for our Volk, for the souls of millions of our workers, our farmers, our citizens! We wrestled like we were fighting for the most precious treasure that could ever exist in this world. What exertion, what sacrifice, what devotion, what fanaticism, what defiance of death has been applied in these years! And if this has led to success, it is not only because I am your Führer, but because you are my followers.

In this hour, do we not once again feel the miracle that brought us together? You once heard the voice of one man and it resonated with your heart, it awoke you, and you followed this voice. You followed it for years without ever having seen the man whose voice it was; you simply heard a voice and followed it.

When we meet here, we are filled with the wondrousness of our coming together. Not every one of you sees me, and I do not see every one of you. But I feel you all, and you feel me! It is the faith in our Volk that has made us little people big, that has made us poor people rich, that has made us wavering, discouraged, fearful people brave and courageous; that has made us fools see, and that forged us together!

And so you come out of your little villages, your market towns, your cities, out of ditches and factories, from the plow you come for a day in this city. You come to get a sense from out of your small environment of the struggle of your life, your struggle for Germany and for our Volk: now we are together, we are in the struggle and it is in us, and now we are Germany! It is such a glorious thought that we are gathered here as representatives of the German nation, and everyone knows it. These 140,000 have one mind and their hearts have one beat; they are all thinking the same thought. This is the fount of our movement's strength, and it leads us through all possible destinies toward the goal that we are striving for, and which is now within our grasp.

It is something wonderful for me to be able to be your Führer.

Who could be prouder of his followers that he who knows that they were moved by nothing other than the purest idealism?

What forced you under my spell? What could I offer you, what could I give you? Together we chose only one thing: the struggle for a great common ideal! We became big and strong in this struggle, and finally we have become victors.

When earlier for many years I had to greet you as my fighters, then today I can also greet you as victors. You have built a new house for our Volk, and you are educating the inhabitants of this house in a new spirit, toward a new meaning. And this should be marked by all those who would like to overrun this state or even to bring it to collapse! If our old enemy and adversary should once again try to attack us, then our battle flags will fly up and they will get to know us!

They will need to recognize that Germany is not their field.

In these many years we have never had any prayer besides this one: "Lord, give our Volk peace within and give and preserve for it peace without!" Our generations have experienced so much fighting that it is understandable if we long for peace. We want to work; we want to shape our Reich, to institute it according to our own thoughts, and not according to those of the Bolshevik Jews.

We want to care for the future of our Volk's children; we want to work for the future so that their lives are not only secured, but also made easier. We have so much difficulty behind us that we can only direct this plea to good and merciful Providence: "Spare our children that which we had to endure!"

We want nothing but peace and tranquility for our work. May others also harbor no other wish, for we have also not hesitated to lay down our tranquility when it was necessary to vanquish our domestic disturbers of the peace. We have not grown old from our fight; we are as young as ever. What the years have added to us, our idealism has sloughed off.

Our new youth already marches with and behind our flags.

We are so happy and so proud when we see it. A new generation of leaders is growing up. What we gratefully accepted as a gift from the selective power of the struggle, this we want to preserve for the future as well through our own hard selection.

Being a National Socialist means being a man, being a fighter, being brave, and courageous, and self-sacrificing. This we will be for all time to come!

Thus, we can look into the future with peaceful repose on this fourth Reich Party Congress since we seized power. We are not careless and reckless; history has taught us too many hard lessons for that. But we are calm and confident. I am, because I see you. I know that there is an unparalleled and unique movement behind me, that there is a wonderful organization of men and women behind me, and I see the endless columns of our new Reich's flags before me. And I can prophetically tell you: this Reich has experienced the first days of its youth. It will keep growing for centuries, and become strong and mighty! These flags will be carried through the ages by succeeding generations of our Volk. Germany has found itself! Our Volk is born again!

Thus, I salute you, my old fellow fighters, my leaders, my flag bearers, as the standard bearers of a new history, and so I salute you here and thank you for your loyalty and all the faith that you have given me these long years.

Thus, I salute you as the hope of the present and the guarantors of the future.

And thus I especially also salute the youth who are gathered here. Become such men as those you see before you!

Fight as they have fought!

Be upright and resolute, shun no one, and do what is right and what is your duty!

Then the Lord our God will never abandon our Volk.

Heil Germany!

AT THE CELEBRATION
OF THE HITLER YOUTH

September 12th, 1936

My German youth!

You have the good fortune to be witnesses to an age as great as it is tumultuous. This is not allotted to every generation. When I recall the youth of my day, and the days of my youth, it seems quite empty compared to what today's times and today's youth have to offer, and the tasks that this age demands and that it demands of the youth. It is truly wonderful to be able to live in such an age and to grow up in such an age. And you have this great fortune!

You do not experience the reestablishment of a state, because you did not know the old Reich. You are experiencing the birth of a great age, which you can measure by a comparison to the world around us! How our contemporary Germany is beautiful and glorious again! Your young eyes will perceive this, too. How glorious and wonderful is this Germany in its order, in its great discipline, in the overwhelming achievement of its work! Can we not feel works growing around us that will equal the best of our German history! We all know it: what we are creating will be able to stand alongside our old cathedrals, the palaces of our old kaisers, the old city halls of our past.

Germany is working again for a great national future, and we are not just experiencing this, but each of us can take part in this work. Perhaps we can see this best if we look toward another country in comparison. Here we have the results of a wonderful order that is filled with a truly fresh life—there this other country is filled with atrocities, murder, and arson, with ruination and convulsion, not with life but only dread, despair, lament, and sorrow.[12] You, too, can measure what a contrast is growing between today's Germany and the world surrounding it! That this is so is not by accident, and not because we laid our hands on our lap and waited for a miracle. The only miracle to which we owe this rise of our Volk is the belief in our own Volk, the conviction that this thousand-year Volk cannot perish, that we ourselves would have to lift it and work for it.

We ourselves have to shape the destiny of our Volk the way we want to see it and live it!

What we are today is thanks to the tenacity of our own will! Providence gives the strong, the brave, the courageous, the diligent, the orderly, and the disciplined the reward for his sacrifice. For many years this Germany did not live, but what we see standing here today, this is our Germany again!

This new Reich formed from immeasurable communal work, from sacrifice and devotion. Its flags were established, the flags of the creed of the Volk's ideal. Thus, millions and millions are working today laying stone upon stone for the great masonry of our national house, our national temple.

But what would this work be if it were tied to the impermanence of one generation? While we fought for Germany decade after decade, many among us became old and gray. This was a wonderful old guard, my comrades. I am one of the happy few in this world who got to know the highest loyalty, highest camaraderie, highest self-sacrifice. This old guard set out on its march when Germany was at its poorest, believing in the eternal wealth of our nation. In the time of their own greatest poverty, this guard gave their dimes and pennies away. This guard came from all classes of our Volk in order to prove that the eternal worth of a nation does not lie in externalities, not in a name, not in origin, not in status, not in wealth, and not even in so-called knowledge! The German heart unlocked itself for me and gave itself to Germany!

The years of struggle did not pass by without leaving a mark on this old guard. But their spirit always stayed lively, just as it was always their

---

[12] Spain is meant here.

unshakeable belief that we must succeed, and that Germany must rise again!

And now, everywhere in Germany, a time of awakening, a time of rising, a time of creation, and of work has come to be. But this alone is not the guarantor of an enduring and thus true resurrection. That Germany has found itself again, this I feel in you; I see it when I look at you!

For a new youth has emerged in you, filled with different ideals than the youth of my time, filled with a holier faith than the generation before us. A new youth has come with different notions, with different conceptions of the beauty of youth, of the strength of youth. I can still see it, the youth of my day. It believed itself to be strong only in pleasure. It expressed its national pride only in the terms of a youth whose young men thought they would become the paragon of their Volk through consumption of the greatest possible amount of alcohol. No, my young friends! Today a glorious generation is growing up! You are a more beautiful picture than what the past asked us to be, taught us to be. A new standard of beauty has emerged. No longer the corpulent beer-philistine, but the lithe, lissome boy is the model of our age, who stands on the earth firmly with straddled legs, who is healthy in body and healthy in soul. And the German girl grows like this beside you young boys, too.

Perhaps this is the greatest wonder of our time: buildings rise, factories are founded, streets are paved again, train stations are built, but above all this, a new German rises! When I look at you, filled with the deepest emotion, when I see your eyes, then I know that my life struggle is not fought for nothing, my work is not for nothing! It will live on in this flag and its young bearers, and a worthy generation will be ready to relieve you.

You will be men, like the great generation of the war was. You will be brave and courageous, like your older brothers and your fathers were. You will be as true as Germans have ever been true. But you will see the Fatherland with totally different eyes than how we unfortunately once had to see it. You will know a different devotion to the eternal Reich and the eternal Volk.

Five years have passed since your leader, my old party comrade Schirach, who himself came out of the Hitler Youth, has taken over your education and formation. Then, a small, weak beginning, and today a wonderful fulfillment! This should be a reminder and an assurance for our future: if we could reach this wonder in five years, then the next five, ten, twenty, and hundred years will really solidify this wonder!

Generation after generation will be relieved of their tasks, and a new youth will always step up here in this city. It will always become stronger, always more vigorous, always healthier, and it will always give the then-living generations greater hope for the future. We want to unite our common wishes for this future. It shall bring our Volk happiness and blessings; it shall let our Volk live and it shall bring to ruin all those who would try to extinguish this life.

We are surrounded by a tumultuous age. But we are not complaining. We are used to fighting, for we came out of the fight. We want to root our feet firmly in the ground, and we will not succumb to any onslaught. And you will stand beside me, should this hour ever come! You will stand before me, beside me, and behind me, and you will hold our flag high! Then let our old adversary try to stand against us and exalt himself again. He may carry a Soviet symbol — but *we* will be victorious under *our* symbol!

THE FÜHRER BEFORE THE
GERMAN LABOR FRONT

September 12th, 1936

At the beginning of his speech, amidst cheering agreement from the masses, Adolf Hitler shared a clear rebuttal of the "great social policy makers of the after-war years."

They may have fed the workers with nice theories and helped increase their income fantastically with the help of the money press, but the workers starved nevertheless, and still the number of unemployed went up month after month. It is not income, *but* outcome *that matters for the workers. But in order to raise the livelihood of the German worker by even just 10 percent, ten thousand factories and businesses would need to produce more. It is a thankless job to have to provide for the livelihoods of sixty-eight million people who are crowded together in an impossibly tight space. Our country can hardly increase production in some areas, and so it is reliant on imports, and must expend extraordinary effort in other areas to make this import possible.*

The central challenge for the National Socialist leadership is to first increase the total volume of our production, so that there can also be an increase in consumption for each individual, because the income of the people only has meaning when it stems from an increase in production. Production alone is true compensation, and not what one earns in money. Every increase in production benefits the whole Volk, and not just a few middlemen. If Germany's production of coal is increased by thirty or forty million tons, then this is not consumed by a few individuals, but by the whole mass of the people. As this increase benefits the people, so the people's living standard is also raised.

Prolonged enthusiastic applause thanked the Führer as he contrasted Bolshe-

vik's destruction with National Socialist construction. The meaning of the National Socialist revolution was to restructure German life, and thus to improve it. Marxism, on the other hand, wants to glorify its revolution through calling for a general strike, through tearing down and destroying life. Afterward, the Marxists blamed their inability to improve the lot of the workers on the fact that they had to build everything back from the ground up. The Bolshevik state is a prime example, because the living standard of its workers is about two-thirds that of the German workers.

If the Ural with its immeasurable wealth of raw resources, Siberia with its rich forests, and the Ukraine with its immense cropland were located in Germany, these would overflow with abundance under National Socialist leadership. We would produce, and every German would have more than enough to live.

Yet the population in Russia is starving because the Judeo-Bolshevik leadership is incapable of organizing production and helping the worker in any practical way.

With their clear example, the Führer pointed out the difference between National Socialist achievements and those of the Bolshevik state:

In Moscow they build a subway and invite the whole world to come and see, and say, "See what we have accomplished!" We do not even mention such feats! We already build our subways in passing, on the side!

In the same time it takes Moscow to build eleven kilometers of subway line, we build seven thousand kilometers of highways; and not eighteen or twenty years after our revolution, but *now*, in our fourth year, and in another four years the whole network will be complete!

The Führer then addressed issues of merit in industry. Whoever wants to lead in industry must be capable. Reality itself is the toughest screening. It should not be someone's length of service that is decisive for a leadership post, but his merit, his intelligence, his initiative, and his vitality. It is an old truism that in the economy, everyone who is incapable fails. National Socialism grounds its principles in this insight.

The betterment of our economic life depends on two factors: first, the tremendous, communal, resolute application of all our strength for this betterment, and second, a better education for people. National Socialism is working on this education. The German Labor Front may be the most tremendous monument of this education in our Volk, the most vibrant expression of this new community. Again and again, we must always hammer it into every single person: you are only a servant of your Volk! Alone, you are nothing; only as part of the community are you anything, and in a united front you are power!

The education of a new, socially conscious man is necessary. This does not happen overnight. This cannot be reached by just a few, but this spirit has to arise out of the whole of the Volk, just as I cannot raise an army in a few days and give it a new spirit. This is a challenge of many centuries. Out of these centuries, a community spirit finally arises, a community attitude, and out of both arise community accomplishments, and a proud tradition grows out of it.

Here it is no different. We called the great national army of labor into being, and it will grow, and expand, and will go forth into the next centuries. Generations will be schooled by it, will march in it, and carry on its ideas. I firmly believe that humanity will become better, not worse, despite everything. Even the Jew will not be able to bring about the opposite. You will become better, you will always understand each other better, you will always increasingly give each other the necessary respect, and our Volk will always polish itself more and will one day represent for posterity this type of the German man, who we believe we see today already as a premonition, and whose first representatives we may already be seeing rising up from our youth today.

Going into detail about this proclamation and the four-year plan, the Führer explained to those who may shrink away from the magnitude of the problems faced:

We will never say that these problems cannot be solved. Problems that are posed can also be solved, and they will be solved! Of course we need daring, gumption, and a lot of strong faith to do this. But it took a lot more daring and much greater faith when eighteen years ago a single man took up the fight against a world of ideas and opponents!

When I say today that we will have solved these problems in four years, this seems much easier to me than it once did to embark on the path from nothing to the head of the German nation. Therefore, no one should come to me with the phrase, "This will not work!" No one can and no one may say this. I do not belong to those men who let themselves be told, "It cannot be done." It *must* be done, because Germany must live.

Of course, we will only solve these problems if we are a united front. If everyone goes his own direction, one this way, the other that, if everyone believes he can be happy in his own way, then of course this will not work. When every German believed he could go his own way, then Germany and each individual German fared very poorly. The same goes for the future. I am gathering together the strengths of our Volk. Sixty-eight million individuals must become one concentrated mind, one concentrated will, one conviction, and one determination. Then these great tasks before us will become laughably small. If I had to imagine that I had to go alone and that all my followers would each go their own way, then I would have to despair, too. But when I know that I forge ahead, and a whole Volk marches behind me, then I do not fear, even if the tasks would be twice as big again!

Then someone can tell me, "We have a cotton shortage!" In four years, my comrades, every factory will be running! We have our own German materials! Someone may tell me we cannot buy enough rubber. Pay attention: factories will spring out of the ground, and one day we will be driving on German rubber! One may ask, "Where will you get the petroleum if you keep advancing motorization in Germany?" We will get our petroleum from our own ground; we will produce it from our coal!

I will never say, "That will not work, so wheels must stop turning, and so the German Volk must starve." No, it *will* work, problems *will* be solved, because they are posed, and because we want them to be solved.

When I see you standing before me as the Front of German Labor, then please, consider the meaning of the word *front*. *Front* means one will, it means one resolve; *front* means one goal and it means one deed!

And this is necessary. Life is very hard for many of our countrymen. Not all are equally blessed by fortune; not all are equally favored. But believe me, the most terrible thing is when the man forgotten by luck loses hope.

When I pose these great problems to the German Volk, I am certainly creating new work and new burdens, and many will say, "We never get any rest; there are always new agendas." You who are of this opinion, do not forget that at the same time this is a glimmer of hope for many millions, that millions who live in the shadowy side of life can believe again that things are moving forward after all. The Führer has worked out a new plan.

We believe that everything will be alright again; we will all get our jobs back. Do not forget that what may seem like a burden to some is an uplift for countless others. There will be a great new confidence, and we will persevere.

We will also preserve Germany from the possibility of someone reaching in from the outside to create chaos and make our solutions impossible. I have had to fight so much in my life, have had so much resistance before me and defeated and eliminated it, that I can only see myself as a fighter anymore. I also know that in the life of nations, only those nations that are ready to encounter any resistance and to fend off any danger can survive. Therefore, I will ensure that we are not a helpless state in the face of the threatening events that may escalate, but that here, too, we can have confidence, hope, and faith in the German future. Just as I created the conditions for a domestic economy by securing domestic peace through the party and its organization, so I will also create the conditions for the happiness of our Volk by providing for our nation's defense from the outside, and nothing shall distract or deter me in this.

I will demand every sacrifice that is necessary to support and protect our Volk; for I believe that the least fortunate man in this world is the one who cannot master his misfortune through his own strength!

And so I salute all of you who are here as fellow fighters of the great front of our economy, which is a part of the great front of our national self-preservation and thus of our German Volk. I salute you, assured that this front will do its duty and fulfill its obligation to help buttress Germany and German life, that it will solve the problems and tasks posed to it, and that it will keep working and doing its part for the preservation and securing of life and for reaching the goal set for our Volk by Providence.

If Germany forms itself into such a front, it will be indestructible. Then the Reich and the nation will be firm, then they will persevere into the coming centuries, and our children will be spared what we had to endure for eighteen years.

AT THE ROLL CALL OF
THE BROWN ARMY

September 13th, 1936

Men of the National Socialist fighting organizations!

We meet here on this field in Nuremberg for the eighth time, and for the fourth time since we took power, for which we fought for fourteen years, and that we did not receive as a present or by chance, but that we earned thanks to our fighting, our discipline, and our order.

Who would have been more justified to seek power in Germany than us, and who would have had more of a right to receive it?

Who would have put the reins of power in worthier hands than the National Socialist movement? But I can also add: who would hold onto them tighter than us?

A part of our movement meets in this city annually for the great demonstration of our party, this exceptional family of fighting men and brave women. We meet here annually to look back at the preceding twelve months, and look each other in the eye and fortify ourselves for the future.

As we look back today, it has been almost four years since that evening when tens of thousands, hundreds of thousands proceeded through Wilhelm Street in Berlin, cheering and enthusiastic, because their movement had finally gained power in the state after an unparalleled struggle. I can ask you, my comrades: was the cheering back then unfounded, or did the voice of the people back then not give expression to what we can now, four years later, call vindicated?

My comrades! I only have two questions:

First: back then I laid out a program for the nation and gave it my promise. Have I kept my promise, or not?

And second: could mortal men ever accomplish as much as we have accomplished?

Yes! A miracle has occurred in Germany since then! Not only the miracle of the economic resurrection, the firing up of our factories and workshops, the miracle of our great constructions, the miracle of our streets. No! The miracle of our humiliated, beaten, downtrodden Volk rising up again, the miracle of such a despondent and self-doubting Volk being upright again!

Today, Germany is on the right track once more. When I look at this whole miracle, I have to bow before the mercy of the Lord, who blessed this fight, and I thank you, my comrades, who made my fight possible.

What would a solitary person be in this world? What would his will be, his intentions, his wishes, and his hopes, if thousands and hundreds of thousands and millions of like-minded people, full of the same determination, devotion, and action, did not join him?

That there was one person in Germany who stood up, who did not despair of Germany, is not as remarkable as the fact that millions found him, that unknown man, and went down the same path with him. This is the miracle of our age, that you found me, that you found me amidst so many millions! And that I found you, this is Germany's good fortune!

I look upon you with proud and happy eyes. Almost four years have passed since our victory, but you have remained what you always were: my old guard of the National Socialist revolution!

There is something wondrous about the founding and formation of such a movement! Now you stand before me again, all in the same shirts, the same uniforms, arranged in rows and columns, and you come from out of the whole Volk; you stand before me as if you were one, and yet you are workers and farmers, craftsmen, and burghers, and students, former officers as well as former enlisted men!

There is something wondrous about the force that called us here and forged us together into a unit in service to our Volk. One day you heard the signal, and without ever having seen the man who gave it, you followed him. How many of you have never even seen me before today, and yet I know you will follow me just the same in the future!

How many of you took part in the Great War! In the hour of fatigue and exhaustion, countless laid down their weapons, and unfortunately also their wills and their vigor, their courage, their determination, and many even their love for Germany. And what did you do, who once also fought in the Great War? You took up the fight anew! Germany had fallen, but in you, it picked itself up again immediately!

And thus, the new Reich was built up with you and through you in all its proud inner security. And I wish that all those who doubt the stability of our government and our state organization would cast a glance at you here. Not even 5 percent of my revolutionary guard stands here, and just as you stand here today, there could be twenty places in Germany where an equal could muster.

Who would ever want to fight against this block of national self-assertion, discipline, order, confidence, and faithfulness?

I know this: I did not create something in vain. It will stand and it will extend into the most remote ages.

And so today we stand in loyal watch over our Volk. All of you grasp the signs of the times. Our old adversary, against whom we have faced off, who we routed and vanquished, who we beat despite his thousandfold numerical advantage, he is trying to stir — not by us, but around us — and he raises his threatening fist against us.

At this point, in light of you, my old and young fighters, I would like to pronounce this: you should not delude yourselves about us! We are ready at every hour!

The world can know that all of us who work — day in, day out, week after week, month after month — on the task of raising our Volk up again, as well as its economy and its culture, have only one wish: to preserve peace, just as we secured our domestic peace. However, it should also be known that we only have one resolution: under no circumstances can Germany ever be surrendered to Bolshevism, whose works we know and which we beat into the ground!

In these weeks and months there are demonstrations taking place everywhere. We read about how, in other countries, incited masses are called up to protest against Fascism, against National Socialism, to demonstrate in favor of Bolshevism, for delivering arms, for fundraising, yes, even demonstrations for delivering people.

I have not yet called for a demonstration, but if I do call for one, there will be one single demonstration in Germany, and then there will not be ten or twenty or thirty thousand undisciplined people demonstrating, but millions and many millions will be afire against the ancient accuser and archenemy of mankind!

I believe I can say this more truthfully in front of you, who are so many of you old frontline fighters, than I can in any other forum: we only want peace because we have been acquainted with war! We want to reach out a hand to the nations; we want to work together with them; we have no animosity and feel no hatred toward them. But Germany will *never* become Bolshevist!

We do not want the fruits of our labor and diligence, the efficiency and activity of millions of Germans, to be destroyed by unconscionable Bolshevik Jews. We do not want for brother to again not know brother, for the one to learn to hate the other, and for the nation—Germany, our dear Fatherland—to perish in this rift. What we have to improve on, this we know ourselves. We do not need any Jews to tell us; whatever men can improve, we will improve! We have never espoused the notion that a people's future is given to it as an unearned gift. We struggle for it, we fight for it, and we will master destiny!

There are two worlds: you can go to another country with its gruesome desolation, fire, murder, ashes, and ruins, or you can look to our laughing, and happy, and beautiful Germany.

How orderly and clean everything has become through our work!

How straight, upright, manly, and strong has our Volk become!

We are ready again to work together for the preservation of our Volk.

Believe me: for me, it is something wonderful to be able to live in this time and to be your Führer and the chancellor of the German Reich!

That I have this good fortune is thanks to all the millions who once believed in me during the worst days; and above all, it is thanks to the hundreds of thousands who fought for me then!

And so, this year we once again renew our old oath of mutual loyalty, of camaraderie, the old common creed to our glorious movement and with it to the eternal German Volk!

Germany, Sieg Heil!

TO THE SOLDIERS OF
THE ARMED FORCES

September 14th, 1936

Soldiers!

You are mustered at this place here in Nuremberg for the third time!

For the first time, the flags of the new Reich are fluttering before you!

For the first time, you hold the new flags of your regiments in your fists!

Thus, we can already see in this outward picture the transformation that Germany — our Germany, your Germany — has undergone.

This transformation is the result of a very great educational effort in our Volk, and no less effort in all other areas of our national life.

We have our Volk's unending activity, its unending diligence, and its unending work to thank for the fact that we are able to stand here today celebrating this day. But all this work would be for nothing if it were not possible for the Reich to secure peace within and without. What fills us with such pride today are the accomplishments of our peacetime work. Our foremost task, then, is to secure and preserve these accomplishments and this work. And if millions of people devote their lives to this work year-in, year-out in factory and workshop, in businesses and in offices, then it is understandable and reasonable that all would be ready to devote their lives to the preservation of all that was worked for.

You, my soldiers, were called for this reason!

Not to serve some frivolous whim of a fanciful chauvinism — but to stand watch over your Volk! To stand watch over our Germany! When I see you before me like this, I feel and I know that this watch will stand firm against all dangers and threats.

The German was always a good soldier. The army you have all grown in carries the proudest heritage of all time. If Germany once collapsed, this was the result of its internal political collapse.

Today the nation is as straight as you, my comrades, who stand here before me. Today Germany is again worthy of a soldier, and I know that you will be this Reich's worthy soldier!

In the Volk, the party, and the armed forces, we are forming a community in which each is indissolubly pledged to one another.

There may come times that are very serious. They will never catch us wavering, fainthearted, and never cowardly! For we all know that heaven is not gained by the half-hearted! Freedom is not kept by cowards! And the future belongs to the courageous alone!

What is demanded of you today is only a small portion of what the past demanded from us. Back then, we fulfilled our duty. But the two years that I demand of you, I give back to you with an extra ten! For each of you will become healthier from this discipline than you were before. What you give to your Fatherland in your youth will be repaid to you in your old age! You will be a healthy generation, not suffocated in offices and factory rooms, but reared in sun and air, steeled through movement, and above all, hardened in your character.

And believe me: Germany loves you as soldiers!

The reverence, the admiration, and the love for our former great army have carried over to you. And you will be worthy of it!

The nation expects no sacrifice from you that you will not fulfill!

Germany will never have to encounter those sad times that we had to live through!

Our Fatherland, our Germany, our home, and the home of our children will be strong and great and happy. It will be able to defend that peace that will secure our lives!

In this hour, we unite ourselves in our commitment to our German Volk and to the millions of working people in city and country in our commitment to the German Reich.

Our Germany: Sieg Heil! Sieg Heil! Sieg Heil!

THE FÜHRER'S CONCLUDING REMARKS
AT THE 1936 PARTY CONGRESS

September 14th, 1936

Party comrades! National Socialists!

For seven days the old imperial city once again stood under the banner of the great political demonstration of our German Volk. We were powerfully made conscious of the deep and enormous transformation of German life. What has marched past our eyes in unison for many days here was the new state, as well as the new man. Whose heart would not overflow again and again when he thinks through the immeasurable transformation our Volk has experienced, and to which we are permitted to be witnesses? How much greater is the happiness of those who have the right to say that their work, and above all their faith helped to wrest this miracle. Once again, we felt the living current of the power that flows from our community!

We experienced anew the beautiful truth of our movement: that we Germans are not only one Volk again, but that the leader and the followers of the National Socialist movement are like members of a big family.

What floated before us for so many years as a visionary plan is now being fulfilled: the international Olympic Games that we celebrated only a few weeks ago in Berlin have obtained a figuration for our Volk that is as profound as it is tremendous and enduring.

Whatever has become of the paltry Party Congresses of the past, and what of our opponents?

This great political, military, spiritual, cultural, and economic demonstration of the nation. And the more the glorious new facilities of the Reich Party Congresses in Nuremberg grow and approach their completion, the more athletic competition will be added.

A new Olympia, though in modern forms and under another name!

Who among you, my German countrymen, who had the fortune to experience these days here with us, has not intensely felt the vindication of this claim, that once many talked about a resurgence of the German Volk and millions clung to this hope? For many it was this that made it possible for them to survive the postwar period. But what was once only talked about, what one could only dream of, and what one hardly dared to seriously believe in, *this* has become a reality today.

A new Germany has emerged thanks to the National Socialist idea and the National Socialist leadership!

You can love it or you can hate it, but no one will change it, and no one can deny it!

This new Germany, which has revealed itself again to us all in these past seven days, is a historical fact. Those outside of Germany who have a realistic enough view, and who do not make their unreasonable desire the master of their thoughts or their hope, do not need to lament that the German Volk's development has taken this turn!

The German rebirth is so deeply and inwardly focused that the neighboring governments will not be touched as long as they themselves do not seek to be touched!

The new National Socialist state lives according to a racial ideal that finds its contentment within the circle of its own blood. National Socialist doctrine recognizes the purpose of the existence of the state to be the preservation of the *ethnos*. It also believes it is the most likely way to solve the problems that arise from the unfortunate discrepancy between the drawing of the borders of the European states and the peoples.

A doctrine that rejects the artificial or even violent denationalization of a people may indeed present the only opportunity for the European states to come to a higher and nobler understanding regarding these problems, without always having to throw the world into new suffering and new injustice through new wars!

The National Socialist state is striving for the political reestablishment of the German people's honor and equal status. It did not announce and advance this agenda in the old bourgeois way, through pompous club speeches, but it materialized it through action. The first and hardest political task laid out for us can today be marked as complete. With the institution of the two-year service, after barely four years of National Socialist government, the German Reich is freed from the worst consequences of that unconscionable mutiny that sought to defame us not only militarily, but morally! Perhaps other nations who were not subjected to a similar misfortune as Germany will have no understanding of the weight that we give to this accomplishment. If, in the future, the world respects Germany's natural rights the same way we intend to respect the rights of other nations, then in this case, too, the National Socialist rebirth is only removing an element of unrest from the world. Through achieving equal rights for the German nation by our own strength, the basis is created for an upright cooperation between the European nations.

The National Socialist state was founded and will be led in the spirit of an ideology that precludes an interest in exporting our politics. We acknowledge every other people's natural right to become politically, ideologically, and economically sound through their own notions and in accordance with their own desires, under the condition that they extend the same attitude toward us.

Many critics in other parts of the world insinuate that we are fanatically chauvinist and spiritually expansionist nationalists or socialists.

The world cannot deny that our nationalism is called National Socialism.

Now, it is not very logical of the rest of the world to assume that a fanatical National Socialist would divulge or even force onto others exactly that idea that forged the ideational and political preconditions for his own national pride.

No: National Socialism is our most valuable German patent.

As National Socialists, we are fighters for this doctrine in our Volk, but we are not missionaries for our political opinions on the outside. It does not matter to us what is explained, believed, or experienced in other nations. However, when we are forced to explain our National Socialist thought to the rest of the world, it is always only as a defense against the constant unprovoked attempts of foreign interference in our internal affairs or against the fraudulent coverage of our doctrine or our intentions!

If anyone has reason to complain about the intolerance of beliefs, then it is us. We keep experiencing attacks from the camps of our ideological opponent, simply because Germany, National Socialist Germany, is going along a different path than what our foreign political opponents see as the correct one.

Why does democracy care if National Socialism reigns in Germany? Democracy does not need to tolerate National Socialism within its own lands, just as we in Germany will not put up with any more democracy. But democracy should finally acknowledge that in the fifteen years prior to the National Socialist regime, the German nation had plenty of opportunity to become practically acquainted with Western democracy's ideas of international fraternity and human happiness.

It totally does not matter to us National Socialists if we are loved or hated by these democracies, whether they see us as equals or not. In fifteen long years, the German Volk has lost its respect for this type of democracy and the brotherly consequences of its true feelings. Today, virtually all stand in the camp of national authority.

There is no desire to refresh the memories of the so upright and beneficial sympathies that world democracy showered upon Germany back then. We have forgotten this, and the world should be happy that we have!

It is then no wonder, if the democratic states constantly honor us with their antipathy, that we would naturally show an equal sympathy to the authoritatively led countries. Another reason for this special sympathy is certainly also that, despite our indifference toward democracy and all its foreign political ideas, we still believe we recognize in these other nations a form of life that is never permanent, but has always been transitional, and we fear this is the case now as well.

And we do not deny the deep trepidation that grips us by the very thought that we may no longer be able to find a way of life suited to a people in this or that country, but rather that they could have fallen victim to that ideology that we oppose to the death with no reservations: Bolshevism.

This mortal opposition is not based on the intransigent rejection of some foreign idea that is contrary to our understanding, but on the natural resistance to an insane and bestial doctrine that violently threatens the entire world.

Besides, it was not National Socialism that sought out a collision with Bolshevism!

National Socialism's first battle against communism did not take place in Russia, but Soviet communism already tried, from 1918 to 1920, to infect Germany. This enemy once tried to find its way into our borders ideologically, and today it is attempting it militarily by gradually drawing its Bolshevik military forces closer to our borders after the failure of its Moscow-directed ideological war against Germany.

We have attacked, defeated, and rooted out this Bolshevism, which the Jewish Soviet terrorists Levine, Axelroth, Neumann, Béla Kun, and others tried to import into Germany. Thus, we have fended off Bolshevism's attempt to revolutionize Germany from Moscow. Only because we know and experience every day that there is no end to the Jewish Soviet rulers' attempt at meddling in German affairs are we forced to view Bolshevism as a mortal enemy externally as well, and to recognize its encroachment as a dangerous threat.

We had to fight Moscow Bolshevism in Germany as a worldview that attempts to poison our Volk and thus destroy it. And we will also fight it as a world power if it wants to attempt to bring the Spanish misfortune into Germany with new and more violent methods. And as we do, we will not let ourselves be fooled by those weaklings who only believe in danger when they are already being devoured by it.

Besides, we did not once fend off Bolshevism because we wanted to conserve or even rejuvenate a bourgeois world. If communism were really nothing but a certain type of cleansing through an elimination of the fouler individual elements in the camp of our so-called upper ten thousand, or of our no less worthless bourgeois stiffs, then maybe we could have seen how it went for a while.

But communism's goal is not to free nations from the pathological, but the opposite: to eliminate the healthy, indeed to root out the healthiest and to replace it with the most depraved.

I cannot make a pact with an ideology that is not concerned with liberating the working people, but rather everywhere it takes power away frees the antisocial human scum concentrated in the penitentiaries, in order to then let these animals loose on a world that has become cowed and bewildered.

Further, we have not defended against the encroachment of this ideology and its victory in Germany because we wanted to block the German workers' path to improvement, but because we did not want 98 percent of all leadership positions to be occupied by ethnically foreign Jews, as in Russia, and because under no circumstances did we want the intelligent stemming from our own Volk to be slaughtered off for that purpose. National Socialism has opened the path to the top for countless of our German countrymen, though under one condition: namely, their obvious capability.

The German worker is not overlooked. Today a man stands at the head of the Reich who was himself a worker barely twenty-five years ago. Former agricultural and industrial workers today occupy countless posts from the bottom to the top. Communism cannot deny that in Russia today, 98 percent of all appointed posts, all leadership positions, are held by Jewish elements, who never even belonged to the proletariat, and who have never earned their bread honestly!

We do not want to let a similar situation come about in Germany. That it would go no differently here is proved by the Munich Soviet Republic. It lasted barely a month, but still it was led by many Judeo-Bolshevik leaders. The only thing left over for the German worker was the honor of writing the execution orders, and to hold those timely deposed Hebrew communist leaders accountable before the German courts!

Based on these racial considerations, in the interest of our German Volk, and not least of the German worker and the German farmer, we National Socialists have taken a stand against Bolshevism.

We also reject this doctrine due to our own more humane approach toward our fellow man. The presentations of our speakers at this Party Congress, as well as the events in Spain, have once again shown the world and our German countrymen a glimpse of the cruelty of Bolshevik methods of war and political maxims. The German Volk is too good and decent for such abominations!

We National Socialists also have a revolution behind us! It was also waged by workers, farmers, and soldiers! And it also defeated and annihilated an adversary. Except we National Socialists are proud that in 1933, as the National Socialist revolution roared across Germany, not a single windowpane was shattered. We are proud that we overcame the assassination attempts and numerous assassinations that communism perpetrated against our people, with a minimum of resistance and without retaliation. And not because we were too weak to stand the sight of blood. As soldiers, we witnessed humanity's worst suffering in the hardest war of all time, while the Bolshevik leaders milled about in Switzerland as cowardly exiles, or raked in profits behind the lines in Germany or Russia as indispensable businessmen. But we led our revolution as we did, and in no other way, because it is detestable to us to inflict more suffering on a person than is absolutely necessary for the security of our regime, just because they are our political opponents. Every civil war is painful. But most painful are those where the poor and incited proletarian workers have to run into machine-gun fire, while their Jewish leaders escape in the decisive hour to their carefully planned foreign estates.

We rejected and fought Bolshevism not because it sought revolution, but because its leaders intended a slaughter like we once saw in Russia and now in Spain, and finally, because we did not want the German people to be ashamed of its history a second time. November 1918 perpetrated enough here. For this is the difference between the Bolshevik and the National Socialist revolution: the one transforms blossoming lands into gruesome fields of ruin, and the other transforms a destroyed and pauperized Reich into a healthy state and a blossoming economy again.

We believe it is a far greater deed to lead five million unemployed, who were betrayed to a gradual destruction, into work again and increasingly reintegrating them into the nation's life process, than it is to burn churches and houses, and to let hundreds of thousands of proletarians, and burghers, and farmers maim and murder each other.

Finally, we rejected and fought Bolshevism for purely economic reasons.

Right now, the world is again hearing harrowing reports of a catastrophic famine in Russia. Since 1917, with Bolshevism's victory, this misery has known no end. The Bolshevik frauds should not blame the weather for their own sins, for this same Russia, which has now been languishing for twenty years, was once one of the richest breadbaskets in the world.

There is eighteen times as much land per capita there than there is in Germany. What a miserable form of economy is that which is unable to let its people live decently under those circumstances. But if Bolshevism is incapable of feeding one non-farmer from nine farmers, then what would have happened in Germany, a country where two and a half farmers have to provide food for seven and a half non-farmers! We, too, are suffering under the changing weather conditions, and much more so, because with incomparably less fertile ground we are much more susceptible to the same weather disruptions. What would have become of Germany and its economy if Judeo-Bolshevik mismanagement had been established here, too!

We fought Bolshevism because its victory in Germany would have certainly relegated half or more of our people to certain death by hunger. If you cannot feed eight people per square kilometer in Russia, then not even ten million would have had the bare necessities for life in Germany under a Bolshevik regime. For our sixty-eight million live on the same area as does not even support five million in Russia!

And we finally reject Bolshevism and fought it because we are socialists, while Bolshevism sees in the worker an object that is good enough to be lead and exploited by his Jewish intellectual leaders, but not good enough to ever lead himself—for we do not understand socialism as the regime of a small group and the forced labor and starvation of millions. Above all, we do not understand socialism as the degradation of the lives of one's people for the benefit of an unconscionable Soviet bourgeoisie and an equally unconscionable agenda.

Besides, the German Volk is so intelligent, and the German worker so educated, that it is an insult to suggest he would have to take his orders from Russia! Moscow stays Moscow, and Germany is Germany!

And we finally fought Bolshevism because we did not want our Volk to once again be led to the butcher's block for a purely Judeo-Bolshevik imperialistic agenda. Bolshevism preaches world revolution, and would have used the German Volk and the German worker merely as cannon fodder for the goal of this world domination. We National Socialists, however, do not want our military might to be used to force something on other nations that they themselves do not even want. Our army does not swear its oath to spread the National Socialist idea to other nations with its blood, but rather to defend with its blood the National Socialist idea and with it the German Volk, and its security, and its freedom from attack by other nations.

We cannot even argue about this with the Jewish communist leaders. Whoever presumes the right to pull strings around the whole world, to incite peaceful people against each other, to organize civil wars, and then, when it goes bad, to leave things hanging and retreat to Moscow, he will lightheartedly utilize the state powers at his disposal for such imperialistic goals.

And everywhere we look today, this Bolshevism is agitating for foreign intervention, for insolent arms deliveries, for money collection, and so forth. The German Volk is one of the best in the world, militarily. This would have been the right death brigade for these bloody goals of the international agitators!

We have averted this danger for our Volk and for others through the

National Socialist revolution. Consequently, we can also observe these attempts in other places with a certain calm. But should the Reich ever be threatened by such an attempt, then with one beat, the nation will remember the National Socialist watchword and in a roaring storm would throw out those who believe they would make easier work of us militarily than they did in these past years ideologically. For in this age of international revolution, you can mark this: in Germany, the German Volk will remain master of its own house! There will be no Judeo-Bolshevik Sovietism!

These are but a few of the contrasts that separate us from communism.

I believe they are unbridgeable. These are truly two worlds that stand apart from each other, and that can never be brought together.

When a Member of Parliament complained in an English newspaper that we want to divide Europe into two pieces, we regretfully have to share some unfortunate news with this Robinson Crusoe, living on his happy British island: this division is already complete! Yes, what's more, this division tears apart from the inside any states that have not made a clear decision toward either one side or the other.

That one does not want to see a thing does not prove its absence. I was laughed at as a mad prophet in Germany for many years. For years, my admonitions and predictions were portrayed as the phantasm of an unwell man.

This was said by those upright citizens who, due to their business, had no use for Bolshevism, and thus also bravely refused to believe in the existence of such a danger. Because the profiteers had no communist leanings, due to their own character and mentality, they also did not want to imagine this horrible possibility in others. Then, when the day came that this danger was unmistakable, it merely caused them to bury their heads deeper in the sand. He who does not see the lightning and hear the thunder may calm his anxious self a bit. But when the lightning was finally so glaring, and the thunder so loud, that even these bourgeois sleepyheads could no longer doubt the danger, then they only had one hope left, which was to not accelerate the eruption of unrest through a rash provocation.

Therefore, they rejected the National Socialist Party and did not want to know anything about our SA and SS, because they might provoke communism, and then it would really go raving mad. These are the peerless bourgeois elements of popular front governments who, if they cannot manage to destroy communism, hope to at least tame it through calmness and meekness, and thus reject any evil adversaries who might embarrass or even provoke it in the end through resistance. For they have to govern! And if they cannot govern against this force, then they must govern *with* it, if possible. Really, communism should be banned, but this is unfortunately impossible with the level of self-awareness of these brave people, and so they instead ban fighting communism. And this is done energetically, as that may give the impression of a strong regime and an even stronger, more upright bourgeois man, who instead desires to tame it with calmness and meekness.

Yes, we were acquainted with them here, these clairvoyants, solid democrats, Centrists, People's Party members, and other political fighters of a bourgeois world who always paired their political might with so much mild wisdom that their resolutions were always measured, and their actions always played out with such cleverness that even a Clausewitz would hardly comprehend.

National Socialism eliminated such weakling elements and thus cleared the field for its contest with communism. Unfortunately, we first had to break through this bourgeois slime before we could hit the real opponent.

Perhaps other nations will also not be spared this task. In any case, we marvel at Fascist Italy, which was able to solve this problem eleven years ahead of us. And we are happy for all those states that are attempting to save their people from this danger in other ways!

We are convinced that sooner or later no Volk will be spared a final and clear decision, despite all the bourgeois will for rapprochement and despite all the so-called political wisdom, because it is not Europe that is divided in two parts, and it was not done by us, but Bolshevism has attacked the foundations of our entire human governmental and social order, our cultural understanding, the foundations of our faith, our moral beliefs, and has thus called them all into question.

If Bolshevism would nurse its doctrines in one single country, then it would not matter to the other nations. However, the principal tenet of this doctrine is its own internationality — that is, the spreading of its doctrine all over the world — and this means taking the present world off its hinges. That a British editorial writer is unwilling to recognize this means about the same as if a humanist in fifteenth-century Vienna denied Islam's intention of spreading in Europe with the suggestion that whoever claimed so was trying to tear the world in two, between Orient and Occident. Unfortunately, I cannot help but notice that most of the doubters of this global Bolshevik threat stem from the Orient themselves.

These world-citizens claim that it is not communism tearing the world into two points of view, but it is whoever notices the fact of communism, and especially whoever defends himself against it! It is not our place to lecture other nations, but it is our place to take to heart the lessons we have learned in Germany. The politicians in England have not yet come to know communism in their own country, but we have. Because I have fought, defeated, and rooted out this Judeo-Soviet theory, I think I can claim a greater understanding of the character of this phenomenon than the people who, at best, have only dealt with it academically.

National Socialists! For fifteen years I have founded, led, and brought to power a movement. In three and a half years in power, I have unquestionably led the nation with even greater success, and have regained it a respected place in the circle of nations. In this time, I have exerted myself to make our Volk healthier, its economy richer, its culture better.

When I consider that twenty-eight years ago I was still earning my bread as a small construction worker, that twenty years ago I was marching as a soldier in the great army, that fifteen years ago I had to grapple against an overwhelmingly superior power with only a handful of followers, that twelve years ago I still sat in a prison for my struggle for Germany, and that only four years ago I had the prospect of coming to power, then the results reached today are at the very least astonishing.

I only reached these results because, in the first place, I put in the effort to see things as they really are, and not as one would like them to be; secondly, because I never allowed the prattling of weaklings to dissuade me from an insight once I had reached it; and thirdly, because I was determined to obey necessity under all circumstances, once I had recognized it.

I will not become untrue to my principles, now that destiny has brought me such great success.

As I was, in the party circles for a decade and a half, the loyal proclaimer of the danger that threatened our Volk, so today I want to speak to the German Volk and to all my followers in all openness about what I am deeply convinced threatens Europe — and also us Germans.

I am tracking the path of Bolshevism's infection of the world today, just as many years ago I saw this infection in our own Volk and warned of it.

I see the methods of Bolshevik subversion of nations, and I see they are getting ripe for overthrow. I have the intense wish that our movement will be allowed to solve the problems we are given again with peaceful work. These problems demand the total commitment, energy, and faithfulness of a leadership and a people.

They are proud tasks, and I know that it is not only my name, but above all the name of our movement that will be immortalized forever by solving them. There is nothing we require more for these great plans than peace. Just as we had to create domestic peace in our nation in order to complete our tasks, these immense projects will only be realized through the preservation of peace in Europe.

I do not need to bolster the renown of the National Socialist movement or the German army through military deeds. Whoever undertakes such immense economic and cultural tasks, and is as determined as us to solve them, can only set his memorial in peace.

However, just as I once had to call the storm troopers of the party, the SA and SS, into being in order to secure domestic peace, I cannot leave external peace up to chance, or the judiciousness or caprice of the surrounding world.

Let our neighboring nations understand that if they respect German independence, freedom, and honor, they will find no warmer friend than the National Socialist Third Reich.

But just as well, let that Bolshevism—which we found out a few months ago intends to ready its army in order to open the gates of other nations to revolution by force, if necessary—let this same Bolshevism understand that the new German army stands before the gates of Germany.

It would be foolish of us not to consider the possibility of a Bolshevik revolution in Europe. Earlier, as party leader, I often discussed and weighed Bolshevism's intentions and prospects with ice-cold sobriety. Back then, I saw its possible development correctly, although I also correctly applied National Socialist strength.

As leader of the state and the whole German nation, I can only speak to the German people with the same sense of duty as I weigh these dangers, which float above Europe to an even greater extent.

If I were of the lowly caliber that my opponents so often ascribe to me, then I could be at peace knowing that Bolshevik subversion's weakening of the states it attacks could be a relief to Germany. I think that as a National Socialist, many bourgeois democrats see me only as a savage. But then as a savage, I am a better European, and in any case, I believe, a more reasonable one.

With anxious concern, I see the following possible development in Europe:

Democracy increasingly subverts the European states, making them internally insecure in judging the given danger and crippling any resolute resistance.

Democracy is the channel through which Bolshevism lets its poisons flow into individual countries, and there lets them take effect until this infection leads to a paralysis of the understanding and of any power of resistance. I think it is possible that then—in order to try to avoid anything more extreme—popular fronts or similarly veiled coalition governments will arise, which will try to eliminate the last organizational and intellectual forces of resistance that remain against Bolshevism in these nations, and may be successful in this.

I am convinced that each successful Bolshevik uprising in a state will have an immediate propagandistic effect in further inciting the masses in other countries and scaring and disheartening the elements of resistance.

The brutal mass slaughtering of nationalist fighters, the torching of the gasoline-soaked wives of nationalist officers, the slaughtering of children and babies of nationalist parents (as is already happening in Spain) will be intended as an example to make similarly-inclined forces in other countries shy away from resistance. But should such methods lead to their goal, and the modern Girondins are displaced by the Jacobins, and the popular front Kerenskys by the Bolsheviks, then Europe will sink into a sea of blood and sorrow. European culture, which, inseminated in ancient prehistory, and that will soon have a two-and-a-half-thousand-year history, will be displaced by the gruesome barbarism of all ages.

I see this danger, and I do not belong to those who faint over it and close their eyes in order to not have to behold it.

I also cannot hide how deep my sympathy is for those in other countries who, in the face of this threat to human culture and civilization, either eliminate or at least ban this danger.

But I would also like to make the most serious plea to the German people in light of this danger to adopt once again that fighting position that we National Socialists had to take for fourteen years before we came to power.

For all fellow countrymen must understand: I am not fighting for myself here. I am only a fighter for our Volk's future, for our beloved Fatherland, for our German people, and especially for our youth, for our children.

At this historic turning point, where fate will decide this way or that sooner or later, I believe it is necessary for all Germans to recognize that — as always and at present — the strength for resistance does not lie in the inanimate numbers of an organization, but in its living substance.

Which of us does not check the news daily during these weeks, on the unhappy country in Southern Europe, where this fight rages as a civil war, which will be decided one way or the other?

We National Socialists are not surprised by what we hear of the fury of the Bolshevik murderers and anarchist criminals. We have always and everywhere known them to be like this. If Germany is, in contrast, a land of peace and happy order today, then this is due not to the inanimate organization of our party or its storm troopers, but to the National Socialist spirit that filled it and led it to victory. What is more natural for us in this threatening time than to return with special fervor to the unshakable ideological foundation of our struggle and of our success?

No one will doubt that National Socialism will defend itself against Bolshevism and annihilate it wherever it attacks under any circumstances. However, as we know this and believe this, we will take measure of the magnitude of this task that will perhaps be assigned to us, and then the old party program will come to life again before our eyes, this program of honor, of social conscience, of national morals, of fanatical fulfillment of duty, of self-sacrifice, as well as eternal resoluteness in action.

When the contest against Bolshevism came to Germany, none of the old institutions decided this fight. No! It was the party, animated by the spirit of the National Socialist ideology, which defeated the elements of subversion and led the elements of order to victory.

How necessary it is for all of us to renew the spirit of this ideology. Today more than ever, the National Socialist state must avow this ideology, which is made for it and supports it, in all its institutions and organizations.

But this ideology cannot only be lip service; if it is going to really protect us in the hardest times, then the life of the state must be filled with it.

In the future, the party must employ the political selection process more than ever, without regard to origin, former status, birth, or wealth, but with the utmost moral obligation and responsibility to the nation. With this, the party has to place less stock in so-called social shortcomings, but exclusively focus on political (that is to say, national and personal) capacity and worthiness.

Our whole state structure must be ruled by the principle that genius, no matter from which social class it comes, opens the door to any position. Napoleon's maxim that every soldier must carry a marshal's baton in his haversack is one of the wisest that men can follow!

Special care has to be taken that a bureaucratic ossification does not place credentials above results, recommendations above worth, and so, ultimately, birth over merit.

We are marching toward tumultuous times with rapid speed. Such times demand men of resolute toughness, not wimpy stiffs. Men will not be measured by their superficial social manners, but by the goodness and toughness of their character in times of the hardest stress.

The party must, now more than before, take care that hard dispositions arise in our Volk, and that there be a relentless war against any trace of that pitiful cleverness that Clausewitz excoriates as the worst symptom of cowardice. We are approaching momentous historic periods, and mere cleverness has never prevailed in such periods, but always brave courage.

The party also has to represent and emphasize the socialist character of today's Reich with the utmost consistency. In such times, we have no use for the well-mannered burgher who thinks only of his business and loses sight of the whole strength of the Volk and its needs. The goal of National Socialism is not Marxist chaos, but it is also not bourgeois complacency. In these last few years, we have made endless strides in the education of our Volk toward a higher socialist communal understanding. National Socialism (that is to say, the party) must always advance here in order to form a tattered and divided nation into a singular, mutually pledged community.

We have to make all our fellow countrymen understand that no sacrifice is too great for this community. We must be hard in the rejection of the useless, and we are determined in carrying out what is necessary.

The party must also continue the theoretical education of the national community, even more than before. The upcoming Winter Relief will be the first opportunity to show our community spirit in a stronger form. We cannot leave it to the individual to decide if he wants to help; rather, he will have to.

But above all, the party has to be the pillar of the optimism that we National Socialists know so well. Every burden can be overcome, and its consequences are easier to deal with than pessimism and its consequences.

Woe to him who does not believe. He sins against the meaning of life.

His existence does no good and becomes a burden to his Volk.

In the course of my political struggle — and unfortunately I have to always emphasize this — it is especially from bourgeois circles that I have come to know these pessimists, who are incapable of faith and any saving deed, due to their pathetic attitude.

And I still experience them today. I have to ask them a question:

What would Germany have become if, in the year 1919, an unknown soldier had not had the faith that he could one day save the German nation from collapse through military preparedness and devotion, through bravery and self-sacrifice?

For what has saved Germany?

Was it the pessimism of a little nagger, this pitiful doubter, this always despondent naysayer? Or was it not the unshakable confidence that the eternal qualities of our Volk would shine through and prevail over the inferior and burdensome? No! It was the miracle of faith that saved Germany! Today, after these historically unprecedented successes, it is more than ever the party's duty to remember this National Socialist creed of faith and to again carry it before it as the holy symbol of our struggle.

For this reason, the party must always again break through to the hearts of the broad Volk, which is the best and strongest pillar of this faith. These hearts alone carry the courage, and bravery, and confidence that even the most primitive beings are given for self-preservation by nature. If the field marshals had always been as brave as the grenadiers had to be, then many battles would not have been lost. And when the politicians are as strong in their faith as the broad mass of a people is loyal, then they are unconquerable as leaders of their nations.

As the last solution in times of worry and inner moral crisis, I have always chosen the path to my Volk. This healthy mass of millions of German workers, farmers, and the middle class has always been a source of strength for me, giving me the courage to defy dangers and to walk my path with firm faith.

Let us all avow these principles and let us close the great circle of our community, strong in trusting our Volk, filled with faith in our mission, and ready for every sacrifice that the Almighty may demand of us. Then Germany, the National Socialist Third Reich, will go through this time of hardship, of affliction, of worry, equipped with the only metal that lets the knight in shining armor survive the battle against death and the devil: the ore of an iron heart.

The experience of these days was wonderful for all of us. The sight of these endless columns of our marching Volk in party and army was uplifting. And it was reassuring to see that it is not dead organizations that march past us, but the pillars of an indestructible faith. Once again we look back, hearts filled with gratitude, at the twelve months behind us.

Once again, we want to humbly tell the Almighty how much we feel His mercy, which has enabled and blessed our enormous work of wresting back our honor, and with it our freedom. Once again, I would like to thank the fellow fighters for the trust that they place in my leadership, and for the obedience with which they follow me.

I also need to thank the countless fighters of the movement for their National Socialist devotion, my countless staff for their tireless service for the reestablishment of our Volk, our Reich, our culture, and our economy, and I would like to especially thank the leaders and soldiers of the army, which will now stand guard over the National Socialist Third Reich and hold watch as it did long ago!

My party comrades!

For the eighth time we again depart from each other and return to our places of work. We will look back wistfully at the hours of this common experience, but filled, as always, with the sure faith that in twelve months we can meet again as the great family of the leaders, officers, fighters, and soldiers of our Volk.

Long live Germany!

THE FÜHRER'S SPEECHES
AT THE 1937 PARTY
CONGRESS OF LABOR

THE COURSE OF THE NSDAP'S
NINTH PARTY CONGRESS

An introduction

As the Party Congress of Labor, the NSDAP's ninth Reich Party Congress, began on September 6th in Nuremberg, the hundreds of thousands of the National Socialist formations streamed into Nuremberg from all over the Reich, which has labored and worked with never-before-seen energy for over four years in all social classes, in cities and villages, in factories and workshops, on sea and on the highways. The rhythm of this working power that reigns over the new Germany also filled the festive hours of this Party Congress, which became a symbol for how Germany united itself under the word of Adolf Hitler into a single great national community of labor. It was a fitting expression of this watchword of labor that many thousands came to the Reich Party Congress by driving on the just-finished Leipzig–Nuremberg Autobahn, where hundreds of laborers and machines still worked along the roadside. This is just one of the Autobahns that now traverse the country like assembly lines of a great German workshop, and that have themselves become a triumph and celebration of labor.

As National Socialism came to power under the leadership of Adolf Hitler, it was not enough to eliminate the communist adversary (and with him the forces of the red undermining of our existence) only in terms of holding power. The international campaigns of Bolshevism played out in a much broader scope than just the revolutionary strivings of the communist sector in individual countries. Bolshevism's attack on the European states is both a political-military one and an economic one. Thus, as the battle of labor initiated by the Führer led to the almost complete eradication of unemployment in Germany after about four years, it was not only a reawakening of all our economic energies, but also a victory over communism. In the very week of the 1937 Party Congress, the unemployment number finally sank below half a million, reaching the prewar level. With this success, communism also lay defeated on the field of the economic battle for the first time in Europe. Its hopes for bringing about the red revolution through labor riots, protests, strikes, and demonstrations by the unemployed, have been conclusively wrecked in Germany by the announcement of this number. They were not wrecked by the police powers of the National Socialist state, but by the victorious waging of the National Socialist battle of labor! They were wrecked by the will to life and the joy in work that newly filled Adolf Hitler's Germany.

The rebuilding of the German armed forces went hand in hand with the waging of this battle of labor, through the Führer's brilliant utilization of all the possibilities afforded by the international political situation. The Reich's outer defense against any attempt by the Red Army to overcome National Socialism by force grew as rapidly as the international plague of Bolshevism was beaten down within Germany. This building up of the armed forces was itself a battle of labor of unprecedented magnitude. It was a battle of labor in which the workers of the armament industry took as much a part as the officers and petty officers and the many hundreds of thousands of young Germans whose deployment as dutiful soldiers made it possible to complete the great feat of turning the hundred-thousand-man army into a national army in an improbably short time.

This fight for our right to self-defense and for security was another great contest with Bolshevism, in that we had to rebuild German arms rapidly enough that Moscow would not have a chance for a bloody strike before we were done. Today, National Socialism once again faces the Bolshevik world revolutionaries' attempts through politics and diplomacy to encircle Germany as well as Fascist Italy.

These attempts are apparently moving in two directions. First, the word has gone out from the Bolshevik Third International and its helmsman Dimitrov to all sections of the Comintern across the world to form a popular front. Hereby the communist organizations are ordered, under every possible disguise, to approach the social-democratic and bourgeois camps of the other parties in order to undermine the democratic states from within, from the center of their own parties, and thus make them ripe for attack. For this reason, Germany viewed the developments in France just months ahead of our 1937 Party Congress with grave concern, as it seemed almost certain that communism would reach its goal. National Socialism likewise attentively observed the events in other countries. First and foremost, National Socialism stood on the side of that nationalist military and political leadership in Spain that prevented a victory for the red revolution in the last hour through a terrible struggle. The official foreign policy of Moscow's Jew Litvinov-Finkelstein became very active on the side of the Comintern in Valencia, and tried to embroil the European states into a new general world conflagration with Moscow's second watchword of "indivisible peace" and "collective security."

All these attempts to keep Bolshevism alive in Spain by way of some collectivist idea, or even to provide it open aid by other European powers, was once and for all rebuked by the Führer in his concluding remarks at the Congress of Labor, as he declared: "In every attempt to spread Bolshevism in Europe, we see a fundamental shift in the European balance."

After the economic defeat of the communist revolution in the Reich, and after militarily safeguarding against a red assault, with this pronouncement Adolf Hitler also placed Germany in the way of the Moscow world-enemy as a definitive political stopping point. With this, the Führer announced, from Nuremberg, National Socialist Germany's will to forever stand against communism internationally as well. He declared Germany's mortal interest in any place where there might be an attempt to establish a new Soviet state.

With the statement that every spread of Bolshevism offsets the European balance, the Führer also lent European politics a more profound relevance. The conversations about the European balance have until now only moved within the frame of those all-too-familiar conferences, which have made this balance into numerical experiments with armament and economic statistics. In contrast to this dilettantish quackery, the Führer's great speech at the Congress was a historic exhortation to European politicians to remember the intellectual and spiritual foundations of European culture, and to not forget that, in this domain, just as in the economic sphere, the Bolshevik attack dissolves and destroys all existing conditions. If a balance has to be maintained in Europe today, then it is the balance between the forces of red destruction and the forces of preservation. But each of Moscow's victories drives the forces of order back and clears the path for the consummation of the world revolution.

The second four-year plan that the Führer ordered at the 1936 Party Congress, and on whose first portion the movement could look back on at the Party Congress, will also be one of the elements of order that the Third Reich will deploy against Moscow. It shall guarantee Germany's economic stability, even if the liberal-democratic world does not yet see the destruction of all economic relations that the Soviet system is gradually spreading across Europe. Germany knows that the time will come when, secured and made independent by this second four-year plan, its Reich can be the powerhouse of the political and economic convalescence of all of Europe. That this will one day be possible is thanks to German labor alone, the greatest strength that the German Volk can deploy for its future, and to which the Führer dedicated this Party Congress of 1937.

And so, in word and deed, through celebration and competition, the new Reich once again grew before everyone's eyes at this Party Congress into a symphony of beauty and strength. But both strength and beauty will always find their origin and their completion in work — in that work that is work for Germany!

— Dr. Walther Schmitt

RECEPTION OF THE FÜHRER IN
THE CITY OF NUREMBERG

September 6th, 1937

The Führer's answer to Chief Mayor Libel's Welcome Address

I am deeply moved by the heartfelt welcome I have received from the citizens of this city and now from you, Herr Oberbürgermeister, and I would like to express my joy and my gratitude to you and to all of Nuremberg. Hundreds of thousands of National Socialist men and women stream into this city for the seventh time, and they will, as always, leave this city strengthened and fortified. Everything that is being created and built in the whole German Reich through diligence and work is finding its perhaps most concentrated expression in Nuremberg right now.

The gigantic plans for the new Reich Party Congress grounds are being realized more and more. The Luitpold Arena was finished this year, as was the Zeppelin Field (but for a few small interior renovations). The foundations of the Congress Hall are laid. The first core of a wall is being raised. The structural work of the wide street from the March Field to the Luitpoldhain is done. The first preliminary work is complete on the March Field, and the artistic architectural designs are decided. On Thursday, September 9th, we will lay the cornerstone for the German Stadium, the most tremendous arena that any people will have ever erected for the training of its physical strength and beauty. Thus, rushing ahead of the rest of Germany, this city will soon receive its eternal imprint.

But just as the building up of Germany can only be the result of unending hard work, the same goes for the building up of this city of our Reich Party Congresses. All these people are creating an immortal monument to the German Volk and to themselves through their work!

That you, Herr Oberbürgermeister, present to me a cast of Thorak's sculpture on behalf of the City of Nuremberg brings me special joy. For this will serve as a perpetual reminder in miniature for me of the wellspring that has its consummation in large scale here.

Therefore, Herr Oberbürgermeister, please accept my heartfelt thanks.

In the belief that the proceedings of the new Reich Party Congress will again increase in magnitude and intensity, I ask you all to salute this venerable city with me, whose name has become a symbol for our movement.

City of Nuremberg: Heil!

The leading men of the state and party enthusiastically joined in the Sieg Heil that the Führer gave the City of Nuremberg. The celebration concluded with the national anthems.

The Führer left the ceremonial hall amidst the sounds of fanfare.

THE PROCLAMATION OF THE FÜHRER AT THE OPENING OF THE 1937 PARTY CONGRESS

September 7th, 1937

Party comrades! National Socialists!

Ten years have passed since the third Party Congress of the movement took place in Nuremberg for the first time. After an arduous, unprecedented rebuilding of the party, we met in Weimar in 1926 to give externally visible proof of the successful reestablishment of the movement.

These were not easy decisions under the circumstances at the time. But how much greater was the responsibility we had to bear, only a year later, when we called together a new assembly in Nuremberg. A big leap from the small Thuringian residence to the great old imperial German city! For the first time, the Party Congress took place before over two thousand people. For the first time, it was followed by the assembly of the militant movement in the now-historic Luitpold Arena for the great SA rally. And although this place has since experienced a many-fold increase in size, back then it appeared so huge to us that many secretly started to doubt that we would be able to fill it. For the first time, on August 19th, thousands and thousands of our SA and SS men stood on the wide expanse in the glimmer of a sun penetrating a wet, rainy morning, and they once again professed their creed to our movement, and to me as their leader. And for the first time, National Socialists proceeded through this very room, in which this proclamation is now being read to you. After several hours of marching, eight thousand old fighters slept here, a mere portion of those who would stand in the great rally the next day.

Much more of what we today take for granted was then already being established.

It was immensely beautiful and touching for all of us to see the National Socialist movement proceed through the wide spaces of today's city of the Reich Party Congress, and to experience the unique forms emerge that have become so dear and familiar to us.

The year 1927 also helped a great deal to give the National Socialist Party Congresses their grand character, which remains today and should continue to develop the uniqueness of its character.

Already in 1927, these Congresses operated under the foremost principle that our party's general exhibition could not be allowed to descend into a parliamentary debate club. Here especially there could be no anonymous responsibility, and therefore no anonymous voting. Our organization's foremost principles had to shine through at our movement's Party Congress more than anywhere.

Always, everywhere, and in all things, the individual man carries the responsibility!

Because of this, the objective work of the Party Congress has always been done in special meetings and briefings followed by the free decision of one responsible person. And at the Congresses, there was the sovereign declaration of the goals and intentions for our work, as well as a great accounting of our tasks in the preceding year. Since then, there have always been three tasks for our Party Congress to accomplish each year:

1. Determining what work has been accomplished, what plans have been realized, and what goals have been reached through the activity of our movement.
2. Announcing our goals and work for the nearer and further future.
3. Initiating our party comrades, who are especially receptive during these Party Congresses, into the theoretical doctrines as well as the organizational principles of the movement, and with them also the whole German Volk.

Only in this way were we able to develop these rallies for ten years, which hold unforgettable impressions in them for every participant, while other groups' gatherings grew into spectacles of the worst kind of squabbling. Thus, the National Socialist movement's Reich Party Congress gradually became the nation's biggest community festival. This year, for the first time, we are adding something new with the inclusion of the athletic combat games and beauty pageants.

Today this all seems obvious. Back then, it was new, and only a very few were able to imagine the whole glorious picture that we now know as this magnificent rally! If ten years ago you could still rightly describe this day as the revolutionary congress of a city-storming party, then today it is the great parade of a German nation conquered by National Socialism.

From the beginning, the intimation of what our Party Congress would become forced us to go against the custom of other parties and find a permanent place for holding our National Socialist demonstration. Back then, many did not understand our decision to always have one place where the party will hold its gatherings. But how else would it have been possible to craft the only space suitable for the biggest rally of all nations and of all times! To do justice to the broadness and magnitude of the movement, you could only develop the vast facilities needed in a single city over the course of years, maybe decades.

Today there can also be no more doubt that we chose the right city. No city would have been worthier for the National Socialist Party's Congress than glorious old Nuremberg. No city had more favorable conditions for having our demonstration back then. But also, it would not have been possible in any other city to establish that enchanting connection between the rich and exceptional heritage of our past and our equally exceptional and glorious present and future.

What Nuremberg has become is a representative slice of what our movement and what Germany has become. A colossal form is in process. Its parade grounds are the biggest in the world. Tomorrow, the cornerstone will be laid for the construction of a stadium such as the world has never seen.

In two years the shell of the colossal Congress Hall will have already been built. As the first granite monument, it will bear witness to the greatness of its motivating idea and the whole facility. A parade and rally grounds worthy of the greatest upheaval in German history, which National Socialism called forth!

My party comrades!

Even the greatest political reshaping takes place against a background of mundane daily routine that does not allow many people to apprehend in what a tumultuous and historic time they live.

In the narrow frame of a modest life, in the clutter of everyday work, the view of the aggregate results of the course of this life is all too easily caught up and distracted. And besides, every success, every victory, and every completed work has to be bought by the application of labor, of diligence, and thus also the care and even suffering of countless individuals.

When we National Socialists conquered Germany, we experienced this fight as one long chain of a thousand tribulations, a thousand sacrifices, and also a thousand failures. But it was so important, for this very reason, to lift the isolated man out of this atmosphere of his own small struggle and its concomitant worries at least once a year, in order to place him in the greater common front and open his eyes to the vast dimensions of the sequence and course of the whole fight, and to show him the proud path that has already been trodden.

The farmer in his village, the worker in his workshop or factory, the clerk in his office — how are they all supposed to be able to see the extent of the entire results of all their countless personal sacrifices and struggles?

Now, once a year, on the occasion of the general exhibition of the party, they will step out of the modesty of their little existences and will see and understand the greatness of the fight and of our successes! Then, many of them might for the first time experience the overwhelming assurance that their worries and efforts on the small scale have not been for nothing, but rather have contributed to massive success, and that even their small and all-too-familiar failures were meaningless compared to the total result of the movement's and the entire Volk's struggle.

And when hundreds of thousands again march into Nuremberg for this Congress, and fill this city like an endless warm stream of life from all the districts of Germany, they will also be able to return home from this exalted place, look back and look within themselves, and they will all be able to say: *We are truly the witnesses of an upheaval the likes of which the German nation has never seen.* Socially, economically, culturally, and racially, we are living in a gigantic change of the times. If we let our gaze venture out past the German borders, we can almost hear the roar of a world in turmoil, filled with fighting and unrest.

If I deal with each of the most important questions of our time, then it is not only to reveal their importance, but also to make clear how we solved these problems in the past, and that we are also determined to solve them in the future!

My party comrades!

We live in a great, historically unprecedented age. Yes, nations have risen and fallen through war or revolution in every century, states have been established or destroyed. But only rarely do earthquakes occur in the lives of nations, tremors that reach into and even threaten or destroy the foundations of the building that is the social order!

And who today wants to ignore or dismiss that we are now in the midst of a battle that is not about the border disputes between peoples or states, but about the question of the survival or destruction of the superior human social orders and their cultures?

The organization of human society is threatened! Not just some state tower will collapse, but a confusion of tongues, a new division of humanity will come over the nations!

What seemed to be solid for all eternity, after a thousand years of development, is now proven to be brittle and weak. All around us we hear the crackling of the fabric of man's existing social contract, and we are already experiencing the crumbling of a few especially fragile structures.

As National Socialism began its historic struggle for the German Volk, it saw this issue as the more crucial and dire one. Wars and defeat do not have as terrible a meaning in the lives of nations as does an inner crisis of the social order.

You can recover from lost wars in a short time. You can often only rebuild a destroyed social order after many centuries. Sometimes a people perishes forever this way.

And there can be no more doubt about this. What we knew as "society" in our time is now not only contested, but partly already so devalued that it can only be a matter of time until the illusion of such a social order is shattered in some catastrophe. There is no durable organization left in human society today whose carrying elements derive their rights only from birth, status, heritage, or especially property. Even supposed "education," such as belongs to a certain confession, can no longer be seen as a factor for creating or holding up society. When the Russian Empire fell victim to Bolshevik chaos, it was only because the forces that once formed and maintained it were no longer capable of fulfilling their mission. The ideas and pillars of this old structure did not prove resilient enough against the onslaught of new notions and certain new doctrines. And in this last year, we witnessed the attempt to further spread this communist confusion in the East and West.

If Germany, like Italy, seems to be a safer and more solid refuge amidst this unrest, then it is only because National Socialism itself found the path to a social revolution without first destroying the existing order with violence, and thus throwing the basis of our political, economic, and cultural life into chaos.

When we recognized the weaknesses of our bourgeois social order, we tried to build a new social structure through disciplined regeneration. The fundamental principle of this work was to break with customary privileges and to put the leadership of all domains of life, but principally in politics, in the hands of a new elite, which would be sought out and selected without regard to heritage, birth, and social or confessional memberships, but exclusively formed on the basis of inner disposition and worthiness.

Building up a new leadership elite in our nation without the devastating chaotic destruction of the existing conditions is one of the greatest deeds in the history of our Volk. This is also a revolution, only without the accompanying lashing-out of the slave masses, gone crazy due to their inability to handle freedom. For it was not a mob that carried out this National Socialist revolution, but a community of the best Germans, Germans from every class, bound to the strictest obedience, loyally devoted, and fighting out of the noblest idealism. But these men's goal was a true revolution, meaning the elimination of a social order that had become impossible (due to its decrepit internal elements), replacing it with a new one. The breadth and depth of this upheaval cannot be better recognized in any place or time than at the Reich Party Congress in Nuremberg.

Is this now a new Volk that marches here, or is it not? Is this Germany still comparable to the old, or is it new? Has this community become firmer and more inseparable, or was the former one more so? And above all: did anyone in the other parties who dreamt of Germany's resurrection imagine it how it is today, or was this vision exclusively in the National Socialist movement and in the fighter's deposit of faith?

It is thus of the utmost importance that we carry out the most meticulous selection process for the leadership of our nation and in all other domains, and that we not capitulate to any resistance or formal limitations. The best that we can offer to the earlier, no longer capable leaders of our social order is the same rights that anyone else would receive. However, in this state, privilege will be granted to virtue, to vitality, and to strength, to courage and resolve, and thus to him capable of leadership.

This can stand in opposition to knowledge, because it would be quite impertinent to claim that knowledge and vigor, courage and insight, boldness and experience were mutually exclusive.

The German nation can take this one sure consolation: the world may begin to burn around us, but the National Socialist state will jut out of the Bolshevik fire like unburnable platinum.

The societal problem is among the greatest we face today. I must distinguish the societal problem from the social problem, because Bolshevism has everywhere only touched the social problem, while it pays absolutely no heed to the societal problem. Bolshevism's social revolution means nothing other than the elimination of the native intelligences of the Volk and their replacement by the Jewish race of parasites. Wherever it comes to power, Bolshevism thoroughly solves *that* problem, or tries to solve it. In contrast, the societal was only seen as the means to an end. The type of treatment the societal problem gets is obvious from the lack of any intention to really come to a beneficial solution on it. Since the Jewish Bolshevik agitators, knowing the understanding and education of the masses of this region, explained the societal problem as exclusively one of income, they have quickly manufactured that tension between income and prices that is convenient for the implementation of the Bolshevik social revolution. While on the one side incomes experience a continual increase due to strikes and terror (while production stays the same or even decreases), on the other side they are forcing a rise in prices.

This process is inevitable because there is no rise in production to offset the higher incomes, and so it must be offset by a rise in prices.

But this rise in prices always gives the natural reason for the immediate raising of incomes, which is always forced by strikes and terror. The just as inevitable consequence is that prices again meet the new, higher income. Because production is further hampered by the strikes and lockouts that are connected with this economic battle, as well as by the general lack of discipline, the decrease in consumable goods must cause prices to rise even quicker than wages as a regulatory factor. This causes discontent to grow without end.

It is easy for the Judeo-Marxist agitators to laud the rise in wages as the work of a socially conscious Bolshevism or Marxism, while blaming the consequent price increases on the accursed intentions of rotten capitalism, the archenemy of Marxism. We see the results of this development in the countries around us: rising wages, declining production, and thus the rapid weakening of the purchasing power of money, as seen in rising prices and currency devaluation.

If Germany can be a calm observer amidst this drama of insanity, then this is thanks to the National Socialist movement, which from the beginning held onto this iron principle: it is not the printed banknote that is crucial in someone's life, but what he is able to buy with it.

But you cannot buy more than what is produced! Therefore, the crucial thing for a nation's general standard of living is the total national production. The goods a nation produces automatically bring in their equivalent in wages, and in this way find their buyers.

It would make no sense to produce thirty or forty million more tons of coal, while reducing the purchasing power of the nation so that you cannot dispense of the coal. Therefore, it is also not right to assume that a shortage in some area is proof of an especially poor economy. No, it is only proof that a further increase in production is needed, because the necessary purchasing power for it is available. What the so-called "ten thousand" consume is totally irrelevant. That is of less volume and worth than what the other sixty-seven million consume!

The fact is that Germany has solved its difficult societal problem, and thoroughly: there is really no more who are jobless in our country.

Quite the opposite: there is a shortage in many areas today, especially of skilled labor. I believe this is a greater social success than to ruin and destroy production in other countries—as was also done here—until finally the so-called proletariat is no less rid of its worries, but in much greater want of work and bread.

We can be all the more satisfied with the results of our efforts because we have been able to keep wages as well as prices almost totally stable. My party comrades, compare this to the results in other countries, and here you will also recognize the correctness of National Socialist leadership. Beyond this, National Socialism has tried, with immense effort, to better and to beautify the social conditions of life.

What our great relief organizations have been able to accomplish will be presented to you with concrete numbers in the course of this week. On the whole though, we can surely classify the activity of the Labor Front in its various arms, the work of the Winter Relief as well as the National Socialist People's Welfare, and finally the complementary work of "Strength through Joy" as the most enormous community effort that has ever happened anywhere. What Bolshevism has to offer in comparison to this is laughable.

Here, too, we will hold on to the foundational principles we have had so far into the future, and here too, it is clear that there can never be the hint of a standstill in this striving. The opposite: the manner in which we will exert ourselves in National Socialist Germany to solve these problems will help raise our individual countrymen to a social conscientiousness whose end result will be a national community in the noblest sense. And this is certain: we are a thousand times closer to this in National Socialist Germany than are the Marxist states, torn apart as they are by class and economic battles.

If we venture from this specialized work into the realm of the general economy, then we also see numerous indications of crisis around us. Only a few years ago, the byword "world economic crisis" still dominated the public consciousness. And almost everywhere—especially in Germany—people were waiting for the miracle of a general collective effort to take care of this international crisis. Back then, and for many years, I warned against this belief that the rectification of this international economic crisis would be accomplished internationally; instead, I stressed that the individual national economies would have to be brought into right order first.

It was also a National Socialist principle that the pattern of continually talking about ending the world economic crisis while committing the most dubious and economically disruptive currency manipulation is something we must reject.

I can ask you now, my party comrades, whether we held true to our values or not. Should we have instead waited longer for this international economic miracle? Was it right to apply our principle even here, that our first help should come from our own strength? As we National Socialists were convinced that our freedom would not just be given to us one day, but that we had to fight for it ourselves, so we believed in the correctness of this principle in economic life as well. In ending the German economic crisis, we always acted according to one dogma: the economy is one of many functions of national life and thus can only be organized in a way that makes it fulfill its purpose; it cannot be organized according to some abstract dogma.

Neither the socialized economy nor the free economy exist as a dogma with us; rather there is only the duty-bound national economy—that is, an economy whose whole purpose is to provide the highest and best conditions of life for a people.

Insofar as it does right by this task without any direction from above and only by the free interplay of market forces, then this is good, and very pleasant for an administration. As far as it is not working toward this proper goal in some area as a free economy, then the leadership of the national community has the duty to give the economy instructions that are necessary for the preservation of the whole. But if the economy should be totally incapable in some area or another of fulfilling its purpose, then the leadership of the national community must employ other means and search out other ways to meet the needs of the general public. But this one thing is certain: here, as in everything else, where there is a will, there is a way.

The National Socialist state's will to secure the economic foundations of the nation had its most acute expression in the resolution that was announced to you all here last year: to make the nation independent from the caprice or insecurity of other nations in many vital areas in a very short time. This resolution is being realized just as surely as the National Socialist state was once realized.

Insofar as private economic forces are sufficient for its realization, they will be engaged with it, but as soon as an impossibility arises for reaching the goal by this path, the nation as such will take over this work.

Let no one be mistaken: a national community that is able to build up a tremendous army, mobilize a gigantic labor service, lead the colossal undertaking that is the German Reich Railway, and do so many other monumental feats, will also be able to, for example, bring German steel and iron production to whatever height is required!

We have already completed other works besides those in the four-year plan! And I would like to assure you, my party comrades, that this work is proceeding at exactly the required tempo under the leadership of Party Comrade Göring!

One thing is certain: there is with us no state-economy ideology, nor a private-economy ideology. In both cases, the ultimate responsibility lies in the same place: the leadership of the nation, meaning the national community itself.

In any case, there is only one single economic question that has continuously filled us with concern. It is the difficulty of procuring our food. Without colonial holdings, the German Lebensraum is too small to guarantee the constant, secure, lasting sustenance of our people.

No other people can point to a greater achievement in this area than us. The numbers that Party Comrade Darré will lay out for you soon are shining proofs for this claim. Still, it is an intolerable thought, to be dependent on the chance of a good or a bad harvest year after year.

Therefore, our demand for our Reich's colonial holdings is one that is founded upon our economic need, and the attitude of the other powers toward this demand is not reasonable.

Germany's former colonies were never stolen from these powers. In a world that today oozes with moralistic phrases, it would be appropriate to also consider this fact!

Besides, this simple and sober fact speaks for German economic management: when we seized power five years ago, Germany's economic life was like a graveyard. Today it is again filled with the rhythm of the creativity and labor of one of the most industrious people on earth.

This is all possible through the authority of today's government, which is rooted in the National Socialist Party.

We are convinced that, especially in the economic realm, our party comrades and all able-bodied National Socialists have the highest duty to blindly trust the Reich's leadership and to comply with its orders, and even just its pleas, without hesitation. For we have a harder fight than most. 137 people per square kilometer are harder to feed than eleven or twelve. We can only accomplish this miracle through the national community's utmost discipline, through everyone immediately recognizing the necessities of the day or of the age. We Germans cannot allow each person to go his own way on this issue! Together, we will be able to solve anything, one way or another. On their own, everyone would become a victim of these communal difficulties.

When I look now at politics, then, my party comrades, I believe there are but a few observations that need to be made for our account in this area. The world around us is filled with wars and rattling sabers! Many nations are filled with unrest, and many states are shattered by revolutions!

After a miserably lost war, after a shameful revolution, after fifteen years of being plundered and extorted, Germany today presents an image of calm, resolute strength despite all this. We have achieved a peace that is defended through our own Volk.

I would like to present three facts as the conclusion of this chapter of German history: 1) The Treaty of Versailles is dead!; 2) Germany is free!;

and 3) The guarantor of our peace is our own armed forces!

Party comrades!

If the National Socialist government had nothing but these three results to show for its leadership and activity, then this alone would already guarantee it a place of honor in the annals of our Volk's history.

We got rid of a diktat that was meant for all time, and in not even five years!

A new military was built up in barely four years. And Germany is not isolated in this today, but is allied with powerful states. The natural bond of common interests between National Socialist Germany and Fascist Italy has shown itself to be a factor for securing Europe against this chaotic insanity more and more in these past months. In the future, it will not be possible to simply step over this community of the will in order to implement the agenda of the day.

Our treaty with Japan serves the same purpose of standing together in defense against the attack on the civilized world that is today taking place in Spain, tomorrow in the East, and the day after tomorrow perhaps somewhere else. Within us all lives the strong hope that other powers will also recognize the signs of the times and strengthen this front of reason and of the defense of peace and of our culture! Even culturally, the National Socialist state stands strong and fortified against a thoroughly insecure world.

During these days, if you walk through this city and see the enormous construction sites, or the already completed assembly halls, then the proud realization will hit you all that, even in this realm, our nation has ended its time of decline, and is currently experiencing the beginning of a great new ascent!

What is being planned in Berlin, Munich, and Hamburg, and is already partly commencing, is proof of a cultural consciousness that is more than a will! It is represented in now-undeniable deeds!

But Germany has experienced its greatest revolution through the racial hygiene that has been systematically addressed for the first time in this country.

These German racial policies will be more consequential for our future than the effects of all other laws combined, for it is these laws that are creating the new man.

They will protect the Volk from losing its earthly existence, as so many sad historical examples of other races did through their blindness to the one important question.

For what is the point of all our work, all our labor, if it is not in service of the preservation of the German man?

And of what value is it to serve this man if we neglect the most important thing, which is to keep him pure and unspoiled in his blood?

Every other failure can be fixed, every other mistake corrected, but what is neglected in this realm can never be made good again. Whether our racial-hygienic work was fruitful can best be judged by oneself during these days. For what you encounter on the streets of this city, *that* is the German man. Come and see for yourself whether he has gotten worse or better under National Socialist leadership. Do not measure it only by the numbers of how many more children are born, but first and foremost, measure it by the appearance of our youth.

How beautiful are our girls and boys, how bright are their expressions, how healthy and fresh their bearings, how glorious are the hundreds of thousands and millions of bodies that have been schooled and nurtured in our organization.

Where are there better men today than those you see here? A rebirth of the nation has really begun through the conscious breeding of a new man.

And this is the most profound vindication for our activity in the past, and the strongest obligation for our will and our decisions in the future. For only he who keeps his Volk healthy guarantees it a future. And so, in this week, we see the new German Volk arising, we see the healthy and beautiful youth, we see the hard frames of the men of our Labor Service, we see the hundreds of thousands of men in our fighting movement, and above all, we experience the proud self-confidence of the soldiers of our young army.

A truly uplifting result of a historic effort!

My party comrades!

In the fifth year since the National Socialist revolution, we can make no more glorious observation than this one: it is good to be a German again, and it is a blessing to live in Germany!

The German Volk, the National Socialist movement, the National Socialist army, and our Reich: Sieg Heil!

THE FÜHRER'S SPEECH AT
THE CULTURAL CONFERENCE

September 7th, 1937

One of the symptoms of the cultural decay behind us is the abnormal increase in art literature. This process very strongly resembles the industrious theoretical affirmations of freedom that weak bourgeois stiffs laud in song and poetical phrases without ever attempting to practically bring it about. They not only believe that they are actually serving or working toward freedom in this Platonic way, no: they find their totally sufficient self-gratification through this activity. Thus, they experience the glorious fact of this condition as a dream, in which they find all the more pleasure in being able to praise it. They patiently carry slave's chains, but speak about the beauty of "freedom." They act submissively, but with warrior-like battle cries, they vociferate about heroism, manly struggle, and victory! But the more they sink into these heroic visions, the more they hate and persecute those who, recognizing reality, confront them with the observation that there is no freedom here and that heroes must first rise up in order to win it!

We experienced this type of bourgeois self-gratification for fifteen years in Germany, and suffered much from it! For fifteen years they wrote and spoke about international law, equal rights, and human rights, and all the while they pretended that their talking and writing would either make this condition into a reality or even prove that it already existed, and in this way they tried — whether consciously or unconsciously — to hide the hard reality from people.

But woe to those who dared to hold cold, hard facts up to this *fata morgana*! Thus, no one hated the marching of the National Socialist battalions more than those who constantly prattled about "national freedom" and talked about "military preparedness." For their struggle was a nice one, first and foremost one without danger, while the goals of others would only be reached through bitter sacrifice. In their world it was enough to talk. But to enter into the other world, one had to act!

The weapons of last resort for these bourgeois extollers of freedom were feather and ink. But National Socialists demanded a thousand privations. But gradually, actual freedom came out of their struggle: a freedom that is not the product of poetical meditations, but the result of hard political struggles, whose elements are therefore not essays editorials, but historic acts and accomplishments. But of course, it was harder to come to March 16th, 1935, or to occupy the Rhineland, than it is to occupy oneself with theoretical treatises in newspapers and literary brochures about the correct form of actual freedom. History will surely only register what is real; that means that it is not political will or theoretical views that are historically decisive, but political accomplishment. This means: *action.*

It is no different in the realm of cultural development. As political regeneration could only come from positive effort outside of literary treatment, so also the cultural rebirth cannot come from editorials, art criticism, art appreciation, or art essays, but needs to lead to a positive cultural effort. What would our art literature do, if past centuries had not provided the objective material foundations for its theoretical treatises? How could humanity in the future speak of an enrichment of its cultural life, if instead of the proliferation of true cultural achievements, all that took place was an expansion of the scope of the literary treatment or appreciation of culture? One cannot speak of cultural politics if it is only understood as the intellectual-theoretical treatment of cultural questions. No: the purpose of cultural politics, as with politics in general, is to lead to new achievements!

These outputs of true creative work will then be collected, and maybe later they can once again be weighed, and in unproductive times they can provide needed fodder for new discussion by the presumably proliferating literati. Certainly, this could not be provided by the so-called cultural-political will, because this is only measurable the moment it distills itself into a deed. Only then does it have substance and only then can it, potentially, lead to the enrichment of the cultural heritage of a people, or otherwise be rejected as unworthy.

Thus, the cultural history of past ages is just the record of cultural achievements, and not the playback of cultural opinions or of cultural will!

What is thought, spoken, or written down in this world can only claim intrinsic value insofar as it, as a purely intellectual work, contributes to the body of intellectual and scientific understanding. Culture is now much too limited in actual achievements, so much so that intellectual treatises count as replacements for the creations lacking in, say, music, architecture, or related arts. Besides, it is utterly impossible to express in speech and writing what, for example, the human voice in song or music overall is able to convey. For this is also a language of nations. Its content and its capacity for expression are as unique as they are irreplaceable. By means of music especially, sentiments can be conveyed that can neither be written nor spoken about with equal intensity! One can gauge how much more wonderful and expressive this language is by the difficulty of learning or understanding it. While the normal, more technical means of expression embodied in speech and writing is easily able to build bridges of scientific understanding between peoples, these almost totally fail at translating many spiritual stirrings and perceptions, compared to music. Thus, the most profound musical wonderworks are only intelligible to a small circle of nations, primarily only those chosen people who — thanks to a common origin, even if deep and prehistoric — still possess the collective antenna for receiving these finest broadcasts of spiritual sensation.

Truly noble cultural achievement is the rarest and most blessed expression of an inner disposition or special talent given to a people, and it is thus also the strongest proof of the higher purpose of a people, already assigned to it in the cradle. For time alone cannot bring forth any work of art besides what men themselves bring forth from out of this inner purpose, and in the way that they see and perceive it, or as their ear hears it.

For example, one of the first artistic stirrings in man has always been the attempt to represent the own *I*, that is, the human body in image and form.

Long before language found the ability to describe the form of the highest earthly creature in words, the creatively disposed man attempted to record and render his impression of himself or his surroundings through drawing.

But here we see how little artistic skill has to do with the actual conditions of man as such, and how much it is clearly the gift of a few capable nations and a few gifted individual people among them. For every creature on this earth must, or should, perceive itself as ideal. But among the human races it is rare that this physical self-perfection is given fitting artistic expression. It is not because the Greek is beautiful that he was able to portray his beautiful body in image and in sculpture, but because the Greek was given the ability to *perceive* this beauty, that is, to *consciously recognize* it, and to imitate it. The masterworks of antiquity are attributable only to this. No doubt there are Negro tribes quite classically beautiful, with well-proportioned physiques, yet they nevertheless lack the higher ability to even approximate their own "I" for us. Thus, a people may be formed to be beautiful (that is, suited to purpose in its physique), but the crucial thing is whether it was given the gift to consciously recognize its own beauty and to represent it correspondingly. But most recognize neither their own appearance nor the forms of their surrounding world, nor are they able to represent this impression in the sense of a creative vision. This should illuminate the great blessing the nations with artistic abilities were given. That this art is only lent to a few races in the highest sense, and not to the majority, can only heighten the importance of these races' worth. For thus the great mass of culturally weak (because creatively sterile) nations confront the few others who, since darkest prehistory, have united artistic perception with the ability of artistic composition.

Not only are the civilized peoples in the minority against the culturally incapable, but even within these nations, there are only a very few blessed chosen ones, to whom Providence has given the intuitive creative power necessary to truly see and reproduce what is seen.

Just as in all realms of life there are always a few individual people who are the trailblazers of new perceptions, the doers of new achievements, so it is in culture. Hundreds of thousands want to possess the same body. Love and passion may lead the millions of feeling creatures of the two sexes to come together or to separate, but only one person will be able to perceive the laws and powers of male and female beauty more consciously, and only one will be able to represent it with a hand guided by a higher power. Only one will be able to represent it so correctly that later generations, educated in the anatomical discoveries made since then, can only be in awe at the wonder of this statue, created over two and a half thousand years ago, which no contemporary anatomist could outdo even scientifically.

But this does not apply only to the representation of the human body or the other visible forms of the surrounding world, no; the power of the creatively gifted individual comes into even starker relief in the realms of music and architecture! The materials used in architecture are almost universally available. In the eternal course of humanity, they stand and have stood available to all peoples pretty equally. The natural need for it was also given equally to all races. And yet how diverse are their solutions! How few nations have become conscious of the possibilities for these materials to better their existence in this time, and how differently they became conscious.

What a distance between the highest musical achievements of a primitive Negro tribe and the *Ninth Symphony* or *Tristan und Isolde*.

What an immeasurable distance between the great radiant constructions of the people of antiquity, two and a half and three thousand years ago, and the pitiful housing of numerous races that live today. Where was time here a factor for creativity? There are divinely gifted individual nations whose capability is just as timeless as the inability of others.

But when we consciously compare these culturally creative races with the others, then we find a measure in the opposite of their achievements. For it is only through opposites that we learn to recognize the great and the small, the light and the dark. Cowards give cause for appreciating heroes, degrees of intelligence are measured against the stupid, and it is through laziness that we first learn to value the importance of hard work. Chaos shows the blessing of order, and the bliss of human culture raises itself above barbarism.

Thus, the civilized peoples are always the opposite pole of the uncultured nations, just as within the nations themselves, the artist stands alone against the mass of people irrelevant or even hostile to art. This is because genius separates itself from the masses by anticipating unknown truths that the masses become aware of only later!

It may also happen that the individual's flash of genius is recognized as a bright certainty the moment this newly discovered truth is announced. But the more genius forges ahead of its time in its thoughts and its works, the harder it will become for it to be understood. The number of those quelled by his insight or his activity will be small, and woe if sloth or indolence are paired with self-seeking against him and his works, and erect an artistic barrier against him. Then centuries may pass before mankind catches up to such a maverick. Because the highest works of artistic genius are usually only rooted in one people, they are generally only given the appreciation they deserve in that same community. Through such a new work, the community is awoken from the sleep of unconsciousness and experiences the naturalness of this now-known insight. As every genius is a trailblazer for the path to the recognition of something real, so the truly great artist does the same. The ancient sculptor, who gave the human body a beautiful portrayal, gave the whole world a representation beyond every description of what is "correct" to subsequent so-called exact science. But this reality is synonymous with the highest purposiveness.

Two and a half thousand years before us, this stone cutter anticipated the human body in such a way, that today after all the insights of our anatomical research we have to say that it was represented according to nature in the highest sense. Therein lies the meaning of what we describe with the word "art." The ability to grasp a reality ahead of time, ahead of the present, by seeing it, and by shaping and representing it with the means specially suited for this. While the normal scientist takes discovered insights and perhaps carefully advances one step and incorporates the new insights, the artist jumps millennia ahead of the insights of his own time. Mankind becomes conscious of static laws two thousand or three thousand years later and now confirms architectural forms that once came from the intuitive apprehension of an individual and already came into being as a work of art. What was granted to a people or a family of peoples as art millennia ago is now proven to correspond with naturally occurring necessary structures that arouse admiration with their beauty. The microscope now discovers these to be the elements of the structure of certain bodies.

Perhaps music's tones will eventually be described as a systematic number pattern of vibrations, and the riddle of its deep power over our souls will be solved. But the artist who lets worlds rise and fall in his tones did not calculate vibrations like a mathematician, but through his divinely gifted apprehension, he intuitively found those accords and harmonies that stir millions of people as the highest art, without the least "why" being understood. And in this sense, the divinely gifted artist is often the pioneer of mankind's path to the deepest and most precise insights, without him ever being conscious of the reasons for and correctness of his intuitions, which are only proven after the fact. For he is perhaps the one who forges furthest ahead of mankind! And thus, his work is to be celebrated as true art, as the highest achievement of his people. This then also belongs to the most valuable treasures of a nation's heritage.

What individual nations accumulate in material goods is wholly meaningless compared to the value of true cultural achievements. Only the thoughtless little stiff cannot grasp the importance of this fact.

If we were to strike out every cultural work that initially seemed to serve no practical purpose from the national inheritance of our people, all in one stroke, the image of our blossoming communal life would be transformed into a desert. For every artistic effort was initially beyond practical use in the comprehension of the average person, but it is one of the additional values that have definitively lifted man alone out of the animalistic sphere. If some magical force removed everything from our own country that was seen as unnecessary or as unprofitable art in the rabbit-horizon of the normal inhabitant of this earth, then our cities would suddenly collapse. Domes, cathedrals, the magnificent buildings of our royal and civic life, museums, theaters — they would all vanish, as well as every last pole of our streetlights or the walls of our homes, the glass from windows and every picture on the wall; in short, nothingness would take the place of our rich and beautiful current world! And then, maybe we would understand the deepest meaning of the phrase, that "man shall not live by bread alone." Thus we cannot imagine the development of our people without artists, or the inheritance of our nation without their artworks, and we cannot squander them! When an economist talks about "national wealth," then we should note that, except for the creative power and vitality of a people, this national wealth lies about 95 percent in its cultural achievements and not even 5 percent in its so-called purely material goods.

As highly as we should value a people's cultural inheritance as a whole, like in other areas, there will have to be perpetual amendment, or replacement and complement to the individual objects and works. To be sure, there are human achievements that can rightly be called "immortal," but these are the results of the creative power of a very few spread throughout a millennium. As the meaning of these works enters into the consciousness of a greater part of the Volk, they begin to spur the more gifted souls toward their imitation. Thus, for every great star in the firmament of art, there is something like a comet's tail of a greater or smaller number of imitators who are inspired by the great work to now continue in the same direction themselves. This is of itself neither indecent nor harmful. For it is a big mistake to believe that geniuses can fall from the heavens in the tens of thousands. They were always solitary, and they will always be solitary. Because of this, the number of their works will always be strictly limited. Therefore those who benefited directly from would have been a very small number. Those working with them, which really means their imitators, ensure that at least a reflection of the one-of-a-kind creation is visible to a greater number of people. Just as the comet's tail gradually wanes in brightness with distance from the comet, finally ending in total darkness, so also a genius's imitators are weaker and weaker images of their lord and master, with increasing distance and with their increasing numbers. Yet they still help fill the need of the broad masses of a people for art.

Thus, chiefly through their work, an artistic status quo gradually emerges that can of course only occasionally be measured against the paragon. But despite this, these works do not have to be bad; to the contrary, as the honestly pursued imitations of a good model, they are a thousand times better than the mendacity of a so-called new art, the only value of which is novelty, never earning the mark of genius on its brow. This more or less solid artistic retinue of a nation will eventually grow so large in the number of followers that at least a portion of the less important will have to fall away, especially if, for example through mechanical reproductions, it is possible to replace poor imitations and original works with better copies of better models. In the course of centuries, when new geniuses are sure to arise who find their own imitators, a perpetual process of the displacement of the artistic status quo will come about. This, however, raises the question of the valuation of the artwork itself.

The natural answer to this question is, in each case, the emergence of something superior, something better. In the course of time, this better thing, even if after the hardest struggle, will force itself through and will displace exactly as much as is required for it to have its requisite space and attention.

This question is much harder to answer when a nation's art world is threatened by the intrusion of a wave of artworks that are not hallowed by the nation's own artistic heights, and thus not justified. We must reject artworks that are merely the attacks of a deeply dissonant, inartistic production which is launched, propagated, and advanced for ideological or political reasons. This has been the case in our own time.

Of all the lousy efforts of so-called "modern art," not even 5 percent could have won a place in the artistic pantheon of the German Volk, had public opinion not been persuaded, even forced, by political and ideologically motivated propaganda that had nothing to do with art as such. How deep the Volk's aversion is to this propagandistic "enrichment" of its art can be seen in people's impressions after viewing the degenerate art exhibition in Munich. Nevertheless, a skillful, cunning Jewish cultural propaganda was able to con our so-called "authoritative custodians of art," if not our healthy individuals, into smuggling these vile concoctions into our galleries, and ultimately forcing it onto the German public.

This was not a natural process of displacement of perhaps antiquated and more or less faded artworks with glowing new works, but rather a rape of artistic sensibilities, and ultimately of the national pantheon of art, by a number of traitors who appeared en-masse and brazenly claimed to be the Promethean creators of a new, "modern" art.

The extent to which this impertinent assault on our national culture and national art succeeded can be seen by the purchases made with state funds.

To cleanse our cultural heritage of these works is a holy duty of our political leadership, which sees itself as the antithesis to these decadent groups that forced these shoddy works on the German Volk!

From this, we are often presented with the urgent need to look critically at the worth of an artwork as such.

When we talk about the worth of an artwork as such, we want to first consider the fact that the great artistic achievements of humanity were ahead of their time, meaning that they were mostly seen as something new by their contemporaries, and only understood by a limited portion, and had to gradually fight their way into the general understanding.

Yes, it is indeed a hallmark of the very greatest artistic achievements that they took a step into the unconscious recognition of something real, and the rest of the world could only gradually follow.

But the right to displace existing artistic achievements can in any case only be granted to those new creations that embody a greater truth, to those that will advance the general insight and understanding of their time!

Certainly, there is sometimes art that looks back, but it is only justified insofar as it brings forth a previously lost racial consciousness.

Then, if artistic development loses its relation to its own blood, its own racial worth and racial sentiment, through alien, ethnically foreign influence, then this original connection can be recovered, and art can be renewed by attaching itself to the creations of a past epoch, in order to start again from there and find the right way forward.

Except for this, every retrogression in art is a mistake, because it leads development back to a previous epoch of the distant past, even if it might equal those previous heights of unimportant races of the past. "Primitive art" of today, or better yet, the art of the primitive in which we only recognize crude caricatures, such as various Negro tribes still make, might be identical with the past artistic creations of our own people. Yes, this is not only probable, but even certain.

The level of these drawings, as I have alluded to in the past, corresponds to the skill of five-, six-, or seven-year-old children, but at the same time also the average level, even the highest level of our people, twenty, thirty, or maybe even fifty thousand years ago.

The purpose of this cleansing of our art cannot be to replace or displace the achievements of an advanced age with the long-exceeded works of a long-past epoch. Thus, when evaluating an artwork, we must remember the principle that it represents a step forward in its time, not a step backward!

Thus, I can very well value a primitive work created two thousand years ago as art, while immediately and sharply rejecting it if a modern "art enthusiast" wants to force it on the world as an expression of *our* age.

Here I see a special danger in the phrases "art consciousness" or "culture consciousness." Art or culture consciousness cannot mean striving to return to outgrown time periods, but it should mean rediscovering a perhaps previously lost path of one's own race-dictated and blood-dictated art and cultural development.

We have to also recognize that the real artist has never limited himself by imposing certain "stylistic" parameters on his creativity, but this only appears so to posterity. The archaic artwork is not the result of the imposition of a certain style of the time, but a result of the greatest achievements of the time, the ultimate expression of contemporary sight and the ability to give material form to this vision. Thus, this art now called archaic was one the highest and most authentic, while its clumsy imitation today is a most inartistic lie.

If the results of the highest artistic dispositions are the embodiments of the furthest anticipations or predictions of something real in the future, then these things that go so far ahead of the general understanding will always only be the works of the rarest phenomena. The highest artistic ability always shows itself through its utter loneliness.

Thus, the true epoch-defining work of art will always be the work of a gifted individual man who clairvoyantly lives far ahead of the rest of humanity, and it will never be the result of a general, average collective effort.

Thus, we can already determine that there will be an eternal dichotomy between the highest genius and the greatest number of the masses. The genius is an individual, and the average remains in the mass. Herein lies the strongest proof of the insanity of so-called "modern art," because it consciously tries to replace the great works of genius with a so-called "work of the masses." This means there is no radiant talent that appears before the people and presents it with the new work of art, but rather only brings forth a host of inferior works fabricated by bunglers who, with their greater numbers, begin to make war against the rarity of truly eternal art!

So-called "modern art" boasts of itself as public communal work. For this reason, it is neither modern, nor certainly art. As far as I'm concerned, there could well be a modern artist, but there cannot be an art of the cohort of 1937 or 1940.

But for the artist who blesses the world with a truly new creation, the knowledge of the kind and techniques of the existing pantheon of art lies deep in his blood, in his understanding, in his faculty. Genius already masterfully commands the available techniques, and grounded in this, it forms his new artwork ahead of its time, which may not win the public's approval for decades or even centuries. The creatively gifted artist with the highest calling masters the meaning and the technique of all that has already come, and out of this he develops his own work.

But these creatively gifted people are the exception. Yet they alone enrich the true pantheon of art for humanity. At the same time, they are the most tolerant admirers of the achievements of the past. They know what they owe to the cultural achievements of the past. Thus they also do not fear being outdone by the past. The opposite: they are happy to be able to place their works in this show of the greats of past and present, and in doing so they are convinced that they will fight their way into a spot in this gallery of their immortal ancestors. Only their followers will then try to make themselves noticed, and their works, which are only average anyway, will compete with each other and with similar works of the past. And here the rule will be that the smaller works will slowly disappear out of existence and human memory, in order to again make temporary room for new ones. Only the truly great stay preserved forever, and it is only their enduring veneration that is secured. And they do not suffer from being greater in number, either!

In judging an artwork, the purpose given to or perceived by the artist and the materials that were at his disposal must be considered.

And here, every artwork is influenced and circumscribed by many forces of its surrounding world. The artist does not live in a vacuum, though very often his fault-finders do! He not only shapes, he is himself shaped. Often the cause for the creation of an artwork, the contract, is already determinative for the result. Contemporary historical attitudes, historical insights, cultural-historical knowledge: all this helps with the formation of a work.

It is impossible to reject the painting of a seventeenth-century master just because his cultural-historical knowledge of Roman life presents numerous anachronisms that we have since become aware of. Here the artwork must be approached from a higher perspective. There should be respect not just for the materials available to a people, but also respect for the cultural context! And this respect must also count when certain conceptions of the present no longer accord with those of the past out of which the artwork arose, or which the artwork represents. Above all, every tremendous artwork carries value in and of itself. It cannot be measured against any other yardstick.

It is impossible to fashion a yardstick in the year 1940 from certain political or ideological attitudes and then use it to measure the ideological content of an artwork of the past to either approve or reject it. Just as it is impossible to individually venerate or damn our physical ancestors according to the attitudes they took to the problems of their own time, so too it is impossible to dismiss a true work of art simply because the ideal of a past world that it depicts or exemplifies no longer agrees with our modern notions, or even opposes them.

Because art often has to turn to the events of its time in its depictions, when the next period came to new opinions, all art of the previous epoch would have to be erased. It is impossible to reject ancient art simply because it is pagan and, in the meantime, the Christian world appeared, just as it is impossible to reject Christian art simply because a few people have since fallen out of full agreement with it! It is wrong to hold the great cultural works of tremendous artistic heroes to the often only very temporary standards of the opinions that briefly rule the day. Only an inartistic creature could try to grasp at such an impossibility. And not only this: this attempt is also disrespectful of our great past as well as historically narrow-minded. Only a disrespectful man would condemn Mozart's *Magic Flute* because its text might ideologically oppose his opinions. Likewise, only the unjust man would reject Richard Wagner's *Ring* because it does not accord with a Christian worldview, or Wagner's *Tannhäuser*, *Lohengrin*, and *Parzifal*, because they on the other hand do not seem to agree with certain non-Christian understandings. The great work of art contains its own absolute value in and of itself. This value is not measured by the yardstick of a temporary notion that has nothing whatsoever to do with the artwork!

If every generation assumed the right to root out the artworks of its political, ideological, or religious past, then surely every political upheaval would mean the immediate destruction of any culture that developed in a different context politically. This is just as unreasonable as it would be unreasonable for a National Socialist economic regime to destroy all material goods that were created or accumulated over the centuries under foreign economic ideologies.

Art is never refuted by literature, speeches, or any writings, but only by better works. Music can only be refuted by music, poetry by poetry, architecture by architecture, dance by dance, paintings by paintings, and never by criticism.

If this were possible, then without further ado, you could simply rip cultural accomplishments out of the pantheon of a people without anything taking their place. But in truth, this would mean nothing but the gradual destruction of a people's cultural pantheon, putting an empty vacuum in its place. But even the most seemingly outdated cultural creations cannot be conquered by a new doctrine, nor the blathering of literary scribblers; they can only be beaten and replaced by new and better achievements.

Thus, the highest law for any evaluation of art is the duty of tolerance toward the truly great cultural creations of the past. An age that is itself great can allow itself to treat the work of their forebears with the respect that they themselves wish for their posterity to have when judging their age. Indeed, it will strive to place its own achievements in comparison with the past and leave it to posterity to evaluate and make the appropriate choice. This will be the mark of a truly great creative age.

It will not be regarded for what it destroyed, but only for what it built and created itself!

Every individual in such an age must remember that it is the exclusive right of genius to form something greater, something better, something new, and the tragic curse of a Herostratus to tear down and burn the old. Thus, when we talk about the judgment of art today, we understand this to include the reverential respect for all sincerely great achievements of our past.

But the best judgment is done through our own highest effort. We are all aware that it is not sufficient to preserve what exists, but that it is now necessary for us to contribute in our own time to our great national cultural inheritance. It is no coincidence that, in the lives of nations, the ages of poets and singers do not always coincide with the epochs of great political uprisings and destiny-deciding global struggles.

This is not only because the poets and singers first have to have the occasion to honor the event or person; rather, what inspires the creative power of an artist can, in tumultuous times, too often fill him with a vigor that compels him to action. The singer does not always carry a sword in one hand and a lyre in the other. All too often, hot-blooded men go the path of warriors in years of storm and strife, when otherwise they would have stayed on the road of the muses. Yes, maybe the highest poetic creativity is only one way of living with a burning heart, which otherwise would have plunged the man headlong into the battle of life. If there seems to have been a dearth of poetic and musical creative power in the past years and decades, then one of the decisive reasons for it is surely that many people who are interiorly musically-inclined are today making history instead of writing it, meaning they have chosen to lead the lives of heroes instead of singing about them.

And the fire-spirit of our youth has, for over a quarter century, found plenty of other outlets to live itself out rather than poetic ebullience or musical creation.

Who knows how many divinely gifted artists found themselves among the two million youthful volunteers with songs on their lips, who in laying down their lives provided a testament of truly musical heroism!

And then National Socialism captured the imaginations of countless people to such an extent that they forgot not only career and job, but even wife and children, in order to fight in the ranks of the new community for the uplift of their people.

Whoever can renounce every last tie to the bourgeois world can also have abdicated living out the artistic expression of his strong ego without him even being conscious of it. After the conclusion of this world-historical battle, the native hot drive for life of these young dreamers will find some other path to express itself.

However, this obligation of bold men toward the more tempting path of action is not exclusively responsible for the shocking dearth of artistic quality in the past decades. This slackening was already perceptible prior to the war, although there was very little heroism to be seen in the bourgeois world before 1914. The reason for this dearth of artistic and especially creative originality was not because of a lack of such things themselves, but much more because of processes that partly prevented their emergence and partly hid them from the rest of the world. It was the curse of the so-called "modern" art world, created and propagated by the literati, which either scared away or suffocated every actually valuable new force. As already explained, genius is only ever an exception and a solitary phenomenon. As such, it has to rise above a certain solid cross-section of the average. It requires a healthy average as its basis and ground. But the highest originality only belongs to a specially favored few. Thus, there is no art that constantly produces something new and original, but there is only a generally acknowledged solid baseline out of which originality can lift itself!

The geniuses do not do this in order to disappear again as the solitary lights of a day, but to be the torchbearers showing and illuminating the way of ascent for others. Therefore, without wanting to be, the artist is almost by definition the master of a school. How narrow the distance between a master and his most gifted students often is can be seen by the difficulty of clearly determining the origin of such works afterward. How often even the most careful investigation must admit of the possibility that a work may have originated from the master or from his school, from the environment he pollinated. But where would humanity be if its enlightened minds only found an audience, but no disciples? There would be no human culture if the geniuses only lit up the sky like meteors and then disappeared again, without leaving any trace. As geniuses, they are the pioneers who not only forge ahead of the rest, but simultaneously pull others toward themselves. This does not change or diminish their glory or their importance. To the contrary, this increases the value of their historic work.

This is the only way that human culture has ever been brought to a higher level, which the broad masses strive to catch up to. Thus, a perpetually advancing current forms, out of which individual natural genius occasionally shines forth to mark out new goals for human striving.

Thus, you can really only demand a valuable originality from the very great minds, while the average, meaning the great mass also active in art, always stays inside the frame delimited by the geniuses.

The decades-long literary attack on this solid cross section only leads to artistic fraud, as the constantly demanded "originality" cannot be delivered by the mass of artists, as such true originality is the rarest phenomenon. And so, these artists mimic originality by brazenly springing backward! And this path backward is certainly easy, and can be traveled by almost anyone, so long as they possess the requisite audacity and shamelessness and are met with the requisite patience or stupidity.

The path from the sacred and sincere labors of our good old German masters to the great painters of the seventeenth, eighteenth, and nineteenth centuries was surely harder than the path from the baseline average of decent nineteenth-century art to the primitive doodle of our so-called moderns, whose products only stand out because they are a couple thousand years behind our time.

This disgraceful retrogression was committed by our literati. They were able, by the constant application of the word "kitsch," to impose such eccentric errors on a well-meaning and decent artistic middle. With arrogance, they describe as interesting or even phenomenal what are in fact shameful steps backward, a collapse of culture such as has never taken place before, and never could have, because such literati have never before had such shameless influence on the visual and performing arts.

It is, by the way, amusing to see how the products of these so-called "moderns" are themselves rightly judged to be the very least "original." The opposite is indeed the case: all these so-called modern artists are the most pathetic and helpless copyists of all time. And they are not copyists of anything decent, but of nonsense! They inflate themselves and complain about the architecture of past ages, despite its immeasurable wealth of forms, while they themselves waste away by parroting some old nonsense until they are in a stupor. How long was it believed that there is a special "originality" in setting doors in a house crooked instead of straight, or sticking on triangular instead of rectangular alcoves, or instead of placing windows static and correctly in front, mounting them unstatic and incorrectly at or around the corner? As soon as such a project was begun, swarms of our younger and older artists pounced on the opportunity of this new but cheap originality and copied it more stupidly and shallowly than the worst of nineteenth-century architects imitating some Renaissance building.

This literary barking against the decent, solid middle was thus one of the most decisive factors in the slow falling away of really meaningful artists who could have pushed humanity forward.

It is undeniable that, in the same measure that art literature grew in the nineteenth and twentieth centuries, the number of really great artists began to decline! Is it not tragic to have to observe that, in the last century, musical geniuses formed a great chain until they were gradually so wiped out in the battle against the intelligentsia, that we are now forced to live in a musical desert? We gained countless employees for the music periodicals, but we lost the creative composers!

When we objectively consider this condition, then we also immediately see the path we have to take in order to regain a healthy art.

Then again, it is not so tragic that, at the moment, fate has denied us that fill of composers who, especially in the first two-thirds of the last century, solidified the glory of German music. They, thank God, accomplished so much that it is an artistic feat for us to at least play their works in the best form for the German Volk.

How many Germans actually have access to the great musical works of our own people or of our related nations? Do we not live in a world where a small coterie of overstuffed parasites hoards the greatest works of art with crippling arrogance, having no other redeeming qualities or skill, while countless millions — interiorly much more receptive people — simply do not have the opportunity to come in contact with these works?

How many Germans even know the great masterworks of our art? And first and foremost, how many Germans were actually brought up to be receptive and understand these works? Is it not a tragic sign of our current age that a hundred years ago cities with barely fifty thousand inhabitants had an opera house with two thousand seats, while today the same opera house — though more limited in seating due to safety requirements—stands in the same cities as the solitary temple of fine musical art, even though the city's population grew twelvefold in the meantime? Given this negligence, is it surprising that the millions of our people have simply lost their artistic qualities, because they never received that impetus in life, which is so often crucial for the later development of an individual? I think that culturally, we can do nothing better for our German history and for our posterity than to treat what the great masters of the past have left us with reverence. And if a very small circle of overbred degenerates no longer enjoys the autochthony of our truly German art and would rather return to the "primitivity" that lies closer to their own hearts, then it is really our duty to lead the broad and healthy Volk to our German art without any hesitation. It is an insult to the greats of our past to assume that they lived, wrote, and composed only for a small class of thoroughly corrupt and lazy creatures. The Volk is too simple and natural to not find enjoyment in the natural greatness of its Old Masters.

Just ask the crowds what makes a greater impression on them after they visit the degenerate art exhibition and then the exhibition of German art, or the works in our museums. Ask these healthy people, and you will get a clear answer. But just don't ask those outwardly and inwardly pallid creatures of intellectual decadence! For these are not the German Volk!

It is therefore the primary duty of the new Third Reich to take good care of the cultural works of our past and to convey them to the broad mass of our Volk. We must do this with sympathy, generously and reasonably, because the man burdened with a full day's work and worries is not always capable of taking on the heaviest artistic problems in the evening, going to bed with them on his mind.

The man who has to wrestle with troubles needs laughter more than the man on whom life only smiles. Therefore, theater should serve the cheerful and not only the serious muse, and surely only a certain percentage of those for whom a good operetta is still a true work of art will understand the last great opera. The crucial thing is that we strive to put our people back on track, through joy and beauty, toward that which is truly profound.

It is no sign of unworthiness if a people clamors not just for bread but also for circuses. To the contrary, it would be a sign of the inferiority of a man if he found his life's purpose and goal exclusively in food and drink.

You can easily judge for yourself whether and to what extent we have been able to raise the German Volk's joy for theater, and for poetry and music. Since the year 1933, there has been a transformation in this area that is itself a revolution. It is not for nothing that one of the largest organizations of all time has come into being with the beautiful goal of giving people the strength to assert themselves through joy, to teach them that life's hardships are to be borne manfully, but its blessings are also to be joyfully pursued.

But whoever prudishly claims to be offended by such an attitude toward life can see from the judicial proceedings of the past months that it is better to give a healthy vital drive its due than to violate God-given nature.

If in some areas the new state seems like it is merely conserving, then in others it is proving to be a creative force. Never in German history have bigger and nobler architectural projects been planned, begun, and completed than in our time. And this is the most important thing, because architecture also determines painting and the plastic arts. Alongside music, architecture is the most elemental art that man has invented. It, too, was defiled for decades. Under the motto of "objectivity," it was degraded to artistic nonsense, even fraud. During the creative poverty of a bourgeois, liberal age, communal buildings shrunk together, becoming ever smaller compared to factories, banks, exchanges, warehouses, hotels, and other such bourgeois concerns. As National Socialism places the community of the Volk above these syndicates, it will also give the constructions of this community precedence over the private. This is crucial. The greater the state's demands on its citizens are, the greater the state must appear to its citizens.

If one talks often about "national economic necessities," then one must consider that these necessities demand much self-sacrifice from the Volk without the community being able to see and understand very well why a higher purpose should take precedence over their own interests.

That is why there has never been a great epoch in a nation's life in which the superior importance of the community's interests has not been expressed through the visible impact of great architecture.

The effect of this has been to give man true community spirit and to establish the preconditions for the creation and preservation of human culture, rather than mere economic striving. This great monumental tenor of the community has helped to erect an authority without which the community could have neither an enduring society nor a stable economy. Whether this authority was rooted in religious or in secular institutions does not matter. The authority that rescued the German Volk in the twentieth century from collapse, which pulled it back from the chaos of Bolshevism, was certainly not the authority of an economic association, but of the National Socialist movement, the National Socialist Party, and now the National Socialist state! Our opponents will intuit this, but above all, our followers must understand: our buildings rise for the strengthening of this authority!

What you see being built in this city, what is being planned and partly already taking shape or even already being completed — in Berlin, in Munich, in Hamburg, and in other places — shall serve this authority!

This is the purpose behind these constructions! And because we believe in the eternity of this Reich — insofar as we can humanly measure an eternity — these works shall also be eternal. This means they should meet eternal demands not only in the greatness of their conception, but also in the clarity of their layout and in the harmony of their proportions.

Little everyday requirements have changed over the millennia, and they will continue to change forever. But humanity's great cultural testaments of granite and marble have likewise stood for millennia. These alone are a truly constant pole among the flurry of all other phenomena. In times of collapse, humanity has looked to these to find that magic power to master their confusion and to create new order from chaos. Thus, these buildings should not be thought of as existing for the year 1940, nor for the year 2000, but just like the dogmas of the past, they should reach out into the millennia of the future.

And if God may let poets and singers be fighters today, then he at least gave these fighters architects, who will ensure that the success of this fight will find its permanent solidification in the monuments of a singularly great art!

The small spirits will not understand this, but they also did not understand our fight. This may embitter our opponents, but their hatred has not yet prevented our successes. But one day it will be clearly understood how great a blessing radiates into the centuries from the architecture of this history-defining time. For they will help to politically unite and strengthen our people more than ever; socially they will become an element of a German feeling of proud togetherness; societally, they will demonstrate the ridiculousness of all our little earthly differences compared to these colossal symbols of our community; psychologically, they will fill our people with an inexhaustible self-awareness, that they are

Germans!

At the same time, these tremendous works will represent the most profound vindication of the German nation's political strength. This state shall not be a power without culture, nor a force without beauty. For the armor of a nation is only morally justified if it is the sword and shield of a higher calling. We do not strive for the brute force of a Genghis Khan, but by forming a socially strong and well-protected community, we, as the pillars and guardians of a higher culture, strive for a Reich of strength!

THE FÜHRER TO THE WORKMEN

September 8th, 1937

My workmen, my workwomen, Party Comrade Hierl!

It is not enough to dream or to talk about a national community. The belief that this community is necessary was around before us, and it is still generally agreed upon. But this community, too, has to be fought for and worked for. How great a blessing this community is can be seen every day when we look outside of Germany toward other nations, countries, and states. This great blessing, which lies in a really cohesive national community, justifies all the exertion it took to get to this community. And here as everywhere, the deed stands far above the word. It cannot be born out of a mere wish, but this wish must transform itself into a will, and this will must translate into action.

And National Socialism's proudest action in the erection of the coming German national community was the founding of the Reich Labor Service!

This Party Congress takes place under the auspices of labor. The accomplishments that have been presented are only the result of untiring labor. Your foremost worker, my comrades, is your leader, Party Comrade Hierl! He hatched the idea, he realized the plan, and from scattered beginnings, he formed this community that we see before us, which is you. And he will continue to lead this community and to develop it further.

Certainly, even this great work is but a beginning. But this beginning is staggering. You, my comrades, have become an indispensable part of our people in these few years. You belong in this state that the party has founded just as much as the armed forces. We can no longer imagine being without you, and we could never get rid of you!

And it is an uplifting thought for us to know that even into the most distant future, generation after generation will shoulder that rifle of peace, the spade, and will step into service with it for our community and for our people. It is comforting for us to know that a new guarantor of Germany's eternal strength, of the greatness of our people and of our Reich, was founded. Today you are no longer a fantasy, you are a tremendous reality! Let the representatives of other nations and other points of view cast a glance here and see what has been accomplished in these short four and a half years, so that they can understand that a new Volk is rising here that is as committed to diligently pursuing its work as it is determined to not let anyone threaten its earthly life or its right to exist. And let everyone understand: a nation is represented by its most valuable forces! Whoever wants to know Germany only has to look at this force here, and then he will get the right impression of the German Volk, the new state, and our community.

And so, I salute you here again, and I am happy and proud to see this effort thriving. You are my guarantor of the implementation of a goal that occurred to me long ago: "One Volk, one Reich, one community, one strength!"

If Germany outwardly shows the might of its self-defense, then at the same time it inwardly shows the strength of its labor. In both, we see the securing of the life of our Volk, to which we belong, and belong proudly.

Our Germany: Sieg Heil!

THE FÜHRER AT THE GROUNDBREAKING
OF THE GERMAN STADIUM

September 9th, 1937

Germans!

In this historic moment, as I lay the cornerstone for the German Stadium, I am filled with three great wishes:

1. Let this enormous construction bring glory and pride to the German Volk.
2. Let it be the eternal witness for a nation united in National Socialism and of a mighty Reich.
3. Let it forever exhort and lead German men and women to that strength and beauty that is the highest expression of the nobility of true freedom.

Herewith, in the year 1937, I declare the opening of the National Socialist Combat Games in Nuremberg.

THE FÜHRER TO THE POLICE

September 10th, 1937

Your leader, Party Comrade Himmler, has just outlined how the position of police officer is the most visible representation of the state authority to the people.

In 1933, the National Socialist government right away tried to make your position easier. By limiting your weapons to exclusively sharp weapons, we took away that most hated and characteristic feature of the November period for the police. Back then, we were convinced that it must be possible to implement the authority of the state and to appreciate the needs of the community of our countrymen without such a humiliating attribute as the rubber truncheon. We had the opinion that there were only two possibilities: either it is enough to invoke the authority of the individual person and the authority of the community, or else it is necessary to forge respect and obedience to this authority using the sharpest weapons. But it is impossible to beat and degrade the citizens of one's own people like a subjugated tribe in a colony.

Today every German knows that the police officer is just as much a representative of the National Socialist state, and with it the National Socialist community, as any other representative of the state. And thus he knows that the police officer approaches him as a friend and as a German countryman just as much as any other bearer of this state authority. But he also knows, for this very reason, that the bearer of this authority is bound to enforce this authority under any circumstances. With this, he also knows that he will not recoil from the ultimate and most extreme requirements.

Conversely, the representative of this state authority knows that the state authority stands behind him, that he will be covered by it in his service to the people and the national community.

In fully stripping the German police officer of his earlier characteristics, we gave the German police a new uniform. Here too, we were guided by the desire to give the police an outward image that strikes everyone as being worthy of representing the state.

Now this shall go one step further. The German police shall be brought more and more into connection with the movement that now politically represents and leads today's Germany. And to that end, you are receiving today's flags from me personally. This shall be an act of the visible integration of the German police into the great front of the militant German national community that marches here.

I know you will carry these flags just as the other organizations that are called to carry them in service of the strength and might of our nation do. In these flags, you will now truly see the symbol of your connection with the German Volk that is shaping its new life underneath this banner.

In this, you will be ruled by two principles: one, as a representative of the state, you will be the best friend of the people. And two, as a representative of the state, you will be the most relentless agent of this national community against any antisocial criminal element that sins against it.

It has to be possible find a relationship and a connection between these two tasks. It is possible on the one hand to be the warmest friend to decent Germans, and on the other hand to be the most merciless enemy and adversary of every enemy of our German national community.

The more German police officers live out these tasks, the more he will not only gain the trust, but gradually also the love of the German Volk. In him, they will see a representative of a perpetually difficult, individually thankless, but as a whole still glorious task, the task of helping strengthen the national body internally, of cleansing it of the incompatible element. First and foremost, they will recognize you as the worthy representative of this national body. Indeed, everyone who visits the Reich from other countries will likely encounter the German police officer as the first representative of the Reich.

And so, today I give you your flags, in the firm knowledge that through them you will become more and more incorporated into that great marching column of the German national community!

Heil Police!

THE FÜHRER TO THE
POLITICAL LEADERS

September 10th, 1937

My party comrades! A part of the political leadership of the German Volk comes to Nuremberg annually, along with a part of the political soldiers, and a part of the armed forces. Many who do not understand the character of our movement might wonder why this rally repeats every year. We, who have been able to experience it for four years now, recognize its meaning and its value. For us fanatical National Socialists, this is the greatest time of the whole year!

How much worry and sacrifice this means for the individual; how hard and difficult it is for so many of you, but also for us, to always come back here. And yet, whenever these days come to an end, we are gripped with sorrow; we feel like children leaving a big party.

For us, these days are a reminder of the time of our historic struggle for Germany. So many among you, standing before you, still know this movement from that time when it was difficult and dangerous to admit to being a member. But for these trusty old fellow fighters, these days are the nicest reminiscence and the greatest reward. Once a year, we personally stand across from each other, as we so often did back then. Once a year you are with me again, as so often during our struggle for Germany. Back then, I could go out into your districts, and each of you knew me. Today you have to come to me, and here in this place we stand together again as the old guard of the National Socialist revolution!

It is a wonderful occurrence that lies behind us and that is coming to fruition in our time. How many of you accompanied me throughout the years in my struggle for Germany. Back then, when we were still mocked and laughed at, your faithful hearts led you to me. You had no idea if I would win. You only believed! Back then, you endured privations and sacrifices, and above all persecution, mockery, and hatred directed at you. What a wonderful road since this beginning! Today, here are the men who once set out to fight a foul system and became the masters of a state.

This kind of victory is truly not given away in history! You stand here before me. One hundred forty thousand political leaders, a part of a great army that today leads and steers our German Volk, and yet, this sector of this tremendous mass already presents an image such as the previous Germany never knew. They once believed they could break the spine of our Volk. It has become stronger and stronger than ever before. But this miracle is the result of equal amounts of faith, courage, and sacrifice, and above all, hard work. What labors have not gone into this result?

We have placed the Party Congress of 1937 under the motto of labor. There are people, especially outside of Germany, who might raise the question, "Why such a slogan?" After four years of setting Germany free, we now have more right than ever to rejoice in our labor!

I know the personal sacrifices that so many hundreds of thousands of my party comrades, and especially my leaders, have taken upon themselves in all the unknown little places. And I know how great this sacrifice is that never receives the light of public recognition. Considering these unknown soldiers of our National Socialist freedom movement, we feel it is a special blessing to be able to meet here in this city year after year. Here each of you is just one member of a great whole! None of you stand here alone! You may be lonely in your villages, in your workshops and factories. Here you sense the common strength and force of one common idea! Here you can judge what it means to be an individual, yet not a solitary one, but the member of a great, proud, cohesive community.

I am so happy that once a year I can know my old fighters are before me. I always have the feeling that as long as a man has life in him, he should yearn for that with which he shaped his life. And what would my life be without you!

The fact that you once found me and once believed in me gave your life a new meaning, and set out a new task for you! That I found you made my life and my struggle possible in the first place!

You know that our old familiar enemy is now preparing himself again to plunge the world into unrest. You know that in his attempt, he will fight with all the weapons we have ever known him to use. But you also know from the get-go that his attempt will fail against the cohesiveness of our movement in Germany. It is a ridiculous undertaking to again try to inject into Germany this sickness that we have already eradicated. But if this attempt should be tried from the outside as opposed to from the inside, then we all know: under the leadership of its party, the nation will defend Germany and will never let it perish!

And our faith attaches itself to this knowledge. It is not the will of Providence to accompany us and bless our wonderful path, and then to let us perish again in the last act. The Almighty has let us go down this wonderful path, and He will continue to bless it. For we are fighting here for a higher law, a higher truth, and a higher human decency.

I can look at the future so calmly today because we have put our house in good order. The German youth is growing up with our ideals and our faith in their young hearts. They will come into our organization and will be consciously raised to be Germans and patriots. They will make their way into the party, the organizations of the party. They will proceed into the Labor Service. Leaving it, they will enter into the armed forces. And leaving the armed forces, they will then really enter into the nation's unified militant front. We have taken precautions that Germany, our German homeland, will not suffer what we had to endure for a decade and a half. Herewith, Germany became an element of calm, a factor of security, and thus a guarantor of peace.

Let the rest of the world understand this! Let them not be misled by those criminal agitators whose only job is to ruin the honor and reputation of nations on paper, and to thus lead them toward belligerence against each other. Let the rest of the world see that the agitators are not in the right, but that, on the contrary, it is a blessing for the rest of the world that, amidst this spreading unrest in Europe, there is a great state in Northern Europe, in addition to the one in Southern Europe, that is consolidated, that is firm, and that will remain firm.

Germany will not be overrun, not from the inside and not from the outside! And I believe this fact is the greatest contribution to peace, because it will be a warning to all those who would try to set the world on fire from Moscow.

So, we look at the coming year with proud, confident trust. Germany will fulfill its assigned tasks! And they are great tasks. You all know the big plans that we have set out to realize. They partly extend across decades, partly across generations. Let the other nations likewise set big goals for themselves! Then it might be easier to understand the longing for peace that grips us Germans. These great future tasks will be solved thanks to the existence of a movement that unites, upholds, and leads our whole nation. You can be proud that you have a part in this historic task!

What is a single one of us? What would he be without the movement? It first gave us our worth! And no matter where the individual stands, as a National Socialist he is irreplaceable!

When these hours and days pass and you return to your districts, your cities and villages, your factories and workshops, then you will look back on this great community experience. Then, at home, you will think about all that came rushing in on you in these days and hours. And then, only with physical and temporal distance, will you be able to measure the whole magnitude of this rally.

For us, this foremost memory will remain: we saw each other again, we heard each other again, and we renewed our old vow. You, my comrades-in-arms, and you, my young new blood: everything for Germany! Germany—Sieg Heil!

AT THE CELEBRATION
OF THE HITLER YOUTH

September 11th, 1937

Youth!

This morning I learned from our weather forecasters that we are currently in a VB weather situation. This is apparently a mix of bad and very bad. Now, my boys and girls: this is the weather Germany had for fifteen years! And the party also had this weather! For over a decade, the sun did not shine on the movement. It was a fight in which we had to hope that, in the end, the sun would again rise over Germany. And indeed, the sun did rise! As you stand here today, it is good that for once the sun does not smile upon you. Because we want to raise a generation not only for the sunny, but also for the stormy days!

I would consider the whole educational work of National Socialism as worthless if the result of this education was not a nation that can withstand even the hardest days. But in the future, my youth, this nation will be you! What you do not learn today you will not be able to do in the future!

We have a different idea of youth now than previous ages had. Once — you do not know this — the young man of eighteen years looked different than he does today. The girl was also raised differently than now. This has changed. In place of a youth that was once raised on pleasure, a youth is today growing up that is being raised on privation, sacrifice, and above all the cultivation of a healthy, resilient body, because we believe that without a healthy body even a healthy mind cannot rule a nation.

Thus, for us National Socialists, the time of the struggle back then also seems beautiful, despite the sun not shining. Yes, maybe one remembers the days of storm and struggle in one's life longer than the days of sunshine. And I am convinced that you, too, will remember this day, perhaps precisely because it rained and you stood here anyway. This is self-evident for us. We only want to fight for and ask Providence for one thing: that it lets our people be healthy and just, that our people is given a sense of real freedom, and that it keeps a sense of honor alive in our people. We never want to ask Providence to make us free or to give us freedom, but only that it lets us be decent enough to fight for our own place in this world, which a free people requires!

We want no gift; we only want the grace to be able to enter into an honest fight! Then Providence will always decide whether we deserve this life or not. And when I see you, I know: this Volk will earn its freedom, and its honor, and its life even in the future!

You have now become the German state's youth. And never will the leadership of this youth be any except the one that comes out of the National Socialist idea and movement! For even today you are an inseparable component of this idea and this movement. It has formed you, it has clothed you, and you will serve it all the rest of your lives! It is a wonderful thing that in you, the educational chain of our people is closed. It begins with you, and it will only end when the German is in his grave!

Never in German history has there been such inner unity in spirit, formation of will, and leadership. Many generations before us have yearned for this, and we are the happy witnesses of its fulfillment.

And in you, my boys and girls, I see the most beautiful fulfillment of this millennia-long dream!

As you stand here before me, so centuries from now the young generations will stand here year after year before the coming leaders. And they will always give their oaths to the Germany that we have won today.

Germany — Sieg Heil!

THE FÜHRER BEFORE THE
GERMAN LABOR FRONT

September 11th, 1937

Party comrades, my German countrymen!

If I have come a little late, it is because of the other various duties that come with this Party Congress. Thus, I have asked my friend, Party Comrade Göring, to speak on my behalf. I also have to be a bit more economical with my voice. With the weather having turned bad and having had to speak a lot outdoors, my voice is somewhat taxed. Now, this is no cause for our foreign press crops to get excited and have high hopes that I have cancer and my voice is at its end. You will still hear it very often and very well. But it does not matter to me which of us speaks. For each of us would say the same. What we have to say is not just some memorized speech. It is the expression of our creed. For its sake, we fought and struggled all these years for power in Germany. And we are also striving today for the realization of this creed. If it is not all accomplished in one day, it is naturally not our fault. All of you will grasp this. Nothing would be nicer for a man than to have the ultimate goal of all his thoughts and hopes be realized within a single month. It would be nice to then be able to simply bask in the sun of what was accomplished. But you know there are so many obstacles. Everything does not come so quickly and so easily. And the worst obstacles are not even the material ones, but the imagined ones — all those obstacles that lie in tradition, in favored customs, in attitudes, in opinions, and above all in good old habit, which is one of the most sluggish things on earth. You can overturn states much more easily than you can overturn habit, because people will all too easily pick their old habits right back up again.

We have all experienced this; you know this because we experienced a socialist revolution in the year 1918. And I do not believe many of you are of the opinion that much of that socialism was realized back then. Everything lagged behind then. But I believe the deepest upheaval has been accomplished by us, despite this sluggishness and despite habit. But of course, it does not come so simply, and so easily, and so quickly. I know well that some will say, "My God, he is the same as he was before. This one has not changed. This one is still so haughty." Or conversely, the others will say, "This one is still the same cad; he has not become civilized at all. This one is just as brutal. He still has such little understanding for the higher economic necessities that we understand." Yes, if all people changed themselves so quickly, then I could go ahead and step down. Then I would no longer be necessary. This requires time, because it is essentially an educational problem. If we presume that we have or will educate all people, then new ones will still come who need to be educated. It is like in the military. Finally, finally a cohort of recruits is brought to the point where it can stand and walk right. And then it goes away and the next cohort comes in, and it starts all over again.

This is not such a big tragedy; quite the opposite. The educational mission is always the most beautiful. For it is an eternal, lasting one. Everything that is accomplished in a moment also usually passes away very quickly. Whatever has to be implemented across generations and also won over generations, that will tend to last a long time. Gradually, this will also become a habit. And, you know, I am hoping for this. As it was previously a habit to be proletarian or bourgeois, so I hope that it will one day also be a habit to be German. This does not come about on its own, but rather must be instilled.

Earlier we already had classes where class consciousness was drilled into them. Now, in certain organizations, we will drill in national consciousness. These are also classes. The Labor Front is such a class. It has the task of helping drill this national consciousness into our German countrymen. It is also a class consciousness, namely the consciousness of belonging to the class of the German people. At the moment this might be uncomfortable for some. But when a recruit first moves into the barracks, some things are uncomfortable for him, as well. He has to be ground down until he loses everything he previously had. And he most often holds onto the very things that he never should have held onto because it is not conducive to honor. How hard is it even to, say, teach him cleanliness? And it is no different for the big things. People hang on so tightly to things that are not worth holding onto. This all has to be brought out. And it is a wonderful task. And when someone says this is not yet accomplished, remember: we are only clocking our fifth year. Now give us a hundred years' time. What can be done in a short time, they must admit we are doing quicker than has ever been done. Streets can be built quickly. Who builds them faster than us? Houses can be built quickly; where are they built faster than by us? Factories can be founded quickly. Yes, where are they founded more rapidly than by us? We are doing all this anyway. But man is the result of yearslong, centuries- or millennia-long upbringing. Unfortunately, we cannot do that so quickly. We are raising ourselves continuously. And so, you must give us time. But this is also the biggest, and far and away the most important task. And you must admit one thing, my fellow countrymen, no matter where you are now. We have at least made an honest effort to begin this, and we have honestly strived to complete this beginning. And if every generation sets about this task with the same holy earnestness as us, then it has to work. And it will work.

This morning I saw a part of the Hitler Youth enter the party. And I have to say: it is just wonderful. This is a glorious young generation that we are receiving. And above all, they are coming from every walk and class of life. And really, you cannot tell these differences by looking at them: they all wear the same brown shirt. No man asks where they come from. But they all look as if they hatched from the same egg. There are children of the proletariat and of the bourgeoisie, and children of entrepreneurs, and of laborers and farmers. But they all appear quite homogeneous. And that is what's wonderful. This is already emerging. And our other organizations, they will help to gradually nurture this. There is the party and its organizations, SA and SS. And then comes the Labor Service. And then comes the military. And thus, the individual German will be molded until he gradually learns to be in close contact with his neighbor. And above all this, the word "ideal" does not hang so heavily. No, no, above all this there hangs a much simpler word: "reason." For this is now very clear. You all are here from every walk and state of life. But one thing is certain. None of you would be here if the others were not also here. In other words, reason teaches us the necessity of everyone's existence. One cannot be without others. And because this is so, it is most expedient to not irrationally organize life in such a manner that we are constantly angry at each other. Rather, reason dictates – if we already have to all live together – that we organize life in a way that is at least tolerable. It begins in the family and it has to carry through to the national community. As far as I'm concerned, let some old nagger tell me, "It bothers me that these proletarians are now valued equally to me." And let the old class warrior proletarian say, "I cannot stand that these bourgeois, these industrialists now also have a say." Yes, both will have to have a say in life. After all, I did not make them. Life made them. They made themselves. This is just a reality; I am just trying to make people realize that it is more expedient to have the common sense to affirm this reality and recognize that it would be irrational to beat each other's heads in. This was National Socialism's theory. You are one people, after all. So act like one. Try to make your life as easy as possible, and it will work. It is not impossible. This is also the point of this great labor organization. It shall also take the class war out of our labor. And in its stead, it shall place the recognition of reason that mind and fist, brow and hand, intelligence and strength belong together for once, because they eternally complement and complement each other. But if one comes to this realization, one must also draw the consequences from this, and we do. And let no one ask me, "Will this work?" It will work, because it has to work. And it will work because, above all, I believe in the German Volk's rationality. And if I did not have this belief, then I would not be standing here, and you would not all be sitting here, and today's Germany would not exist. One must have faith in reason and nature. Almost twenty years ago now I set out with this faith. What did I even have except faith in the reason and the worth of my German Volk of all classes?

And I further believe that it is good that the people gradually become closer to each other in such a movement. Otherwise, they do not come together so easily. Only then will they get to know each other. Maybe then I would not be standing before you. I would certainly not be standing before you had I not been a soldier, and had I not as a soldier received the absolute faith in the worth of my people, my countrymen, and the worker. For you yourselves know how often one could hear from bourgeois circles, "Oh, these people aren't worth anything; it's the rabble." I have always said this is not true at all. These are comrades. I have often experienced it. These are the comrades who, God knows, have so often put their lives on the line for Germany. These are a bunch of decent men. These are a bunch of men who are prepared, if necessary, to lay everything, even their lives, on the line for an ideal—and it is indeed for an ideal that one goes into the battlefield for Germany. I was convinced they were wrong. Our people has value. You are wrong about the German worker. You do not know him. You did not care to know. You never made the effort to have any care for his concerns. Neither could he come to you. Of all people, you left it to the Jew to seem to pretend to care for the German worker, or to give the impression that he could ever care for the German worker. From this common experience I became convinced back then: this is not so! And we must carry this common experience into our whole lives, forever. Then the individuals will more and more recognize that there are great communal works and communal interests. They will realize that all these individual people fulfill their duty somewhere, and are irreplaceable in their own contexts. They will know that their activity benefits everyone. And ultimately, this is the point of the German Labor Front. And if someone says to me, "Sure, but are you not viewing the world too idealistically?" Then I can only say, "Esteemed sir, if I had not had this idealism, then our current condition would not be reality." Above all, do you really believe that one can get by in this world without idealism? I believe not. The final test, we know, is the test of a people, even tested in resistance, if necessary. Yes, this is a test of idealism. What do I expect here? I expect heroism! What is heroism? I expect men to be ready to give themselves up so that others can live. Is this idealism or is it not? Do I expect idealism, or do I not? Would it not be shameful if I expected that others be idealists, that they would be ready to sacrifice themselves if necessary, while we, the leaders, have no need for idealism? I believe the leadership must lead from the front here, too. It too must have this belief. It also must think idealistically. The people will obey a leadership all the more if it senses that an ideal is not just demanded of the people, but that the leadership also believes in this ideal. I believe in this ideal of my united German Volk.

AT THE ROLL CALL OF
THE BROWN ARMY

September 12th, 1937

Men of the National Socialist militant movement!

Ten years ago, on almost the same morning, we gathered here for the first time. Today, not only has this place expanded, but since then the movement has become something else. Where thousands once stood, there now stand tens of thousands. But one thing remains the same: the spirit that once led you here. We have a new Germany — not because, as many before us believed, that only the Lord could make us free, but because through this movement's struggle, the Almighty could again consecrate someone in the fight for freedom.

That Germany stands before us today is the result of the National Socialist movement's struggle. It ripped Germany out of the deepest discouragement, despondency, and insecurity, gave it firm courage again, strong faith, and an unshakable security. The men of the National Socialist militant organizations stood at the forefront of this transformation, in spite of the desires of countless enemies.

Earlier it was easy to talk about how we should fight with spiritual weapons while the enemy more resolutely broke the spirit with the use of brute force. If it were about the spirit alone, then Germany would have never sunk so low; the spirit has always tried to enable, demand, and do the right thing among us. But a conspiracy of meanness and malice stood opposed to the spirit of reason, and violence rose against it. It did not want reason and understanding to enter into our people. And when the first men stood up with me and behind me to preach the new reason of a national community, we were opposed by the interests of national fragmentation. And they did not oppose us with spiritual weapons, but with the brute force of violence.

Back then, we National Socialists and frontline fighters rose up against this, and we were determined to meet this violence against reason with the violence of reason. And the Storm Division was this force for reason, a firm fist against whoever dared to sabotage and prevent the battle of the spirit and of reason with violence.

And now you know: this struggle of a decade and a half—in which we slowly broke the resistance of our foes with National Socialist fists, conquered place after place, eliminated the red terror, and only then cleared the way for the spirit—is your historic work!

And this struggle not only demanded its bloody sacrifices, but first and foremost interior spiritual sacrifices. How many of you had to live for years, as if ostracized, in a Germany that no one loved more than you. Many of you had to win this fight by losing positions and income. Many also suffered from a lack of understanding. Yes, even family ties were torn over this great duty to serve the nation according to one's will and conviction. For years, these National Socialists not only faced the violence of organized mobs, but these mobs also had the state authority behind them. It often seemed hopeless to stand against this conspiracy of malice, unreason, and violence.

When this miracle did succeed, it was due to the firmness of our party's faith, and primarily the loyal men that stood behind me, even if they did not know me or had never seen me. Together, we all only had one thing in common: an unbridled love for our people and an unshakeable faith in its resurrection. And today Germany is truly resurrected, and this is our achievement!

It is rare in history that one generation's struggle meets with such success. But more happened than just the resurrection of our people: a historic, singular reshaping took place. And as I already explained at the beginning of this Party Congress, it is not assertions that are decisive, but facts, and this reshaping of our national body is also shown and grounded in facts. One of the strongest facts lies in you. You very visibly demonstrate the transformation of our people into a new form. What a tattered mass once stood before us, and what a solid block our people has become today! Ten or fifteen years ago, the people could hardly understand one another, and today the German nation follows one command, one order!

Man in his earthly life requires outward, visible symbols to be carried before him, which he can strive toward. This holy symbol has always been the flag for Germans. It is no piece of cloth; rather, it is conviction and creed, and consequently duty.

In the long years of our struggle for the German people against their adversaries, the flag that is now the German Reich's flag was carried before you. The standards of our struggle back then were unassuming and faded, totally unrepresentative, and yet how we loved our flag, which had nothing to do with the collapse of our nation, but which appeared to us like the sunshine of a better German future! How the tens and later hundreds of thousands of our party clung to and rallied to this flag!

Sometimes we still see these old battle standards of our party today, all washed out and faded, and yet they remain beacons for us all. They accompanied us in a time of fantastic struggle, the likes of which have not been seen in any other country. Today they are raised as a symbol of the state that we won and the German national community that we won.

When I give you new standards, you will see nothing in them but the continuation of our old battle standards, and you will follow these standards with the same loyal devotion with which we all once followed our old flag.

The flag is really more than an outward symbol. When everything begins to falter, a glance at it will set a man aright once more. He will regain his composure and recognize his holy duty. And this is perhaps more important today than a couple years ago. The enemy that we once drove out of Germany by our fists is once again threatening us from the outside. We are again seeing the signs of our old adversary throwing the nations into confusion. What then could be more necessary than that we all now rally to this symbol of victory? And we know that in this struggle, only this symbol can be victorious for all time in Germany. It is not only the symbol of our struggle and our victory; above all, it is a symbol of our blood!

Men! Many of you were already standing here ten years ago. Back then, just as now, the sun was trying hard to shine through the cloud cover. What a transformation since then! Only ten years later, and the German Volk has experienced its most profound transformation in many centuries.

In this, you can see what faith, confidence, bravery, courage, loyalty, and obedience can accomplish!

As you now receive these new standards, see in them the symbols of these virtues!

Together we are everything. Following one command we are unconquerable; dissolved into individuals we are nothing. But even in the future, we want to be Germany!

TO THE SOLDIERS OF
THE ARMED FORCES

September 13th, 1937

Soldiers!

You are gathered here on this field, on the great day of our nation, for the fourth time. Much has changed since then, nothing for the worse, everything for the better! Germany is more beautiful today, bigger, and above all stronger than it once was. You yourselves are the visible proof of this strength!

In a few weeks, a portion of you will leave the barracks and return to civilian life. Two years of service to our nation and our homeland you gave us. You did not only give these two years to Germany, but these two years were also given to you! For in these two years, you not only became soldiers, but first and foremost, you became men, men of whom the nation has reason to be proud and of whom it is immeasurably proud today!

Through the developing military, it has become possible not only to win Germany's freedom from the outside, but also to begin and complete the great works you see within Germany today. But above all, through it we can secure Germany's peace in a time of unrest and general danger.

Weak nations have never been blessed with peace; only the strong have that luxury. That Germany is strong again today is thanks first of all to you soldiers!

Germany loves you and is proud of you, for in you, it sees the carriers of an immortal and glorious past. You have just as much reason to love

Germany, for you can also be proud of your people, of your homeland, of our German Reich!

Germany — Sieg Heil!

THE FÜHRER'S CONCLUDING REMARKS AT THE 1937 PARTY CONGRESS

September 13th, 1937

Party comrades! National Socialists!

The ninth Party Congress of the National Socialist movement comes to an end in a few short hours. For eight days, the German nation once again has stood under the spell of its greatest celebration. What hundreds of thousands could experience themselves or behold with their own eyes was also followed closely by millions of Germans within and beyond the Reich with no less rapt attention. When else would there be a better opportunity to be convinced of the reality of the new German state, besides its greatest and most demonstrative expression this week?

We always look back on what we experienced and search for a comparison with earlier times. And again and again, everyone is struck by the realization that these rallies so far exceed the frame of all previous experiences in their form and in their urgency, that they can only be compared to each other. They were not created according to any known model, but their idea and their organization have always exclusively belonged to the National Socialist Party.

Already in the time of the party's struggle for power, it lent these rallies their characteristic traits, and it has since developed them further to such depths and heights that each year seems impossible to outdo. And yet we believe that we can see another enhancement in the Reich Party Congress of Labor over that of the year 1936. More than before, the magnitude of National Socialism's educational mission came to the fore at this

Party Congress. That synthesis of strength, beauty, and spirit is striving toward its realization.

In this week that lies behind us, the nation was shown a concentrated image of the colossal spiritual and material labor of the past twelve months, just as it was shown the first results of the new physical education of the new German man. The rhythm of this magnificent demonstration of national strength and resolve, of intellectual cultivation and order, is so gripping that no one who came to these days or even just followed them with an open heart could tear himself away. This truly has nothing to do with that superficial, shallow patriotism that has unfortunately been claimed as a national strength in past decades but was really just hollow pretension. What sometimes almost shook us to the core this week was the ideological-national creed of a new generation, and more than once, hundreds of thousands stood here and were no longer part of a political rally, but of a solemn prayer!

Who could claim that this is only the effect of form? No, the forms we see here are only the outward organizational expressions of an idea.

But this assessment is a happy one for everyone, as we get closer and closer to reaching our ideal. Just as National Socialism once caused a spiritual revolution in our people, it is also revolutionizing the image of the appearance and demeanor of the German man. In a few decades, these rallies will meet all the expectations of our new political creed; the enhancement of combat games that were added for ideological-political reasons will help form the type of the German man: hard, steeled men and graceful, beautiful women shall be here year after year in the coming centuries as the living proof of the success of the National Socialist mission!

This will be the final rebuttal against what is believed by many even among us, but especially by outsiders: namely, that this new Germany is a rebirth of the old.

You, my countrymen who were fortunate enough to have experienced these past eight days in Nuremberg, you must have at least unconsciously sensed that what you see playing out before your eyes has never been before. It is not a rebirth, but something new and something unprecedented in German history. Never has the intellectual agenda and formation of our will been so identical with the natural duties of political self-assertion as today. Never before in the German Volk has its ideology been the same as the eternal laws of nature and as the nation's necessities for life. Never before has the ideological alignment been so uniformly focused on the perpetuation of our people, and never has such a clear concurrence been found between intellectual orientation and physical form.

Who thought this miracle was possible ten or twenty years ago, except for the faithful of our movement? Have these developments not far outpaced even the boldest hopes that were once pronounced in the "nationalist circles"? Who from those old ranks must not admit with deepest satisfaction that our people was given a strength that far exceeded all previous imaginings?

However, we must acknowledge that such a mobilization of a nation's mental and physical forces is only possible in a suitable time and environment. One of the tasks of a truly great movement is the duty to understand those conditions that caused its own existence and created the preconditions for its development.

In the sluggish times of German bourgeois liberalism there could have never been such a gigantic increase in the strength and consciousness of such a mission in our people. Just as the body develops its highest vitality when it fights off some threatening sickness, so also our people experienced the greatest boost of its latent energy when its existence was threatened, even endangered!

My fellow countrymen, in view of this demonstrative show of our movement's and our people's strength and might, do you not all sense that such a mobilization of mind and body can only have been the result and the consequence of an urgent situation? When don't some of us mull over the idea of what might have happened if fate had given us an easy and quick victory in the year 1914? What we all strove for with burning hearts back then, seen from a higher perspective, may well have been a great misfortune for our people. This victory would have likely had very tragic consequences, because it would have prevented us from gaining those insights that, looking back today, let us recognize what kind of path Germany was on. The few clairvoyant watchmen would have been relegated to ridiculousness. That state that was only grounded in and carried by military power, being totally incognizant of the importance of our people's blood and source of strength, would have sooner or later become the destroyer of its own existence and its own life source! The forces that we have been able to see take hold of the victorious countries would have taken hold of us. Instead of being pulled back from the abyss after a catastrophic convulsion, we would have all the more certainly been killed gradually by the creeping poisons of the internal subversion of our people! We can really see the truthfulness of the old saying: sometimes the deepest love of Providence for its creatures is expressed through chastisement!

The hardship of that collapse led to the National Socialist idea, and with it, the political creed that restoration must take the shape of an internal regeneration of our people, not just the outward reestablishment of the state! The National Socialist movement also has this hardship to thank for its unique organization. Only in an environment filled with enemies could the party have developed those militant forces that were prepared to wage the decisive battle for power. And it was only thanks to constant persecution and oppression that the first and best selection process took place, which has given our nation fanatics of the people's movement instead of the previous weak politicians.

Thanks to this hardship, the movement not only gained the might to take power in the state, but also those strengths necessary to successfully implement all its thoughts and intentions. Now, led by the National Socialist Party, the German Volk has stepped into the place of the National Socialist Party. This German Volk now stands across from the same forces as the party once did.

The same enemy that called us into being and that continually strengthened us in the course of this fight stands against us still today. He employs every lie and every violent act to reach his goals.

This is no longer a conflict over decrepit dynastic interests, or the correction of national borders, or little economic interests. No, this is a fight against a true global sickness that threatens to pollute the nations, a contamination of nations that is remarkable for its internationality.

We know the reason for this, because it is not a Russian sickness or a Spanish one, just as it was neither a German one in 1918, nor a Hungarian or Bavarian one in 1919! Neither Russians, nor Germans, nor Hungarians, nor Spaniards are the pathogens of this sickness; rather it is that international parasite of nations that has spread itself across the world since many centuries ago, and that in our own time is back to its full destructive potency.

Only someone who is biased could close his eyes to the fact that there is an undeniable common thread that runs through all the diverse phenomena of the collapse of nations' political structures and lives, of their economies or their traditional cultures. Only someone who desperately wants to stick his head in the sand can fail to see what the actual spiritual inspirers of this international sickness themselves openly and unashamedly admit!

It requires a blessed naivete to deny Bolshevism's international and revolutionary character in a time when Bolshevism itself hardly lets a day pass without proclaiming its world-revolutionary mission to be the alpha and omega of its program, the very foundation of its existence! Only a bourgeois democratic politician could refuse to accept that these are the proclaimed principles of this global movement. It was not National Socialism that first claimed that Bolshevism is international; Bolshevism, as the most logically consistent interpretation of Marxism, solemnly declared this itself!

But if one of our Western Europeans still denies that Bolshevism is international and pursues the same goal everywhere with uniform international means and methods, then we can certainly expect that next we will hear from the mouth of this world-wise man that, analogous to this, National Socialism's program must not be intended just for Germans, and Fascism also not for Italy! Still, I would regret it if they do not want to believe us. I am also sorry that they do not even want to believe Bolshevism when it claims and proclaims all this itself.

In any case, whoever has no clue of this worldwide danger, and especially whoever is not allowed to believe in this danger for domestic and foreign political reasons, will only too easily be able to purposefully ignore everything that might be a sign of the imminence of this world danger! For example, he will not see that, at this very moment, constant revolutionary convulsions are occurring across the globe. Because he does not want to see, he will not see that these convulsions are all triggered and directed from one headquarters. Perhaps he will not be able to deny that all these revolutions march under the same flag and the same star! Yes, that they even have this cloth of their revolutionary symbol delivered from Moscow! But still, he will refuse to consider, much less openly admit, that this all might be happening intentionally!

Such a bourgeois will not be able to deny the constant economic battles that are slowly leading to a total breakdown of production, the lifeblood of their states. He will also not be able to wave away the fact that all these fights proceed according to one uniform formula, that all their instigators went to the same school, and that their financial support all comes from one state. Still, despite all this, he will refuse to accept that there is one deliberate intention behind it, because this does not fit into the models of understanding and thinking of his bourgeois political complacency.

Such politicians will also not be capable to deny that the Mr. Dimitrov who suddenly appeared in Spain, the Mr. Dimitrov who co-directs the Third International in Moscow, the Mr. Dimitrov who worked to incite the Bolshevik revolution in Berlin, and finally the Mr. Dimitrov who committed the assassinations in Sofia are all the same person. This cannot be doubted. The bourgeois democrat politicians see in this nothing but the random coincidences of the various political adventures of a wanderlust-filled private gentleman who is active sometimes here, sometimes there, but who by no means has any higher mission, and certainly not a consistent plan! For such an assumption, insofar as it could ever be spoken of, will never fit into such politicians' jumbled thoughts, or the clean conception of their worldview.

Party comrades!

As National Socialists we are completely clear on the causes and conditions of the fight that is currently throwing the world into unrest. To begin with, we grasp the magnitude and scope of this struggle. It is a colossal, world-historical event! It is the greatest danger to human culture and civilization since the collapse of the ancient states.

This crisis cannot be compared to some run-of-the-mill war or one of these ever-present revolutions. No, this is about an all-encompassing general attack against the existing social order, against our intellectual and cultural world. At the same time, this attack is also directed at the substance of the nations as such, against their internal organization and the racially endogenous leadership of the national body, as well as against their spiritual life, their traditions, their sciences, and all other institutions that give essence and character to the lives of nations.

This attack is so comprehensive that it puts almost all functions of life within the scope of its activity. We cannot foresee the duration of this fight. But it is certain that the world has not seen a similar process since the rise of Christianity, the triumph of Islam, or the Reformation. Though they took place primarily in the religious realm, these great ideological conflicts of the past influenced and pulled all aspects of life into the sphere of their battles, and the same is occurring today through the worldwide Bolshevik revolution!

It works like a creeping national poison and does not make room for any recusal! Just as in other ages individual men or nations could not escape such catastrophes or world-shaking revolutions simply because they had different opinions or intentions, so today no one can save themselves from the political danger of communism by simply denying its existence or refusing to recognize its dangerous effects!

I readily believe that the statesmen of the democratic world will find no joy in troubling themselves with the communist problem. But this is not up for discussion. They do not need to want it, but they will have to, or democracy will come to ruin anyway. This global plague will not ask permission to replace the democracies with Marxist dictatorships; it will simply do it. Unless it is prevented from doing so, that is. And this prevention will not be through a friendly refutation of this force or by a more or less solemn rejection; rather this prevention can only occur through the immunization of the nations against this poisoning, as well as through fighting the international disease vectors themselves.

This immunization is all the more necessary because the fates of individual nations are tied together in our interconnected Europe. Yes, not just that: because Europe is a community of nations and states that has formed together over centuries and mutually pollinated and enhanced one another, the infection of one state in this community is not only burdensome to that state and at most somewhat interesting to the others; no, it is crucial and dire for them all.

You cannot stick healthy children in a school with those afflicted with an infectious disease, and you cannot have a useful, blissful long-term coexistence in Europe if there are those among us who, afflicted with infectious toxins, make it no secret that they seek to spread their sickness to the healthy ones!

As far as Germany is concerned, similar to today's Italy, we have become immune to this danger. This means that, like Fascism, National Socialism has endeavored to remove those weaknesses from the organism of our Volk that would have allowed the infiltration of Bolshevik poison. For this reason, National Socialism has not viewed its task as the shallow restoration of an earlier condition — one which was then already incapable of saving itself from the Bolshevik poison anyway — but instead it has undertaken a deliberate internal restoration of our national body. That is to say, it did not place the state and the government in the center, but the Volk and the nation. How right we were in doing this work, as opposed to a deliberate policy of bourgeois or monarchical restoration, can best be measured by the impressions left by the proceedings of such a rally as you have experienced here in this city these past eight days.

Despite the constant attempts of the Moscow organization of criminals to smuggle their agents and their subversive materials into Germany, Germany is as safe as a large part of the rest of the world is unsafe, in our opinion. And nothing is better suited to compel us to bind ourselves to the National Socialist idea with all our strength than the clear recognition that we stand in the midst of a world that has gradually fallen out of its former political and economic framework.

What others cannot see because they do not want to see, we must unfortunately declare as a bitter fact: The world finds itself in a condition of increasing turmoil, which is without a doubt intellectually and materially arranged and led by the authorities of Jewish Bolshevism in Moscow.

When I deliberately portray this problem as a Jewish problem, then you know, my party comrades, that this is not an unfounded assumption, but a fact proven by undeniable evidence.

It is in man's slothful nature to assume that the conditions of his time have always been the same and so will forever stay the same. The more limited one's capacity for actual historical perspective, the less able he will be to look backward and figure out the necessary implications for his future.

The weak man is especially marked by his reluctance to think through developments whose outcomes might be undesired, because unpleasant. Thus, it is always easiest for these weak natures to assume that the given conditions are not only those of all time past, but surely will also be the conditions for all time to come.

Opposed to this sloth and fear in historical thinking is our historical responsibility: namely, the sense of responsibility felt by all those who not only know that the lives of nations proceed according to natural laws, but who are also able to draw an accurate picture of the causes or conditions of their own or another nation's rise or fall from their historical understanding. These will also have a true understanding of the causes that lead to the formation of a people and its political manifestations. First, they will understand that the river of human development is an uninterrupted one, and that its ultimate source is humanity's God-given drives for reproduction and self-preservation, which are especially well developed in humans. This dutiful investigation will further discover that human self-preservation generally can go no other way than the one prescribed in the rest of nature. The same elementary drives and forces of self-preservation belong to all creatures. These determine the struggle and the path of man's life.

It indicates a lack of historical and scientific understanding to assume that this understandable drive for self-preservation can suddenly be erased or brought to a standstill after a certain number of revolutions around the sun. Only then could one try to put the prescriptions of the League of Nations in the place of the law of omnipotent nature, which has stood since the beginning of life on earth. But as the iron natural laws of self-preservation have been definitive for man's struggle for existence so far, they will also be so for all time to come.

If this struggle for life has long been a static one, then processes like the formation of peoples, the founding of states, and any great community developments will likewise proceed according to the same principles.

We know today that the complete structure we call a "state" was artificially constructed over the course of millennia. To wit, it was not the result of the signing of a general, voluntarily entered social contract, but rather the result of a developmental process, which found its beginning and its fulfillment through natural right—namely, the right of skill and might, of willpower and heroic disposition!

All our European states grew from originally small racial cores, which were nevertheless the really powerful and formative factors of this entity.

This fact can be seen most starkly when we look at states that even in our own day still have not reached an equilibrium between the formed and led masses, and the formational and leading forces, maybe because this equilibrium was not even intended. Russia was one of these states. A very small, ethnically non-Russian, non-Slavic ruling class turned Russia from a mishmash of small and miniscule communities into a real colossus of a state, which seemed to be unshakeable, but whose great weakness was always the discrepancy between the quantity and quality of its ethnically non-Russian ruling class and the quantity and quality of the national Russian element.

Here a new racial core was easily able to infiltrate and attack. Ethnically camouflaged, they presented a contrast to the official state leadership. Here this tiny Jewish minority, by appropriating the leadership of the proletariat to itself, was able to not only force the previous social and state leadership out of its position, but to systematically root them out.

But for this very reason, the Russia of today is fundamentally no different from the Russia of two or three hundred years ago. It is the brutal dictatorship of a foreign race that claims and exercises total lordship over the actual Russian people.

If and when this state-building process comes to its completion, one could view this process like every other similar historical reality and come to terms with it. But insofar as this Jewish racial core is striving toward the same outcomes in other nations as well, and is using Russia as a base and bridgehead for further expansion, this Russian problem has become a global problem, which will be addressed one way or another, because it must be addressed.

My party comrades, you know the path of this most remarkable phenomenon of our age.

Without being called forth, the Jewish race infiltrates a people, and next tries to secure a certain economic influence by establishing itself as a foreign merchant class occupied with commerce and trade.

After centuries of this process, the economic power of the infiltrators gradually gives cause for a severe reaction on the part of the host nation. This natural defense only accelerates the Jewish attempt to feign an assimilation, which eliminates the surface of attack and, beyond this, allows them to gain direct political influence in the country in question.

Due partly to economic interests and partly to inborn bourgeois inertia, the dangers of this development are missed by many. The warning voices of influential or spirited men are ignored, as has always been the case whenever the prophesied consequences are of an unpleasant nature.

Thus, this Jewish racial community—though operating in the language of the host nation—starting from their influence on trade, is always able to get more and more influence on political development. And this community moves about in the courts just as much as it does in the opposition. To the extent that they are able to rattle the dynastic monarchy, which is certainly gradually weakened for other reasons as well, they shift their interests more to the promotion of democratic movements. But democracy then provides the preconditions for the organization of those terroristic entities we know as social democracy and the Communist International.

While democracy gradually suffocates any living will to resist with a thousand formalities and above all the cultivation of the weakest possible representatives of the state, the avant-garde of the global Jewish revolution develops within the radical movements.

Social and economic weaknesses help make this subversive attack by the exclusively Jewish-run Communist International easier.

And so, this stage repeats the same process as the previous one. While one part of our "Jewish fellow citizens" immobilizes democracy, especially through the influence of the press, or even infects it with toxins by coupling it together with revolutionary forces in the form of popular fronts, the other part of Jewry already carries the torch of Bolshevik revolution into the midst of the bourgeois world, without needing to fear any effective defense. The ultimate goal is the final Bolshevik revolution, but this does not mean the establishment of a government for the proletariat by the proletariat, but the subjugation of the proletariat under the leadership of its new foreign master.

As the agitated, frenzied, and insane mass, aided by the antisocial elements let loose from the prisons and penitentiaries, root out the natural, indigenous intelligence of the nations and leave it to bleed out on the scaffolds, only the Jew remains as the carrier of the last, albeit miserable, intellectual knowledge. For this must be remembered: this race is not an intellectually or morally superior one, but is in both cases thoroughly inferior! For unscrupulousness and a lack of conscience can never be counted as equal to a sincere and brilliant disposition.

Take a look, my fellow countrymen, at Jewry's importance in a commercial respect, and then take another look at the truly valuable inventions and great works of humanity that come from creative imagination, brilliance, and honest work. If the maxim ever applies that not analysis of facts, but the creation of facts is decisive, then it certainly applies to judging the actual value of Jewry. It may occupy 90 percent of all intellectual positions in a country, but it has not discovered, created, or cultivated the elements of knowledge, culture, or art. It may bring commerce under its control through certain manipulations, but the fundamentals of commerce, which are values, were not discovered, invented, or developed by Jews. Creatively, it is a thoroughly untalented race.

Thus, if it is to ever rule somewhere long-term, then it quickly has to root out the previous intellectual elite of the other nations. Otherwise, it will shortly be subject again to a superior intelligence, because first and foremost, as far as actual accomplishment is concerned, Jews have always been fumblers, and will ever remain fumblers.

How has National Socialism dealt with these arrogant incompetents? As democrats, they did not even master the potential that lies in democracy, and as social democrats they did not command the masses. As interested parties in our economy, they could not prevent its collapse, and neither were they able to reach their hoped-for goals as communists after this collapse. And all of these aims failed only because a discerning National Socialism deliberately stood in their way.

This is why we National Socialists are so confident and convinced of the indestructibility of our state. Certainly, we see the rest of the world as very endangered, because it deliberately closes its eyes to this issue and does not want to see that the dictatorship of the proletariat is nothing other than the dictatorship of Jewish intellectualism.

In the past year, with a slew of staggering statistical evidence, we have shown that in today's Soviet Russia, over 80 percent of leadership positions are occupied by Jews. In other words, the proletariat is not dictating; rather, it is that race whose symbol is the Star of David that calls the shots. We have compared this to the situation in Germany, where, through the work of National Socialism the most capable minds are sought out and readied for leadership without regard to person, origin, or wealth. Back then, the Jewish global press wrote about a whole lot, as did the press of Soviet Judea, but not a word was mentioned about this statistic of the entirely Jewish leadership of the so-called "state of workers and peasants." They had to be silent about this. Here there was nothing they were able to lie about or hide away, and there was the danger of enlightening the other nations!

We experienced this ourselves in Germany. Who were the leaders of our Bavarian Soviet Republic? Who were the leaders of the Spartacists? Who were the real leaders and financiers of our communist party? Even the most sympathetic democratic gentlemen cannot deny or change this fact: it was always and only the Jews!

And that is how it was in Hungary, and also in those parts of Spain that have not yet been reconquered by the real Spaniards!

Therefore, there can also be no doubt that in all countries it is not the Fascists, but the Jewish elements who try to shake democracy. And further, it cannot be doubted that the destruction of national production serves as a means to this end. For when someone tries to destroy the national economy of a country through certain methods and bring about a shortage of goods, then this can only be in the hopes of politically exploiting the resultant discontent.

For decades in our country, this Jewry used the Marxist parties of the proletariat as a battering ram, and not against the parasites of our national and economic life, but the opposite: in service of the parasites, and only ever against national production. It worked on this national economy so long until there were finally seven million jobless people lying in our streets. And all this in the hopes of using these seven million to build up its Bolshevik revolutionary army! With them, it hoped to root out our national intelligence, just as is being attempted in Spain and has already been done in Russia.

The Jew, as the leading element of "social justice," leads and organizes this fight, but not a single Jew is attacked in this fight as a disloyal element. Only in those places where there is no longer any indigenous leadership do the Jew's final fruits begin to ripen. The most wretched leadership that is humanly possible then starts to mutually kill itself off and root itself out, like in Soviet Russia.

If someone wages this seemingly pro-social global battle in order to ultimately only subjugate the other nations under the leadership of this race in the form of a brutal dictatorship, and meanwhile strives to spread this process across the world, then such developments do not only concern the directly affected, but also everyone who is indirectly threatened.

This counts for Germany!

We could make a sufficient study of how necessary it is to come to grips with this problem from this past year.

As you know, this Jewish Bolshevism went into open revolution in Spain, by way of democracy, in a similar process. It is a massive inversion of the facts to claim that the Bolshevik oppressors there possess legal authority and that the fighters for a nationalist Spain are the illegal revolutionaries.

No! In General Franco's men, we see the real and above all the lasting Spain, and in the usurpers of Valencia we see the international revolutionary troop bought and paid for by Moscow, which today has its sights on Spain, but tomorrow perhaps somewhere else.

Can we be indifferent to these events?

I would like to make a few brief observations.

In the press of our Western democracies and in the speeches of some politicians we hear again and again about how far-reaching the natural scope of the interests of these powers is. It seems quite obvious to the representatives of these states that their interests should include every ocean and also every state in Europe, and beyond Europe, practically everything in nature. Conversely, we experience immediate outcries of insurrection as soon as someone outside this circle of international propertied powers even says a word about their interests that lie outside of their borders. In view of this hubris, I would like to explain this.

We continuously hear the claim from England and France that they have sacrosanct interests in Spain. What type of interests are these now? Are we talking about political or economic interests? If political, then this would make as little sense to us as if someone were to say that they had political interests in Germany. Who governs in Germany is no one's business but ours, so long as we do not intend to carry out hostilities against other states. But if England and France have certain economic interests in Spain, then we will readily concede this, only we must state that we claim exactly the same economic interests. In other words: National Socialist Germany follows the Jewish attempt to globally revolutionize Spain with rapt interest, and for two reasons.

First, just as England and France do not wish for the balance of power to be shifted in Europe either to the German or Italian side, so we also do not wish for a shift of power in the direction of the proliferation of Bolshevism, because if Fascism reigns in Italy, this is a purely Italian national concern. It would be stupidity to assert that Fascist Italy could only be given direction or orders from the outside.

It would be even stupider to claim that Fascist Italy is a component of a larger, higher international Fascist organization. Just the opposite. It is rooted deep in the character of Fascism and National Socialism that these are political doctrines whose ideology and activity lies only within the borders of their respective peoples.

Likewise, it is certain that a nationalist Spain will be national (that is, Spanish), just as it cannot be denied that Bolshevism is consciously international and has only one central office, while everything else is only a branch of this office.

Just as England and France pretend to be troubled by the thought that Spain might come to be owned by Germany or Italy, we are equally upset at the possibility that it might be conquered by Soviet Russia! This conquest does not need to occur through Soviet troops, but it is accomplished once Spain becomes a section, an integrated component of the Bolshevik Moscow headquarters, a franchise that receives its political directives as well as its material subsidies from Moscow.

In every attempted spread of Bolshevism in Europe, we see a fundamental shift in the European balance of power. And just as England is interested in preventing something contrary to its interests, so we are interested in the same regarding *our* interests!

We must therefore decline to be lectured on the nature of such a Bolshevik shift of the balance by statesmen who do not have the knowledge of this topic that we have, and who have not had the opportunity to gain the practical experiences that we unfortunately did gain.

Secondly, but no less significantly, such a Bolshevik political shifting of the balance of power is also an economic development, which can only have catastrophic consequences for the closely tied European states.

The first result of every Bolshevik revolution is not an increase of production, but the total destruction of all existing economic value as well as all economic functions in the affected countries. The world does not live by occasional world economic conferences—as experience has taught—but it lives by the exchange of its goods, and thus primarily by the production of these goods. If the production of goods is gradually destroyed in individual states by some criminal insanity, then world economic conferences cannot spare us from the consequences. Rather, the consequences will reach those countries that are safe from Bolshevism within their own borders, but which, by the nature of their economic situation, had important economic relationships with the affected nations.

We have all kinds of experiences in this area. The moment that Bolshevism broke out in Spain, its entire national production was so damaged that there was an immediate halt to a really valuable exchange of goods. When someone rejoins us with the claim that other countries were still able to do good business with Spain, this is because of the payment of their deliveries in gold, which did not get its value through Spanish Bolshevism, but was simply the representation of value that was created earlier by nationalist Spanish labor and effort, and then stolen and sent out of the country by Bolshevism. This is not the basis for a durable and solid economic exchange, because this can only be founded in the exchange of real values, not on the activity of traffickers or dealers of stolen goods!

Bolshevism completely destroys the production of actual value. And—as Soviet Russia proves—even after twenty years, it cannot bring it back into order, despite reducing their workers to the status of dogs! This may be of no interest to rich Great Britain. Perhaps England is indifferent whether or not Spain becomes a desert or economically plunged into the chaos of Bolshevism. Maybe England is really only thinking of this Spanish question politically. But, for us Germans, who do not have the option of shifting our trade to our own global empire, Europe as it is today is a requirement for our own existence. A Bolshevized Europe would make our state's trade policies impossible, and not because we would not want to trade, but because we would not be able to have any trading partners.

Thus, this is not an opportunity for theoretical contemplation or moral concern for us, nor is it a problem to be solved internationally—for the amount of respect we have for the international institutions does not allow us to believe for one second that their empty talk could provide practical help—no, this is an *existential* question.

We know very well: if Spain had ultimately become Bolshevik, perhaps this wave would have spread through the rest of Europe, or still might—and Bolshevism itself certainly claims so and definitely wants it. If this occurred, it would be a severe economic catastrophe for Germany.

We have to engage in trade with these countries, and we have to do so out of naked self-interest for our own survival. This exchange is only possible if these countries produce goods under normal, well-ordered conditions. Should this stop due to a Bolshevik catastrophe, then Germany would also fall into hard times economically.

We are all aware that in the case of such a development, the League of Nations in Geneva would muster about as much strength as our own German Frankfurt Parliament once did. We can already see today how little such international help can be relied upon.

Barely after the Bolshevik uprising began in Spain, not only did its trade with Germany immediately tank, but over fifteen thousand German nationals had to leave this land fraught with internal turmoil. Their businesses were plundered, German schools were destroyed, many of the community buildings were set on fire—all the wealth of these hardworking people was annihilated in one stroke; the rewards of years of honest work, gone. I do not think the League of Nations will reimburse them for this. Knowing this, we cannot go to the League with any plea. We know it has its own problems and tasks. For example, it has had to work hard for years to support various Marxist and Jewish emigrations in order to keep them alive!

I am only describing what the case is! We thus have a sincere interest in seeing that this Bolshevik plague does not spread further in Europe. Apart from that, we have of course had plenty of disagreements with the nation of France historically. However, somehow and somewhere, we all belong to the same European family of nations, especially if we all look deep within ourselves.

And so, I believe we do not want to miss any of the actually civilized European nations or wish them away. We have not only provided each other with plenty of anger and sorrow, but also a tremendous mutual pollination. We gave each other models, examples, and guidance, just as we gave each other plenty of joy and many beautiful things. If we are fair, then we have every reason to admire each other more than to hate each other!

Global Jewish Bolshevism is a totally alien entity in this community of civilized European nations, and it has not contributed anything to our economy or our culture except confusion. It cannot put forward a single positive achievement at an international exposition of European and global life, only charts of fraudulent figures and rabble-rousing posters.

I do not want to forget to answer those who ceaselessly speak about the necessity of improving global economic relations and international solidarity, and who now complain that — in their view — National Socialist Germany is deliberately trying to isolate itself.

I have already expressed how greatly mistaken the statesmen and editorialists who sincerely believe this are. It is forcefully refuted by practical reality. We have neither the desire nor the intention to be political or economic hermits! Germany has in no way isolated itself, not politically, and not economically! Not politically, because to the contrary, it has strived to work together with all those who have the goal of a real European community. We categorically refuse to be grouped together with those whose agenda is the destruction of Europe, and who make no secret of this agenda!

Even if we ourselves feel safe from this destruction, it still seems like a self-contradiction to enter into accords of European solidarity that actually seek to destroy this very solidarity.

To refuse affiliation with these elements thus does not mean we isolate ourselves, rather it means we secure ourselves. And all the greater is our determination to come to agreement with all those who not only talk about solidarity but actually want it, and by this I do not mean a negative solidarity of common destruction, but a positive and constructive one.

The accusation that we seek economic isolation is even more insane. I believe our trade figures are the best contradiction of this silly ungrounded opinion. Even if our trade were to not increase, this would be something we merely tolerate against our will; we still would not be seeking economic isolation.

However, economic isolation would inevitably come the moment that Europe fell to Bolshevism. We are currently experiencing the comedic farce of the press in countries that always think they have to persuade us to be more involved in the world economy, screaming the moment they find out, for example, that we are doing business with nationalist Spain, that we deliver machines and so on to nationalist Spain, and that it sends us raw materials and food. Well, here we are doing what these apostles of the global economy keep wanting! Why the sudden outrage over this? No! We know the true causes of this all too well.

They are angry that for once we in Germany are prepared to categorically refuse to import those Marxist toxins that have already once brought us to the edge of the abyss. This is a commerce that we certainly refuse. They are angry that we are not only not isolating ourselves, but that we have, in fact, found a firm interdependence with states that have leaders who have similar ideals and think and act similarly. Here, I can only repeat that no other orientation is possible for Germany. We are more interested in Europe, as some other countries need to be. Our country, our people, our culture, our economy grew out of the European condition. We must, therefore, be the enemy of any attempt to bring an element of subversion and destruction into this European family of nations, either individually or as a whole.

Besides this, it is simply an intolerable thought for us Germans that this Europe could be directed and ruled from Moscow, of all places. If this hubris is tolerated as a political necessity in other states, we can only look on in amazement and regret. But for us, in any case, the very notion of taking directives from such an inferior world is just as ridiculous as it is outrageous. The uncivilized Judeo-Bolshevik international guild of criminals insolently demands to rule Germany, an old civilized European nation, from Moscow. Moscow stays Moscow and Soviet Russia, as far as we care, can stay Soviet Russia. But our German capital city will be Berlin, and Germany, thank God, will always stay Germany!

Do not be mistaken about this: National Socialism has banned the Bolshevik danger from the inside of Germany. It has ensured that a bunch of exiled foreign Jewish literati do not dictate over the proletariat, meaning the German worker, but that the German Volk finally has self-determination and its own leadership. And it has made our people and our Reich immune to Bolshevik infestation.

In light of this, it will also not hesitate to act against any renewed attempt against the sovereignty of our people with the most decisive means.

We National Socialists grew up in the struggle against this enemy. In fifteen years, we have intellectually, ideologically, and materially destroyed it in Germany. Neither its countless murders, nor its other atrocities, nor the support it once received from the Marxists then in power in the Reich were able to prevent our triumph. Today, we will diligently guard against any such danger coming into Germany. But should anyone think they carry this danger into Germany from the outside, then they should know that the National Socialist state has also forged the weapons it needs to crush such an attempt with the speed of lightning.

The world will not have forgotten that we are good soldiers. They can trust that we are even better soldiers today. And let no one doubt that the National Socialist state would defend its existence with a very different fanaticism than the bourgeois state of old!

The age of the German Volk's parliamentary weakness is over, and will not return. We all have the same great wish, that fate will give us sufficient peace and time for our internal regeneration, allowing us to complete our great work of building ourselves up, and to complete this in a Europe that has come back to its senses. We do not intend to force our thoughts or ideas on anyone else, but let no one try to force his opinion on us! First and foremost, let that criminal Moscow Sovietism finally refrain from spreading its barbarity and trying to bring us to tragedy! The time when one could demand anything from a defenseless people is over. The bombs that fell on our armored ships did not only hit the ship by the name of *Deutschland*, but they also experienced that retaliation from the real Germany that from henceforth will be the immediate answer to any such attempt. A few months ago, England still had no sympathy for this act of self-defense.

It is interesting to see how quickly the British public tossed its own standards overboard and adopted the position we had. Of course, this time it was British ships that were the targets of red submarines.

Today Germany stands behind its armed forces just as its armed forces stand before it. It is no longer an abstract concept; it is a Germany that millions of people carry deep within their heart with faithful love as a sacred treasure. Never in our history has the German Volk been more unified in one state as now. Previously there were always differences and prejudices based on tribal, denominational, or dynastic (and later, party) reasons. The time of prejudice is over. The millions of our people are unconditionally devoted to National Socialism and the National Socialist state today.

Ideology and national discipline are working together. Political will is strengthening the spiritual guidance and political leadership of the nation. That this has also found its necessary complement in the interior and exterior posture of the German man is nowhere better demonstrated than at the Party Congress in Nuremberg. Here, for eight days, you have witnessed living proof for the success of a truly world-historical effort and accomplishment.

When we first met here in this city as National Socialists ten years ago on the occasion of a Party Congress, we were a small community of partly misunderstood, partly notorious idealists. And back then we had a vision of a new state that would be the official representation for an interiorly rejuvenated German Volk. Here, ten years later, Volk and state have merged to become that prophesied entity.

As so many countries around us became afflicted by those revolutionary forces that we knew even then, or suffered under their subversive and dangerous agendas, our Germany not only gained confidence in its government's mission, but also became convinced of the correctness of its way of thinking and its agenda.

Hundreds of thousands marched past here in these past days, all uniform and orderly, like grenadiers of the very best regiments. But this is not the crucial thing. They were not forced to come here; they were compelled by the inner harmony of their souls and the shared alignment of their wills to present this wonderful image of unity. You have seen hundreds of thousands before you like this. Yet they are only the vanguard of this great army of the German Volk, which marched here with us in spirit.

Every National Socialist who stood here as a fighter in the arenas or who marched on the streets was accompanied by the heartbeat of countless of his comrades in the villages, factories, and workshops, who belong with him; even if they could not come to Nuremberg, they stood by him in spirit. Thus, in reality Nuremberg was not experienced by a hundred thousand political leaders, or a hundred thousand SA men, or forty thousand workmen, or the part of the Hitler Youth that we saw here in these days; it was experienced by the millions of men and women of all the enormous organizations of our party: the entire German Volk. We only saw the forefront here.

And likewise, our National Socialist armed forces, the entire military of our German nation, stands behind the soldiers who are now departing here. You have seen only the tip of a spear that shields our homeland and that is our very own.

That Germany rose to such glory again is not a miraculous coincidence, but all aspects of this uplift are the result of just as much deliberation and courage as diligence and labor. What unfathomable achievements are contained in the seventeen years that have elapsed since the founding of our movement. Today, it is so easy to admire this result, but so hard to comprehend the labor, the sacrifice, the diligence, and the energy that were necessary to reach these results! How many men is even just a hundred thousand! They stood here group after group, standard after standard, company after company, battalion after battalion, regiment after regiment. Behind them there are millions of comrades and soldiers, and this was all called into being in just a few years from almost nothing, from confusion and decay.

Indeed, even this tremendous demonstration in and of itself is the result of unfathomable labor. Do you understand now, my party comrades, why, in the light of such a radiant achievement of human skill and hard work, we gave this celebration the name of the Party Congress of Labor?

I cannot close without thanking all those who gave their labor and their help; those who, through their work, make it possible for me to carry out the tremendous project of establishing the Reich. I know that hundreds of thousands, even millions of men and women have, according to their knowledge and conscience, given the utmost to save Germany.

One man's strength is used for building up the Reich; the other man's strength is used on his group or his company. Political leader, officer, official, fellow fighter, or soldier — at the conclusion of such an event, all of them can reach out a hand to each other, knowing that they did their duty to their people.

And likewise, we must extend our deepest gratitude to the countless German women for their compassionate help, and above all to the German mothers, who give this generational struggle its ultimate meaning and its most beautiful significance through the gift of their children.

May Almighty God help us in the future, as He has helped us thus far, to always fulfill our duties, and to always be worthy of our people and its history.

In just a few hours the trains will roll out toward all the German districts with the hundreds of thousands of participants. The farmers and their sons return to the villages; workers, professionals, and officials step back into their plants, their offices; the soldiers return to their barracks, and the youth to their schools. But all of them will remember this great demonstration of the National Socialist Party and state with burning hearts.

They will take with them the proud feeling of having again been witness to the interior and exterior rise of their people. And let them be conscious of the fact that with this, the hope of millennia and the prayer of many generations, the confidence and faith of countless great men of our people, have achieved their historic realization.

The German nation has received its Germanic Reich.

THE FÜHRER'S SPEECHES
AT THE 1938 PARTY CONGRESS
OF GREATER GERMANY

THE COURSE OF THE NSDAP'S
TENTH PARTY CONGRESS

An introduction

On the February 20th, 1938, in a great speech before the Reichstag in which he dealt with all current problems of German politics, the Führer said:

We feel deep and sincere satisfaction at seeing a series of European states strongly striving for real neutrality. We believe that with this we are seeing an element of increasing security. But we are also seeing the painful economic and demographic consequences of the disordered European map caused by the insane Treaty of Versailles. There are ten million Germans included in just two of our bordering countries. Until 1866, they were still unified with the whole German Volk in a single constitutional covenant. In 1918, they fought shoulder to shoulder with the German soldiers of the Reich in the Great War. Against their will, the peace treaties prevented unification with the Reich. This is itself painful enough. But there can be no doubt in our view about one thing: the constitutional separation from our Reich cannot lead to a removal of a group's rights, meaning the general right of national self-determination. This was, by the way, promised to us in Wilson's Fourteen Points as a condition for the armistice, and it cannot be ignored simply because we are Germans! In the long run, it is intolerable for a self-respecting world power to know that the heaviest suffering is being inflicted on its countrymen for their sympathy and connection to the greater Volk, its destiny, and its worldview! We know very well that there can be practically no European border configuration that can please everyone. However, that makes it all the more important to avoid unnecessarily abusing national minorities and adding to the pain of political separation the pain of persecution for belonging to a certain nationality. As has been mentioned, it is possible to find paths to balance and to relax tensions, if there is good will. But whoever uses force to prevent such an easing through balance will one day inevitably bring about a war among the nations! It should not be denied that, as long as Germany itself remained powerless and defenseless, we had to simply accept many of these constant persecutions of German people beyond our borders. Just as England represents its own interests across the entire globe, Germany will also represent and defend its interests, albeit on a much more limited scale. And among the German Reich's interests is the protection of those German countrymen who are not in a position to secure their human, political, and ideological freedom through our borders!

These explanations of the Führer came after a discussion on February 12th at Obersalzberg, to which Adolf Hitler had invited the former Austrian Federal Chancellor Schuschnigg, where he gave the Führer reassurances about his support. Only a few days later it became apparent that he did not intend to keep his word. Just the opposite. He believed that he could cut National Socialism out of Austria once and for all through a popular referendum that he suddenly announced, and that was to be held just three days after that. A referendum was supposed to give cover for his despotic regime in the eyes of the "great democracies" of the West.

The terms of his electoral decree were a brazen challenge to the entire straight-thinking and German-thinking Austrian population. A storm of outrage went through the country at the chancellor's breaking of his promise. The National Socialist Volk rose up in every district. The battle was decided in the evening hours of March 11th. Schuschnigg stepped down the following day, after one more dishonest broadcast, despised by the entire Volk. The troops of the Third Reich marched across the border on the morning of the 12th, with the population showering them with flowers. In the afternoon, the Führer entered Linz greeted with unimaginable cheers. On the 13th, he made his entrance into Vienna, of which foreign observers noted that no emperor has ever experienced a triumph so splendorous. The old German Austria was freed from foreign rule and systemic hardship. The Greater German Reich, this dream of many centuries, finally found its realization under Adolf Hitler's flag of the National Socialist revolution.

The tenth Reich Party Congress, the Party Congress of Greater Germany, was filled with the echoes of this tremendous historic event. What all of Germany experienced in the cheerful tempest of those March days came to life again at this Party Congress. Whether it was Oberbürgermeister Liebel greeting the Führer at the ceremonial welcome in city hall as "the creator of Greater Germany, the liberator of the German Austria," or Reichstatthalter of Austria Seyß-Inquart putting the insignia of the First German Reich—the crown and crown jewels of the Holy Roman Empire—into the care of Nuremberg at the opening ceremony at the Katharinenkirche, or Chief of Staff Lutze including the martyrs of Austria for the first time when he read out the movement's list of dead at the opening of the Party Congress, or the Führer's deputy praising Austria's standards and flags as symbols of sacrifice, faith, and victory, or the first words of greeting at the assemblies of the Labor Service, political leaders, Hitler Youth, Brown Army of the SA, SS, NSKK, and NSFK, and finally on the day of the Armed Forces all being addressed to the comrades from the Austria, who could previously only secretly sneak into the NSDAP's Reich Party Congress in limited numbers, but could now proudly stand side by side with the other districts of Greater Germany: a flaming arch of burning thoughts and wishes stretched across the whole political celebrations of National Socialist Germany in Nuremberg toward the seven districts of Austria, affirming the German unity that the Führer's deed of March 12th created a millionfold.

Austria's return to the greater German homeland was not made possible by a war or by an international court. For the first time in history, a Reich was founded not by the strength of arms, but by the force of hearts. The National Socialist idea was the sole conqueror, and it tore out the boundary posts that separated Germans from Germans. This was also the first time that the party stepped across the border to take a part in framing European politics.

In his great proclamation at the start of the Party Congress, after having given a proud accounting of the past years, the Führer said the following:

> As the flag of the new Reich was carried forth on the morning of the March 12th, it was no longer a symbol of conquest, but a symbol of a unity that had long encompassed all Germans. The battle flag that our young armed forces carried into the districts back then became a symbol of faith in victory for our brothers in their hard struggle for Austria. Thus, for the first time, an idea conquered and unified a people.

This idea gained its organizational form in the NSDAP. Thus, it is always the work and mission that are shown to be the foundation for all success in the great moments of the Reich's destiny.

What the party's work has already richly and solidly grounded and secured in the political realm is still partially awaiting fulfillment in the economic realm. Here, the Führer also gave clear directives in his proclamation. Since National Socialism has eliminated millions-high joblessness down to the last man in the matter of a few years, there are two other worries that affect the nation's economic life: the shortage of skilled industrial workers and the shortage of the rural workforce. But the great successes of National Socialist economic policy in the last year have been securing the German Volk's absolute nutritional freedom, and the outcome of the four-year plan. The Führer explained:

> The German national economy as a whole is being built up in such a way that it can be totally independent from other countries and can stand on its own two feet at all times. And this worked. The idea of blockading Germany can now be buried as a totally ineffectual weapon.

With these words, Adolf Hitler also touched on the activity of certain foreign circles which, in an unabated frenzy, predict a coming world war — especially during this Reich Party Congress. They have their most eager accomplice in the Czechoslovakian president, Dr. Beneš. Since the Anschluss, he has implemented a systematic policy of constant provocation against the German Reich, apparently for the purpose of securing business for the international warmongers. The Czechoslovakian regime seemed to think that it could only preserve the existence of the Czecho-slovakian multi-ethnic state through a general catastrophe. The Führer's statement that a blockade of Germany would be henceforth ineffective undercut one of the most vital aspects of this circle's machinations.

Every last corner of the Congress Hall was filled on Monday, September 12th, as the Führer began his great concluding speech for the first Reich Party Congress of Greater Germany, and along with the twenty-thousand in the hall, uncounted millions across the Reich, and in many foreign states whose stations carried the speech, listened through loud-speakers with bated breath to hear what Adolf Hitler had to say to the world. Adolf Hitler opened once again by reminding his followers of the eternal principles of the National Socialist movement, as he so often did during the difficult and decisive years of struggle, and he elucidated that in this hour as well, the enemies of National Socialist Germany are the same as in the party's earlier times of struggle. After that, sharply saying "I am speaking of Czechoslovakia," Adolf Hitler gave a devastating account of the cynical terroristic policies of the Beneš system. Sentence after sentence, the Führer was interrupted by the tumultuous cheers of the crowd.

Among the majority of peoples being oppressed in this state are 3.5 million Germans, so about as many people of our race as, for example, Denmark has in its total population. These Germans are likewise God's creatures. The Almighty did not make them to be delivered unto a foreign power that despises them by a Versailles construct. And He did not make seven million Czechs for them to watch over and patronize 3.5 million Germans, or to abuse and torment them. When 3.5 million members of a people of eighty million cannot sing what song they like because the Czechs do not like it, or when they are beaten bloody only because they wear stockings that the Czechs simply do not want to see, or when they are terrorized and mistreated because they use a greeting that the Czechs find unpleasant even though they only greet each other this way and not the Czechs, or when they are hunted and chased like wild animals — then this is irrelevant to our esteemed representatives of democracy, possibly even agreeable, because it involves 3.5 million Germans. But I can only tell these representatives of democ-

racy that it is not irrelevant to us and that, if these tormented creatures can find no state and no help for themselves, then we will
provide them with both. The deprivation of these people's rights
must come to an end!

And then the Führer announced to the German and the global public
what measures have been taken in the past months to give weight to
Germany's legal point of view regarding the Czechoslovakian government:

> Firstly: the previously announced increases of the army and the air
> force were greatly expanded by my order and immediately imple-
> mented. Secondly: I ordered the immediate expansion of fortifica-
> tions in the West. I can assure you that since May 28th, the most co-
> lossal fortifications of all time are in the process of being completed.
> The German Western Fortification will be complete before winter.
> Its defensive capabilities are already fully assured. After its comple-
> tion, it will include a total of seventeen thousand bunkers and tank
> traps. Behind this front of steel and concrete, which consists of
> three lines, and in some places reaches a depth of four lines or fifty
> kilometers, there is the German Volk at arms. I have ordered this
> most enormous effort of all time to serve peace. But I will not, un-
> der any circumstance, sit idly by and watch the continued oppres-
> sion of our countrymen in Czechoslovakia. By no means do I want
> to let a second Palestine be created here in the heart of Germany
> through the diligent efforts of other statesmen. The poor Arabs are
> defenseless and abandoned. The Germans in Czechoslovakia are
> neither defenseless nor abandoned. Understand that.

As the Führer concluded his speech to the ever-growing cheers of the
Germans, everyone knew, especially the Sudeten Germans, that this
German suffering would be eliminated in a short time. After this speech,
events unfolded in short order: on September 15th, British Prime Minister
Chamberlain visited the Führer at Obersalzberg in order to learn Germany's stance on the Czechoslovakia issue. A few days later, on the 22nd
and 23rd, this was followed by a second conversation between the Führer
and Chamberlain in Godesberg. There, Adolf Hitler gave the prime minister a German memorandum to pass on to the government in Prague. In

this memorandum, the Reich demanded that the Czechoslovakian military clear out of the Sudetenland by October 1st, 1938. On Monday, September 26th, the Führer spoke again to the whole nation in the Berlin Sportpalast to underscore this German demand. On the 29th, the four-way discussion between Adolf Hitler, Mussolini, Chamberlain, and French Prime Minister Daladier took place. Its result was an agreement between the four powers on settling the Sudeten German issue. It determined that, pursuant to Adolf Hitler's demand, the clearing of the German areas was to begin on October 1st. On the 1st, at 2 o'clock in the afternoon, the first German troops crossed the former German-Czechoslovakian border in the Bohemian Forest between Helfenberg and Finsterau, bringing freedom to 3.5 million Sudeten Germans. This tremendous work is complete. What no man dared dream is reality. The ten million Germans the Führer spoke of on February 20th belong to the Reich again today. What was just a distant dream before then was accomplished in a mere eight months.

The meaning of the first Party Congress of Greater Germany was, in an exceptional way, doubly fulfilled. It was the Party Congress for the return of the old German Austria into the Reich, and at the same time it became the Party Congress where the Führer proclaimed the Sudeten Germans' right to self-determination. From this historic rally, the work of liberating these 3.5 million German people began, and it was completed barely three weeks later.

— Dr. Walther Schmitt

RECEPTION OF THE FÜHRER IN
THE CITY OF NUREMBERG

September 5th, 1938

In this hour in which the bells of Nuremberg ring in the tenth Reich Party Congress of our National Socialist movement, I would like to extend to you, Herr Oberbürgermeister, my deeply felt gratitude for your welcome and the exceedingly heartfelt reception that the people of your city have prepared for me.

Once again, the National Socialist Party and its unified German Volk find themselves gathered in this city to summon the strength for the coming year's labors and tasks through the experience of these uplifting days and these hours of the affirmation of our community.

Nuremberg, this old German imperial city whose time-honored glory is so deeply connected with the character of our new Reich, reminds us National Socialists of fond memories of the glorious years of our movement's struggle. Fifteen years ago, within the walls of this city, we had the first German Day, and since then it has seen many of the movement's pugnacious and glamorous Party Congresses. You, Herr Oberbürgermeister, have alluded to the special significance of this year's Party Congress. This year, for the first time, we are all happy to have our fellow countrymen from the returned German Austria among us, united to the Reich.

In no other German city does the past and present of the Greater German Reich come together in such a symbolic unity and expressive power as in Nuremberg, the old and simultaneously new imperial city. This city, whose walls the old German Reich deemed worthy of bearing its imperial insignia, now possesses these symbols anew, which testify to the might and greatness of the old Reich. Today, Nuremberg is the city of the Reich Party Congresses, the expression in stone of German might and German greatness in the New German Reich!

As I thank you, Herr Oberbürgermeister, for this reception, and ask you to convey this thanks to the whole city. I salute Nuremberg of the Reich Party Congresses once again with our old call:

Nuremberg — Sieg Heil!

THE PROCLAMATION OF THE FÜHRER AT THE OPENING OF THE 1938 PARTY CONGRESS

September 6th, 1938

Party comrades! National Socialists!

This time we traveled to Nuremberg more deeply moved than before. For years, the Reich Party Congress has not only been a festival of joy and of pride, but also of inner reflection. The old fighters come here in the happy hope of being able to see their old acquaintances from the days of our struggle for power. And so, the comrades-in-arms of the greatest German revolution always meet again in this city. For the first time this year, the scope has broadened so much more. The National Socialist Reich has taken in new countrymen. Many of them find themselves among us for the first time here in this festive hour. Many others are immersed in the magic of this incomparable city and these sublime hours in the streams of our surging movement. Others, as members of the militant organizations, will march in with their brothers from all over the German Reich for the first time, and will most sincerely renew their vow to never again be separate from this greatest of communities.

This year in particular elicits memories in us all! In these months, twenty years ago, Germany's internal collapse began. The external enemy did not break our front, but the creeping venom within us started to undermine it. The weakness of our half-hearted leadership became the cause of the greatest national and state catastrophe in our history! Only a few months later, Germany seemed lost forever. The time of our deepest humiliation and shameful indignity had begun. A year after this catastrophe, a new symbol arose out of the chaos of misfortune and despair. Providence called me forth to carry it. The National Socialist movement's first Reich Party Congress took place four years later. This was fifteen years ago, and there in Munich the men and women from all over the German Reich met, whose flag would become the flag of the German Reich barely ten years later. Since then, this rally of an awakened nation has been repeated nine times, and now we are meeting for the tenth!

But, my party comrades, what has become of Germany in that time! Today, does it not seem as if Providence had to let us walk this path in order to refine us and ready us for a greater community of Germans, which shall for all time be considered necessary for the existence of our people? Looking back on the times behind us on the path to National Socialism and the rise of our Reich may seem dreamlike and unreal to many. Perhaps one day there will be talk of the great miracle that Providence did for us. But let it not be forgotten: at the beginning of this miracle there was faith! Faith in the eternal German Volk!

When I first set out on this path as an unknown soldier of the war that took me to the summit of this nation and to you here today, it was only my own faith in the value of my people that enabled such a foolhardy decision. Today I must say that it was good that in the years of my youth and of my military service, I only had the opportunity to get to know my people, for this alone gave me faith, and I persevered in the memory of it through all difficulties and perils. If instead of knowing the people I had only known its intellectual elite, its bourgeois political leadership, its commercial morality, and its political and human frailties, then I may have also doubted the German Volk and its future. The thing that lifted me out of these bitter days and weeks of collapse was not the knowledge of the political or military leadership, or the intellectual classes, as far as individuals, but the knowledge of the German musketeers, knowledge of the German frontline soldier, and knowledge of those millions of German workers and farmers that form the steel core of the German Volk. I have this faith alone to thank for the courage to begin this tremendous struggle and to unswervingly believe in its success from the first day. For there could be no doubt about this: the human and moral value of the nation's leadership then did not even approach the value of those led. Ninety-nine percent of the courage and bravery was with the musketeers. The Reich and the Volk's leadership could not claim even 1 percent of it. But I resolved to give the Reich a new leadership that would possess the same fundamental values as we expect in the Volk, and that we saw amply present in it. A ruling social class proved its inability to lead on and before November 1918. Thus, I saw the problem I had to solve quite clearly. A new leadership organization had to be built. Every notion of saving the nation with the old force relied on believing, against all logic and experience, that a proven weakness would suddenly transform into a strength. For over four years, the German Volk laid down a proof of its worth that had never before been demanded in history. Regiments reported for duty and bled out without wavering, batteries fired to the last officer and man, ship crews held tattered flags up in their fists and sank into the waters with the song of German faith on their lips. This valiant demonstration of an eternal heroism was met with the shocking cowardice of the Reich and nation's leadership. While a front of heroes proved their worth a thousand times over, the leadership of their homeland could not muster the strength for even one similarly great and bold deed. Bravery was only with the musketeers, and all cowardice was concentrated in the organized political leadership of the nation. Any attempt to set Germany right again could only succeed if this political leadership class was first rooted out and eliminated. To do this, we first had to find a new method of leadership selection. This ruled out any possibility of shaping the history of Germany within the frame of the old parties. In those nights when I decided to become a politician the fate of the German parties was decided.

My party comrades, as I make these observations in light of the general improvement of the Reich, I must take a stance against those who always see obstacles blocking the future but at the same time seem to view the path traveled by the nation and Reich in the past as something obvious. Today, in this festive hour, let me emphatically state that in years past, during the movement's establishment and of the struggle for power and for Germany, we were neither understood nor supported by this world. They thought that the attempt to make brave courage and a sense of responsibility the leading currency of the German Reich would cause trouble, because they automatically held any boldness to be unreason, while they saw the traces of wisdom in every act of cowardice! Sure, they thought the virtues of courage shown in the past were valid, but they were above such primitive impulses in the current day. They talked about Prussianism, but they all forgot that Prussianism was not founded by some birth certificate, but exclusively in a peerless conduct. They cited the names of the great Prussian heroes and tried to invoke them whenever possible, yet they refused to recognize that all their cleverness fit into the chapter that the Prussian Clausewitz dismissed under the blanket term "cowardice." Thus, they also had no appreciation for the unknown fighter who tried to finally apply the frontline soldier's courage to German politics, and who raised up a party for this purpose, which became the most appropriate and the only political representation of this frontline soldiery.

They did not understand, or did not want to understand that a political leader — and the entire political leadership of a nation — requires a solid character, strong heart, bold courage, the highest sense of responsibility, reckless decisiveness, and dogged tenacity, and that these all are more important than supposed abstract knowledge! But because they did not see it as important, their organizations, being pervaded by their spirit, were consequently in no state to solve the internal and much less the external problems. What they saw as fragmentation in the founding of the National Socialist movement was actually the beginning of the greatest cleansing and simultaneously the greatest unification of our history. A new selection process took effect. The emphasis of intolerant platform points caused the shedding of those with tolerant natures. By being hawkish and aggressive, we drew in ever-ready fighters. That is how I began to collect my old guard, which has not left me since — with very few exceptions. And when I mustered my guard in Munich for the first time for that Party Congress, it was indeed small numerically, but it represented all Germany by its values and worth. This was the first movement that did not carry the banner of any class, sectarian, professional, or economic interests, or of loyalty to a certain tribe or form of government, but only of one faith: Germany!

When we look back today at those first days of our struggle, after so many years, then we must tremble at the recognition: what a tremendous turn of destiny! What did Germany look like during this first Party Congress? Trodden down, despised, disgraced, economically ruined and plundered, given over to insanity domestically, and occupied in the Ruhr region and vast parts of the west!

And today? We are all struck by the question and its answer. Yet still, we should never forget: throughout all of this, our Volk has always remained the same. The Volk of 1918 was none other than the Volk of 1914, and the Volk of 1923 was the same as that of 1918 and of 1938. It is the same men and women. How can we explain this riddle?

My party comrades!

One thing has changed since then: the German leadership has changed. National Socialism built it up through a ruthless process of selection. As far as it still stems from the years of struggle, it represents a peak value that cannot be replaced through any external or material political or military efforts. This leadership became the pillar of the German rise. The miracle that occurred between 1805 and 1813 was no different. The Prussian men and women in the age of the Battle of Nations at Leipzig were the same as those in the days of Jena and Auerstedt. The difference then was that a weak state and military leadership was replaced within a few years by a heroic leadership, and their names were von Stein and Blücher, Scharnhorst and Gneisenau, Yorck and Clausewitz, and thousands of others — these names explain the miracle of Prussia's rise. One day, Germany's rise cannot be seen as anything else either. The National Socialist Party is the central pillar of this rise. It completed the tremendous work that had to be done for Germany to regain the strength to resume its place in the world.

It had to break and root out the other parties; it had to declare war on the world of class and status prejudices; it had to ensure that all resolute and capable Germans could make their way to the top without regard to birth and origin. It had to cleanse Germany of all the parasites for whom the Fatherland's and the Volk's misery became an opportunity for their own enrichment. It had to acknowledge the eternal values of blood and soil, and raise the observance of these to the ruling law of our lives. It had to begin the fight against the greatest enemy that threatened to destroy our people: the international Jewish enemy!

Its task was to cleanse the German Volk, our race, and our culture from this enemy. It had to put an end to the disunity of public opinion. It had to take hold of all means of governance, the press, theater, film, and all other means of propaganda, and it had to orient these toward one goal. It also had to secure the social fundamentals of this new national community, and to put the economy in service of the nation, and above all, it was its duty to establish a new central and universal authority. For, if there could be any hope for saving Germany, it could not be through a hodgepodge of contradictory opinions, through letting obnoxious know-it-alls and nagging critics "live and let live!" It had to protect this authority not just from the attacks of individuals, but much more from the vapid attitude of large social circles of those superiors and wiseacres for whom

freedom was only the permission to live in service of one's personal interests, without any regard for the decline of freedom for others. In these
things, it could not flinch against the great front of all bourgeois and
Marxist unreason. It could also not give in to the attempted influences of
all those who may have hoped to use the movement to recover from their
own financial or political inadequacy.

The movement had an immense agenda to fulfill. And today, after fifteen years, we can proudly state that the National Socialist Party has fulfilled the hopes that were placed in it. Indeed, more has been done
through it than anyone could have expected. It began to actualize its
agenda item by item. We have a strong state authority, a mighty military
protects the Reich by land, sea, and air, the economy is ensuring the German Volk's independence and freedom, and culture is once again serving
the beauty and greatness of the nation. It won the nation's freedom in an
unprecedented struggle. In exactly the measure that the German Volk
became worthy of its freedom through its increasing unification in National Socialism, it was able to loosen chain after chain of that treaty that
was intended to annihilate our people. You all know the historic dates.
One day they will be written gloriously in the book of our people's history. Most importantly, they will stand as proof for all time that prudence
and vigor are not mutually exclusive concepts.

A few weeks ago, an English paper wrote that I had a burning desire
to enter into a pact with several states because it would otherwise be impossible for me to appear at this year's Reich Party Congress. I did not
and do not have this desire. I appear before you, my old party comrades,
not with a pact, but with the seven new German districts of my old homeland. It is Greater Germany that appears for the first time now in Nuremberg. As the insignia of the old Holy Roman Empire have now returned
to this old German city, they are carried here and accompanied by 6.5
million Germans who today unite themselves in spirit with all the other
men and women of the German Volk. All of them, today more than ever,
are happily aware of belonging to one great indissoluble community.
What burdens the individual in this community is carried by all. But what
all must bear will thus be all the easier for each individual to carry.

The return of Austria to the German Reich presents us with additional
tasks for the coming year. The movement is politically mature in this region as well. Its economic integration into the great circle and tremendous
rhythm of German life will proceed quickly. A few months ago I ex-

pressed the confident hope that we will be able to eliminate joblessness in this region of the Reich in three to four years. Today I can already delineate this expectation more precisely: the unemployment crisis in the Austria of the Reich will be totally overcome by the end of next year. At the moment, we are suffering from only two real economic worries: one, the worry of having a sufficient skilled industrial workforce, and two, the worry of having a sufficient rural workforce

If other states want to see this as the long-sought-after sign of an economic weakness of the Third Reich, then we will gladly endure this weakness of a shortage of labor, and we will let the democracies keep the strength of their unemployment. If the shortage of labor is the only economic difficulty to be seen in Germany, then it is thanks to two facts:

One, by the grace of God, we were finally given a bountiful harvest this year. Through the energetic measures of our Party Comrade Göring, it was possible to enter into this year with a large reserve, despite the poor harvests of the past years. With these reserves and with the blessing of this year's harvest, we will be delivered from any food worries for years. Still, we want to remain frugal. We want to amass a reserve of bread cereals that will protect us from any hardship under any circumstances.

Two, the four-year plan is gradually beginning to have more and more observable effects. What I once supposed has now become real: after the German economy and above all the German inventors were presented the necessary National Socialist goals, the skill and genius of our chemists, physicists, machinists, and technicians, our industrialists and organizers, reached unforeseen, astounding results.

If it was necessary at the beginning of our struggle in 1933 to put as many Germans as possible to work, no matter of what type, then today it is necessary to replace as much primitive work as possible with machines. Our qualitatively great workers will thus gradually be led away from simpler tasks toward higher ones suited to them. Alongside other measures, saving labor will also help alleviate the shortage of agricultural labor. Finally, this will lead to a further increase of our production, and this, as I constantly repeat, is the crucial thing. If over 7.5 million people could be integrated into the workforce of the Reich, now including Austria, then a tangible increase in production proportional to their additional income must be guaranteed. For, the problem of eliminating unemployment is not a problem of paying wages, but of providing corresponding purchasable products. The German Volk has no gold currency. Thanks to the efforts of our enemies, and even if in a painful way, we have been released from the absurdity of a so-called gold currency and gold backing. But it is therefore all the more important to give German currency the only real backing that, as a condition for its stability, ensures a constant purchasing power, namely increased production. For every additional Mark that is paid in Germany, an additional Mark needs to be produced. Otherwise, this Mark is a worthless piece of paper, because, lacking a corresponding production, it has nothing to purchase. This primitive National Socialist economic and monetary policy has allowed us to keep the purchasing power of the Mark stable in a time of universal monetary con games. The urban man's wage or salary only has any meaning if he is able to buy the groceries produced by the farmer, and for the farmer only if he is able to get the products of industry and craftsmanship. Thus, it is National Socialism's economic belief that the only true increase in income is an increase in production. This means the greater allotment of goods made possible through it, and not handing out worthless rags of paper. And it is perhaps one of the National Socialist movement's greatest accomplishments that it made these simple and natural, but unfortunately often unpopular principles ever more commonly accepted by the whole people. While at the same time incomes and prices are chasing each other up in wild haste in the democracies, and their total production constantly sinks, National Socialist economic policy offers an example of constantly increasing production, and a picture of continuously rising consumption, and a stable currency.

If the whole nation of such a great people produces, then the tremendous consumable goods will once again be available for the people's consumption. For one can save up or hoard money for a long time, but not manufactured goods. Be they foodstuffs or wares, they scream for consumers. In calling on the German Volk to continuously raise production, it automatically becomes necessary to supply these consumable goods to the Volk in this cycle. The goal of National Socialist economic policy is not to raise a people to laziness and a lower living standard, but to make it hardworking and its living standard as high as possible. We want to produce so many goods through our hard work that every German can and will have an ever-increasing portion of them. But this process requires a lot of political prudence. It can only work if a whole people keeps the interests of all in view and also serves all, as in a close-knit community. If the National Socialist state would let the economy run the course it once did, then we would also have continual fights, strikes, and lockouts, and with these also a constant reduction of production and, as reward, a seeming increase of incomes, resulting in the devaluation of the currency and consequently an inevitable sinking of the standard of living. It is a sign of our people's intelligence and insight that it grasps this National Socialist economic policy and happily serves its aims.

Apart from that, my countrymen, I ask you to consider the following. Whatever the future holds, one thing is certain: we cannot predict what shape economic relations will take. Because if other nations get the idea to destroy their production instead of raising it, then, lacking trade goods, global trade must sooner or later collapse. Thus, it is all the more important to keep one's own economy in good order, and this will be the best contribution to the betterment of the world economy. It will not be propped up by seemingly learned but really vacuous phrases from democratic statesmen. At most, it could be pollinated by fixing the national economies of the democracies that are slowly dying off. As long as these statesmen continue to prefer chiding authoritative states with empty universal phrases over managing their own production, they are doing nothing to restore the global economy, but are indeed actively harming it. For its own part, Germany can certainly say that, thanks to its constantly increasing production, it has become not only a growing exporter of its own goods, but also a growing importer of foreign goods. Though this is said with one qualification: the German national economy as a whole is being built up in such a way that it can be totally independent from other countries and can stand on its own two feet at all times. And this has worked. The idea of blockading Germany can now be buried as a totally ineffectual weapon. The National Socialist state has taken appropriate steps based on the experience of the last war. And now as before, we will hold to the principle that we would rather be limited in some area or another than be dependent on other countries. Above all, this determination will always be at the forefront of our economic activity: the nation's security always comes first. Its economic existence must then also be fully materially secured through our own necessities for life and our own living space. Only then will the armed forces always be able to protect the Reich's freedom and interests. And then Germany will be the most desirable friend and ally for anyone. I say this on the occasion of the tenth Reich Party Congress, safe in the knowledge that Germany's days of isolation are over, politically as well as economically. The Reich has gained great and strong world powers as friends.

My party comrades!

The Bolshevik nation-destroying danger is rising over this world more threateningly than ever. A thousand times over, we can see the effects of the Jewish pathogen of this global plague. Here I can say, for myself and I think for all of us, how deeply happy we are about the fact that another great European world power has found its own way from its own experiences and its own resolve to represent the same opinions, and has taken far-reaching actions in response, with remarkable determination. Though the development of the Fascist and National Socialist revolutions arose out of distinct needs, and though both of these historic upheavals emerged independently, it is so joyous for us all to find that our attitudes and stances to all the vital tasks of our time have the same spirit, to which this world's unreason and destruction always bring us closer together. At the same time, this spirit orients both nations toward the inside. How we will once again see our happy, beaming youth here! How we will see the hundred thousand young men, tanned and healthy to the core, and how we will then become aware again how this might be the greatest achievement of our revolution. A new, healthier German Volk is being raised here, and not through empty words and theories, but through an invigorating reality. The passion and love of millions of German women has once again grown up into the child, that wonderful youth that we see marching past us in thunderous and roaring cheer during these days. Whoever takes all this in has to admit that life is worth living in this world again for a German. A healthy people, a politically sensible leadership, a strong military, an economy striving upward, and above all a blossoming cultural life. That is why we thank all those fighters that have gathered here and that accompany us in spirit from the past or the present; it is why we thank the men and women of our movement, and thank the soldiers of the armed forces of the National Socialist state.

But our greatest thanks go to the Almighty for the successful unification of Austria with the Third Reich.

He has granted the nation a great blessing, and the Reich a great success, without it being necessary to commit the blood or lives of our countrymen. May Germans never forget that this would have never been possible without the entire nation's strength united in National Socialism. As the flag of the new Reich was carried forth on the morning of March 12th, it was no longer a symbol of conquest, but a symbol of a unity that had long encompassed all Germans.

The battle flag that our young armed forces carried into the districts then became a symbol of faith in victory for our brothers in their hard struggle for Austria.

Thus, for the first time, an idea conquered and unified a people!

For us and for all who will come after us, the Reich of the Germans will forevermore be Greater Germany!

THE FÜHRER'S SPEECH AT
THE CULTURAL CONFERENCE

September 7th, 1938

Even the National Socialist movement's most obstinate opponent must now find it very difficult to overlook or deny this new regime's successes, at least in certain domains, as they did up until a few years ago. The actions speak for themselves. The creation of an internally cohesive German national community, the reestablishment of German confidence, the strengthening of German power, the expansion of the Reich's territory — all this cannot be talked away or denied. Despite all their prophecies and barely disguised hope, there was no economic collapse. Despite the insufficient territorial conditions, we have secured food and consumable goods for our people. The battle against unemployment ended in a victory that is baffling to the democratic countries, as the problem seems to be mostly unsolvable for them. The four-year plan is proceeding in scientific research and increased production, which the rest of the world views partly with admiring recognition, or with bitter silence. Even in the area of general social welfare they must look on with concern at the accomplishments of the new Reich. Yes, in some places it even seems like the recognition is dawning on them that National Socialist Germany has gained the approval of the German Volk to a much greater extent than the governments of the democratic plutocracies enjoy from their own populations. The sharpest rebuke that national Germany still receives despite all this, from inside and from without, comes from the circle of those that have nothing to do with the German Volk or with the interests of other nations:

the camp of international Jewry.

In making this observation, I am disregarding those international press organs whose dishonesty is more stupid than it is mean. In their Jewish hatred for the German Volk, they grasp for such witless claims and libel, that by a few weeks later even the most simpleminded can offer them a rebuttal. The only area where they still believe they can successfully challenge the Reich is in the cultural sphere. There they try to complain about Germany's cultural decline through the always successful appeal to the sentimentality of the democratic global citizens, which is unencumbered by any true information. They are complaining about the censorship of those proponents of the November Republic who forced their unnatural and deplorable cultural features on us, and who have now played out their part.

Because this refers essentially to Jews, who are by no means closer to our Volk than they are to the English or French, and who in fact should fit much more nicely into the democracies on account of their being refined global citizens, one would assume that our reckless ejection of these "divinely gifted," "culturally pregnant" elements would be seen as a welcome gain. Yet that is not how they feel. As worked up as they are about the impoverishment of German cultural life, they are so coolly cautious about the acquisition and admission of these Jews, who they allegedly hold to be so pure, so culturally superior. From this, we can conclude that the excited lamentations from the international gazettes about the collapse of German culture are an obvious sham, like so many other revelations from this world. But thankfully, here as elsewhere, positive actions speak louder than any negative criticism, even though the period of National Socialism's government is very short, seen from the perspective of cultural work. We Germans can justifiably speak of a newly awakening cultural life today, and this cultural awakening is not proven by mutual compliments and empty phrases, but by the positive documents of creative power. German architecture, sculpture, painting, theater, and so on all provide the documentary evidence for an artistic period such as we have only rarely seen in history. And if the Jewish democratic press still wants to impertinently try to invert the facts from top to bottom, then at least we know that in a few years German cultural achievements will have gained the world's attention and estimation to a much greater degree than even our work in the material domain already has.

The buildings now rising in the Reich will speak for longer and with much more power than the mumbling or of our democratic international cultural critics. What the fingers of these pathetic wights write will, like so much else, be completely forgotten — perhaps even unfortunately. But the colossal works being constructed under the banner of the cultural establishment of the Third Reich will one day belong to the inalienable cultural inheritance of the Western World, just as the great cultural achievements of the past are for us today.

Of course, it is not so important if and how foreign nations react to our cultural work, because we do not doubt that cultural works, being the most delicate expressions of blood-determined disposition, cannot be understood or much less appreciated by people or races that are not of the same or related blood. We will not worry about making German art and culture palatable to international Jewry. We know that if a Jew has ever had or will ever have a disposition for our German-Aryan culture, it could only be because somewhere, by coincidence or by mistake, a drop of foreign blood once entered into this wandering Jew's genealogical tree, which begins to act against the Jew in him. But the great mass of Jewry is, as a race, wholly unproductive culturally. For this reason, this race is understandably more drawn to the manifestations of primitive Negro tribes than to the culturally superior works of truly creative races. Thus, as already stated, this international Judeo-Bolshevik circle's approval or rejection of our cultural policies or our actions, and their opinion on the value or worthlessness of our achievements, is not only unimportant, but totally irrelevant. Much more important than this is our own people's attitude. The Volk's participation or refusal is for us the only valid judgment of the correctness of our cultural activity. And with this, I would like to make a distinction between the Volk — the healthy, full-blooded and loyal mass of Germans — and an untrustworthy, because only partly blood-related, decadent "society." Sometimes it is thoughtlessly described as the "elite," while in reality they are the disoriented cosmopolitan emission of a social misbreeding, contaminated in blood and mind.

I make a distinction between the natural, primitive, healthy sensibility of the Volk and the witty arrogance that vaunts itself in being different from the normal people, and thanks and praise be to God that they are. When I talk about the real Volk, no one will deny that in just a few years, we were able to forge an inner connection again between German art and this German Volk. Millions and millions of Germans sit in our theaters and enjoy the language of our poets and the sounds of eternally beautiful music.

These same millions stand before our buildings in adoration and are happy to be able to show their pride for these great and noble national achievements. The Volk approves of our new monuments. Hundreds of thousands rush into the galleries of our art exhibitions and follow the work of our painters with equally rapt and approving attention. In this, we can see the proof of the correctness of our new German cultural policies. Though every divinely inspired cultural work owes its creation to only one individual, this flame that leaps out of this individual is a revelation that everyone carries unconsciously within themselves. The moment the individual lets it out into the public, it belongs to everyone, because it had always belonged to everyone. It does not need to be talked into them or intellectually illuminated for them. It is as if millions of people had been waiting for this proclamation of this subconsciously intuited artistic revelation. There occurs this synchronization between the feeling and perception of the Volk and the manifesting or uncovering artistic act; the Volk sometimes all too easily keeps the acts but forgets the creators. A nation's greatest buildings are so many temples of glory for them, but they are all too often silent witnesses for their forgotten, unknown masters. In these works, we see something almost divinely willed and self-evident. Thus, the individual creative artist's disposition is in harmony with everyone's dispositions.

This deep inner accordance between the healthy core of a people and their great cultural works stands in stark contrast to that art that only serves as masturbation for the maker or—as is much more often the case—a collective event between the producer, consumer, and dealer of the artwork. The dealer is the one who benefits materially, if not culturally; he arranges the important relationships between the producer and the consumer, meaning he organizes art criticism, which has nothing to do anymore with the appreciation or evaluation of art, but that sees its sole purpose as increasing the marketability of the artwork. We had decades to be able to observe these art-makers' industry, or rather racket, in Germany. It will be totally forgotten in a few years. This industry's inferior morality corresponds to the quality and thus the longevity of its products. The people had no interior connection with these processes. Sure, if a decadent social class sees it as the highest proof of their worth to have nothing to do with the people, then this is useful to this type of art industry, at least as long as this social class controls society's material means.

Because in the end this is all that matters with such fraud. But where it is not possible to constantly avoid the people (because the sole holders of financial means are within it), then concessions will have to be made, like it or not. Otherwise, the people would begin to protest. It certainly never bought those crazy paintings. These could only be pawned off on a financially rich but culturally stupid class of social climbers, bourgeois stiffs, or decadent airheads.

The theaters, for example, had to be filled by the people, and these gradually became empty. Exhibitions lost visitors. The broad public took no notice of the meaningless public buildings. But not because it had no disposition for art and no interest was available; the opposite: it had no interest because it was the healthy core of our people that still possessed an unspoiled attitude. We know from plenty of examples from the past and even from plenty of positive signs of the present how much the people can be involved with the artistic achievements of a time. The great masterworks of ancient architecture, sculpture, and painting were counted as national patrimony, even holy relics. This was not due to some commercial value analogous to the market prices created by our modern dealers. No, it was due to the interior connection through which an entire people, meaning back then an entire state, followed the birth and becoming of such a work.

And this was no different in the great epochs of medieval art. In such ages, the great artist was the darling of the people, the only real king by divine right, because through him the otherwise silent soul of a people experienced the power of a God-given utterance.

Thus, it is only too understandable that not only has the people always had an interior connection to its real art, but conversely, the artists have always had a deep connection to all that the people experienced, to what captivated the people in feeling, thought, and action. And this is said not just in the pictorial sense of providing the poet, singer, or fashioner with the motifs to explore, from the course of the individual man's life of fortune and misfortune, wealth and poverty, highs and lows, love and hate, or of delivering the subjects for the sculptor, painter, or dramatist to describe, and lift heroes from the struggle of the people.

No! Art was always obligated to the entirety of its age. It had to serve and obey the spirit of its age, or else there was no art. Yes, even more: beyond this, it was in service of the mission of its age and thus it helped to design and shape it. The essence of its action does not lie in the purely contemplative rendering of content and process, but in the striking demonstration of the forces and ideals of an age, be they of religious, cultural, or political origin, or a newly formed synopsis that has its roots in the recognition of an eternal law, which may have theretofore been disguised as a mere theory, an unknown or intuited force that nevertheless ruled the whole being and life struggle of that age.

Thus, Hellenic art is not just a formal representation of Greek life or Greek landscapes and people. No, it is a proclamation of the Greek body and spirit as such. It does not produce propaganda for a single work, for the subject or the artist, but propaganda for the Greek world as such. A cultural ideal arises before us that, thanks to its art and our own blood-related origin, still today presents us with a gripping vision of the most beautiful epoch of human development and its most enlightened proponents. And in the same way, Roman art testifies to the imperial power of the Roman world. It is no coincidence that the same Roman art's character becoming alien coincided with its social degeneration and the consequent collapse of its empire.

Likewise, we see that Christian art was the herald of an age. This age's entire being, its imagination, its thoughts and its actions found their apt expression in Christian churches, sculptures, paintings, and music, as well as every other artistic representation of public life.

Thus, today's art will also be the herald and proclaimer of those sentiments and views on life that rule this age. And not only because this age assigns the artists these tasks, but because the execution of these tasks can only be realized if the character of the spirit of the age reveals itself in the artist's understanding.

Christianity's mysticism, in its most introverted age, promoted an architectural form that not only contradicted the spirit of the age, but the opposite; it actually helped achieve that mysterious darkness that encouraged men to obey the rejection of the world. The nascent protest against the centuries-long oppression of the freedom of the soul and will immediately finds the path to new forms of artistic expression. The mystical narrowness and dimness of the cathedrals began to yield, and spaces widened to let in light according to the freer spiritual life. Mystical half-dark yielded to a growing light. The nineteenth century's tentative, unsure transition finally led in our own time to that crisis that had to end one way or another. The question was whether Jewry would be able to topple the Aryan states with its Bolshevik assault and root out their blood-determined ruling classes, which would also mean destroying the culture that grew out of the same roots. If the duke falls when his mantle drags him down, then the mantle is brought even lower by the duke's demise. All these processes do not play out in discrete events, and likewise, the dethroning and destruction of the Aryan states and their indigenous leadership by the global Jewish enemy does not happen in a few weeks or months; it is a long process that eventually comes to a head like other historical events, at which point the coin will decisively fall on one side or the other.

Jewry waged this battle for power in our own state for over a hundred years, gaining control over numerous institutions while destroying or at least eroding others, and finally even trying to arrange cultural life according to its own racial needs. The art of this period was an apt expression of the political tendencies of the time, and as these tendencies were toward decomposition, art likewise decomposed. Art's manifestations corresponded to the political worldview that calls for the ferment of decomposition of nations and races, as Mommsen described Jewry.

If National Socialism had not prevailed in Germany in the last hour and vanquished the Jewish enemy, then the Jews' deliberate political and human debasement of our people, as well as the debasement and alienation of our art, would have proceeded according to their plan. It is natural that, after our victory, German art (and only since then can we really call it such again) once again heeds its inner impulse from that ideational world that the National Socialist revolution has helped make ascendant. The purpose of the National Socialist revolution is by no means the destruction of the traditional values of our historical life; it also cannot be the purpose of today's German art to express a negative attitude to the past. Rather, it must add its own new contribution to the total cultural inheritance of our people, which is really only the collected cultural prowess of our genotype. For there is no new culture in this world, just as there is no new language or new people. A nation's culture is the collected wealth of the cultural creations of millennia. The greatness of a cultural age cannot be measured by the amount of earlier cultural achievements that it rejects, but by the extent to which its own cultural contribution can be expected to be seen as valuable by posterity, added to the cultural treasure, and then passed on. It is understandable that in the course of a people's historical development, its contact with other or related peoples leads it to a continual enrichment not only of its abstract knowledge, but also of its cultural treasury. And this is not meant in only a material sense, as in the acquisition of artworks, but also even more from the cultural pollination that results from contact with such a related surrounding world. And this is never a disgrace, because in the long run, a people will only take on and keep seemingly foreign cultural artifacts if their creators and possessors were or are similar in blood, even if separated in language, politics, or time. To contribute something to this collective cultural inheritance made up of one's ethnicity's own creative power and work has to be the pride and the ambition of every decent age and contemporary person, and in doing so, we should be under no illusions: just as only a fraction of all the past's works made their way down to us, only a fraction of our work will be carried into the future.

The only crucial thing is that this fraction of such a great quantity of production possesses the utmost quality in the individual works.

In this way, a people's cultural path is similar to the firmament's Milky Way. Single suns shine forth out of myriads of pale entities. Planets and suns are composed of the same substance and obey the same laws. All of a people's cultural labor must not only have one mission, but must be done in the same spirit. Therefore, the geniuses must not be an abnormality, but the transcendent exceptions — that is, their works, being inherently superior, must gain such brightness that they outshine all works of the same kind, and thus shortly put the mass of healthy people under the spell of their luminosity. Consequently, it is not only the state, some other community, or the individual that commissions art, but above all, the tasks of art are determined by the perceptions and understandings of the whole spirit and way of life that rules a people at that time. They also determine the real purpose of the task, and the artist must serve this inner purpose. His work thus becomes more than an objective completion of the assignment. As it is born, it contributes to, even helps shape, the spirit of the assignment — that is, the substance, will, and goals of its time.

It is always the sign of the inner giftedness of a true artist to be able to express this collective will of an age, which grips him as well. Perhaps this is most easily visible for everyone in architecture. Here it is immediately apparent how much the commissioning of a work already determines its inner feeling and outward form. The religious, interior-oriented mystic world of the Christian Middle Ages found forms of expression that were only possible, only useful for this age alone. A Gothic stadium is just as unthinkable as a Roman train station or a Byzantine market hall.

The way in which the artists of medieval and early modern times artistically solved the architectural tasks assigned to them by their time is simply astounding and admirable. This does not imply the absolute correctness or incorrectness of that age's way of life in and of itself, but it speaks to an artwork's correct response to the inner conditions of this age. As far as attempts to relieve a world are concerned, it makes sense that the artistic solutions would be found in the thoughts that animated that world. And so, it is conceivable that in, for example, the religious domain, people will still reach back to the vocabulary of forms of an age in which Christianity as a worldview seemed to suffice for everything. Conversely, the expression of a racially-determined worldview will not hesitate to reach back into those areas of the past that possessed a similar freedom of spirit, of will, and of perception. Thus, it is understandable that the artistic manifestation of European conceptions of the state cannot look to irrelevant — because foreign — cultures, as for example East Asian cultures. Instead, it is immensely influenced by the witness, the documents, and the memories of the enormous imperial power of antiquity, which still lives on and confronts us as an intangible force in our imagination, even though it was killed well over a millennium ago as an objective force. Indeed, the closer the modern state approaches the imperial idea of that ancient world power, the more its cultural tastes and expressions will affect modern culture. The age of the attempt to establish a Napoleonic world empire is also the age of empire. However, the mercantile purposes also influence the orientation of architecture, as does public hygiene. But despite this fact, we cannot allow architectural projects, which are to be the product and symbol of the National Socialist age, to be determined by anything outside of the character, attitude, and agenda of our age. And here it is important for the public commissioners of art not to let the nature of their commission allow for the spirit of their age to be falsified, thus allowing the foundation of their own ideological existence to be put into question. National Socialism is a doctrine of cold, hard reality, and of the sharpest scientific insights and their logical ramifications. Having opened the German Volk's heart to this doctrine, we do not want to fill it with a mysticism that is outside of the purposes and goals of our doctrine.

First and foremost, National Socialism may be a people's movement in its organization, but it is in no way a cultic phenomenon. Insofar as we used certain traditional methods to enlighten and win over our people, this is the result of insights gained from experience, and helps serve our purpose. It is also useful to retain these as customs later. But they have nothing to do with the methods and forms of expression that may have been borrowed from other points of view that have previously made use of the term "cult." For National Socialism is no cultic movement; it is an ethnic-political doctrine that grew out of exclusively racial insights. Its purpose does not lie in a mystical cult, but in the care and leadership of the blood-determined German Volk. For this reason, we do not have cult temples, but Volk-Halls; we do not have cult sites, but rally and marching grounds. We do not have cult groves, but sports arenas and fields. Our assembly halls are not mystically dark, like cult sites, but they are bright and let light into their beautiful and practical buildings. And inside them, there are no cultic activities that take place, but exclusively rallies of the people, rallies of the type that we have learned to hold in the long course of our struggle, and to which we are accustomed and desire to keep holding in the future. Thus, the movement cannot tolerate the infiltration of mystically disposed occult explorers of the beyond. They are not National Socialists, but something else, and in any case something that has nothing to do with us. The most important part of our program is not mysterious intuition but clear insight and a public creed. Insofar as we place the preservation and perpetuation of a God-created being in the center of this insight and this creed, we are serving the preservation of God's creation and thus the fulfillment of God's will—and we do this not in the secretive twilight of a new cult shrine, but in the open sight of the Lord. There were ages in which half-dark was necessary for the effectiveness of the epoch's doctrine, but today we inhabit an age in which light is the fundamental necessity for our success. Woe if the movement or the state begins to give unclear orders due to the infiltration of mystical elements. It is already enough if this unclarity lies in words. It is already dangerous to commission a so-called "Kultstätte," because it already provides the imperative to later concoct so-called cultic games and cultic activities that have nothing to do with National Socialism. Our cult is exclusively to care for what is natural, and thus what is willed by God. Our humility is the unconditional obeisance to the divine laws of existence that have been made known to man. Our law is this: brave fulfillment of our duties. But we are not responsible for cultic activities; the churches are! But if someone believes that these, our duties, are not enough for him or are not agreeable to him, then he can ask his own god to go ahead and make it better. In no case can National Socialism and the National Socialist state task German art with anything that is not grounded in our worldview. We can also not task art with anything that is impossible for it to fulfill. The artists themselves should not try to solve problems that are beyond the domain of creative power.

I mention this because it is infinitely important, for once a false path is embarked upon, depending on the circumstances, it could render a whole century artistically barren. Someone commissioning art who fails at setting the right tasks is equally as dangerous as an artist who fails to find the only possible correct solution, for both are deluded by false notions. False goals given out by the public commissioner can only too easily lead to a false ambition to form things that cannot be formed. For example, the artist who truly lives within our time — and only he alone will be able to create great things — will be unable to provide a satisfactory solution to an ideologically false request. Because the request to build a cult room is outside of the character and goals of our age, it will be impossible for the artist to create the right form for it. What led to captivating architectural achievements in the Middle Ages, when Christianity was the default way of life everywhere, would fall entirely flat today, as National Socialism is beginning to shape our destiny. Thus, it is impossible from the get-go to give German architecture a task that cannot be completed by the National Socialist artist. The discrepancy between the commissioning of such a work and the actual effect of a so-called National Socialist cult room is appalling, but this is not just due to the failure of the artist, but the failure of the one who commissioned it. He forgets that the architect cannot succeed in building something that lies beyond the task of his time, and what is more, for a purpose without use. For, what is the point of this cult room, what purpose does it serve, what happens there? Besides dull boredom, nothing!

Architects can only accomplish truly great things if they are given truly great tasks appropriate to the age in which they live. To stray from this principle will make them unfruitful; their solutions to the tasks will be contrived, fraudulent, wrong, and therefore meaningless and worthless for both the present and the future.

Likewise, you cannot task music with something that lies outside of its capacity. Music, as an absolute art, obeys laws that are still unknown to us. The reasons for harmony and dissonance we do not exactly know at this time. But what is sure is that music is the greatest designer of feelings and perceptions that moves our soul, and it seems to be the least suited to satisfying our mind. Thus, it can be all too rare that an intellect and a musical ear meet in the same body. The mind expresses itself with language. Music reveals a world of feelings and moods that are difficult for language to describe. Thus, music can do without any linguistic interpretation, and it can of course help deepen the emotional impact of any spoken statement by its accompaniment. The more music leads to pure illustration, the more important it is that the action it is emphasizing is conspicuously added. Beyond the pure action, the ingenuity of the great artists will add additional mood and effect that can only be reached through music. The singular highpoint of this art of creating a basic and comprehensive musical character as mood was reached by the great master from Bayreuth. However, there have been a number of other divinely gifted musicians who have been able to give certain dramatic works a striking musical core and overall expression. The great symphonists try to give more general moods, but also require an introduction to certain general linguistic reference points for their audience.

But it is impossible to give musical expression to an ideology or a science. It is possible to paint a picture of a time with the help of available musical works, but it is impossible to try to musically interpret or deepen certain scientific or political insights or processes. That is why there is no musical party history and no musical ideology, just as there are no musical illustrations or interpretations of scientific insights. That is exclusively for language. And it is now the task of our poets or thinkers to gain such command of our language that they do not just express any of their insights plainly and abruptly to their fellow men, but go beyond this, so that they can master the shape of the sound that lies in language and raise it to art. We Germans can be proud to have a language as beautiful as it is rich, though certainly a difficult language. To learn to master it is a wonderful task, and to use it is an art. To express the thoughts of our worldview in it has to be possible, indeed is possible. To represent them musically is neither possible nor necessary. It is nonsense, then, to think one has to or even could give an interpretation of the party's history in the musical introduction of, let's say, a political conference. In such a case, there would certainly need to be accompanying text to make the composer's thoughts comprehensible to the audience. But this is, as I have said, totally unnecessary, though it is necessary to apply the general laws of the development and leadership of our national life to the domain of music. Music should not bring people to baffled shock with a technically complex and confused whirlwind of notes, but instead must captivate their hearts with the intuited and deeply felt beauty of its tones. Intellectual understanding does not have to be the mentor of our musicians, but an overflowing musical soul is required. The maxim applies here: "when the heart is full, the mouth overflows." In other words, whoever is pervaded or overcome by greatness, beauty, or pain, by the suffering of the age and of his people, can—if he has a gift from God—bare his soul through music. As always, technical ability is the outward precondition for the revelation of the interior disposition.

I find it urgently important that our musicians take these things to heart. The past century has let countless musical geniuses appear in our Volk. In previous speeches, I have attempted to elucidate the reasons for their gradual drying up. It would be bad if National Socialism conquered the spirit of the age that led to the fading of our musicians, only to then provide the wrong goals and aims, thus leaving or even leading music down a wrong path, just as bad as the one lying behind us.

Whether music or architecture, sculpture or painting, one thing should fundamentally never be forgotten: every true art must give its work *beauty*. For our ideal lies in caring for what is healthy. Everything healthy is right and natural, and everything right and natural is beautiful.

Today it is just as necessary to find the courage for beauty as for truth. The global enemy that we confront has written the destruction of beauty as well as the destruction of truth on his banner. He was able to portray the affirmation of natural feelings as partly dumb, partly laughable, and partly even as cowardly. He ridiculed, laughed at, and tainted all great sentiments and virtues of character. He was able to make many lose their courage to avow their own people, much less to defend it. Finally, it was not only considered unwise to fight for one's people, but even cowardly, while the real cowards who left their community in the lurch could be praised as brave heralds of a new ideal. And countless members of the genteel social circles fell victim to this psychosis due to the emptiness of their souls. Partly from fear, but partly all too willingly, they subjugated themselves to this Jewish terror. In the first decade of our National Socialist struggle, it took great resolve, a brave heart, and constant courage to represent the belief in the eternal ideals of our people, and to promote these and openly call for action. It is likewise our task now to find the courage for true beauty, to not let ourselves be fooled by the partly daft, partly shameless blathering of decadent literati, who try to smear the beautiful as kitsch and call the sick and unhealthy interesting, noteworthy, and remarkable.

Once humanity starts going down this path that leads away from the eternally beautiful, it will shortly lose any measure by which to judge human cultural effort. The art world will then be like a madhouse, where lunatics stammer and scribble, and an epoch characterized by the wonderful blossoming of humanity will come to an end in insanity and decay.

It is therefore a great and uplifting task to curb this cultural decay through really nurturing music, theater, sculpture, and painting, but especially through architecture. And along the way we must strive to ensure that the artists not only create, but that the Volk is educated, that its eyes will always learn to see clearer, that its sense for beautiful and noble proportions develops and deepens, that its ear becomes finer, and its understanding grows — not only for artistic achievement seen from afar, but for the small, fine details.

In this way, we will slowly raise ourselves to true artistic conscientiousness. This will best prevent any slide into a noxious, arrogant satiety. It will widen and sharpen the eye and educate the ear to perceive the wonders of artistic work in the limitless world of the small. It will help to one day allow the entirety of the Volk to take part in the creation of our tremendous national artworks, seen even in the individual fine details. And only then will one be able to speak of a truly new epoch of art. Then posterity will be able to report about the wonder of a time when, in the midst of one of the most enormous political renewals of history, unaffected by the war and confusion of the world, culture in the German lands began to blossom most beautifully.

With proud reverence, our people will guard the works that we are adding to the eternal treasure of German culture.

THE FÜHRER TO THE WORKMEN

September 7th, 1938

I greet you men of the Reich Labor Service for the fifth time here, and you maidens for the second time!

For the first time I can greet the workmen of my own homeland!

With this, you are not only symbolically, but actually a part of the great front of the new German community, which has no more beautiful symbol than the spade, which has become the token of our National Socialist community.

You are fighting within Germany for the expansion of this community and its spiritual deepening. But you are also fighting for the defense of the Reich and its independence as your spades work new ground and secure old Reich territory!

Today your spade stands in the heart of Germany, in the north, in the east, in the south, and in the west, in service of the security and preservation of the Reich!

You are also helping raise a new generation to be well-grounded in the soil of their homeland, in health, strength, and in fortitude. You yourselves are a flesh and blood expression of German virility, such as we wish it to be in the future.

Sunned and steeled — that is the German youth of today!

We are proud of you!

All of Germany loves you!

You do not only carry spades, but beyond this, you have come to carry the Reich!

You represent the noblest motto we know: "God helps those who help themselves!"

I thank you for your labor and work! I thank your Reich Labor Leader for the gigantic work of building you up!

As the Führer and chancellor of the Reich, I am happy to see the sight of you, happy about the spirit that inhabits you, and happy for my people, that it has such men and women!

Heil to you!

THE FÜHRER TO THE
POLITICAL LEADERS

September 9th, 1938

Party comrades!

I greet you at an especially festive time for us National Socialists. Fifteen years ago the first Reich Party Congress took place, and in September of that year the first German Day in Nuremberg. Back then we already entered into this city by the many thousands, yet it cannot compare to the enormous parade of today. Since then, everything in Germany has transformed.

Only one thing has remained the same through these fifteen years: our faith in Germany, our love of Germany, and our unswerving confidence in the resurrection of Germany!

There are some among you who experienced those former days. Many others joined us in the following years. But altogether, you are the most reliable and loyal followers a Führer could ever have! In these fifteen years, fate has shown us this not once, but a thousand times; you yourselves have proven it!

It is too easy to be enchanted with this new Germany, and how many there are that now see this Reich as something to be taken for granted, although they contributed so little to its birth and becoming. You alone, my party comrades, know how hard this struggle was, which our opponents deemed hopeless. You gave everything that could be expected from friends of the Fatherland, in suffering and in sorrow.

You never once doubted Germany's future in these fifteen years. And above all, you granted me your steadfast trust. I would be ungrateful if I could not experience anew each year, at least during these days in Nuremberg and at this hour in front of you and among you, the joy of being allowed to stand before you, just as I stood as a fighter before you in the long years and countless assemblies, seeing you before me as I have seen you so often. It is necessary that we each recognize each other. I recognize you, and you recognize me!

For the first time, I can greet the comrades-in-arms of Austria among you, my loyal old revolutionary guard! They stand among you, my old fighters, and they can no longer be recognized as separate. The same brown uniform, the same flag, and above all, the same mind, and the same loyal German heart! They are the same fighters. For, as long as the political fighters have fought in the old Reich, they were also fighting in Austria. Just as the fighters in the old Reich had charge against a world of obstacles, so also do the fighters of Austria! They also rose out of suffering and sorrow, and have now entered into our great German national community, our Greater German Reich for all time!

You all will have the feeling of how strong this community is. And exactly in this time, when there are clouds in the firmament, I see it as doubly joyful to think of the million-man guard of imperturbably fanatic National Socialists, whose spiritual tip of the spear is you, their leadership!

Just as I could blindly rely on you in the long years of our struggle for power in Germany, I know that Germany and I can rely on you now!

You were tested and hardened in these long years. You yourselves know what power inhabits a community that, indissolubly consolidated within itself, carries a strong faith in its heart and is determined to capitulate to no one!

And so, you make it easy for me to be the Führer of Germany!

All those who have been counting on the collapse of our movement for fifteen years have been mistaken! It emerged stronger from every hardship and danger! And all those today who are counting on Germany's weakness will be just as mistaken!

When I speak to you like this, I do not see the 140,000 political leaders that stand before me. Rather, you are the German nation! A people is no greater and no lesser than its leadership. Our leadership shall be good — this is our promise to the German Volk!

And with this pledge, you shall again depart Nuremberg and return to your districts and circles, your regional groups and outposts, your market towns and villages, and there in the coming times, you shall not only be unshakeable pillars of faith for our movement, but also of the Greater German Reich that you represent today.

Germany — Sieg Heil!

AT THE CELEBRATION
OF THE HITLER YOUTH

September 10th, 1938

Youth of Germany!

Every year I greet the million-mass of all our German boys and girls in the Reich through you here!

Last year I pointed out to you all what a great fortune it is to have been born in this time. Back then we did not yet know what enormous things this year would add to German history. You are the witnesses of a historic event that does not get repeated often, even over many centuries. You yourselves were fighters for this new greater Germany. You have always carried in your hearts what has today become reality.

Joining us for the first time at this Reich Party Congress of National Socialism in Nuremberg are the young boys and girls from Austria, which now is and will be a part of Germany forevermore. It was not coincidence nor talk of brotherhood that brought about this triumph, but knowing and living out our movement's commandments. It is to the National Socialist movement's eternal credit that, in the time of its people's deepest humiliation, we did not for one moment lose our faith in this future development, instead nurturing this faith and teaching the Germans to live according to its precepts.

What could this old Germany offer the future in its inner fragmentation? Does anyone believe that this old Germany could have created what is now a reality? A new movement had to come to educate our people and make it fit for service! And if all National Socialism ever accomplished in its historical existence was to reach the 12th and 13th of March, 1938, then this alone would be enough to justify its existence for a millennium!

But I believe this is only the beginning of our beneficial movement. There is immeasurable work laid out for us. However it may be, we will only solve our problems with a unified body of the people, which does not arise from wishes and hopes, but from education. Only through education can we create the German Volk we need, and that those who want to shape history in the future will need. But the German Volk will not be educated in its dotage, but always in its youth. And that is why I am so proud and happy when I see you!

Year by year, the picture you present gets more beautiful. It is really a proud joy to think of the German future now. We already know the old tried and true men we have in Germany.

It is our proudest certainty that the German youth will live after this best of German manhood and the best German womanly ideal!

And for this reason, I also know that our future is forever safe and secure, because the German Volk will endure and stand fast!

It is the same Volk as the one I knew in my own youth. It is the Volk that is more united than ever before, that now understands its life's purpose, and that is forming a community of destiny in life and death to fulfill this purpose.

You are in this community of destiny! You will grow into it and one day you will carry it. One day Germany's strength will be measured by your strength. And I am counting on you blindly and confidently!

When Providence takes me from my people, I will leave the coming Führer a people that is solidly united, forged together like iron, that can never be separated and torn apart again, that will stand together unswervingly, happy in good times and defiant in sorrow!

You, each boy and each girl, are the living guarantors for this!

Whoever has trusted in the united German Volk has always had the greatest success in Germany! You are that German Volk!

AT THE ROLL CALL OF
THE BROWN ARMY

September 11th, 1938

Men of the National Socialist militant movement!

First I would like to greet those comrades among you who have stood by our movement for years in loyalty and devotion, without being able to give outward expression to the desires of their hearts by being among us. This year, Providence has made it possible to realize the dream of countless generations. Even in this part of the Volk, the National Socialist movement helped consummate destiny. I greet you, SA men and SS men of the newly joined old Austria!

We all recognize how great their sacrifices were to be able to stay true to our ideal. We also recognize the great pride and joy that must be filling their hearts right now in view of this powerful, visible demonstration of the unity of the German Volk. What is standing here is the best group of political fighters that the German Volk has ever had.

Our times require us to remember that it was not vague hoping, but strong fighting that brought National Socialism to power. And we also must remember that it is determined to defend its position and the position of the Reich it has created under all circumstances!

As you marched today, the old standards were carried before you, the old standards that were given to the SA at the first Reich Party Congress fifteen years ago. Hundreds and thousands have followed them since then. Their spirit and the spirit of their bearers have stayed the same: they are symbols of the glory, the power, and the strength of the National Socialist faith and of the Reich that it conquered!

Today you receive the new standards, and they will perfectly take the same place as the old. But I also expect that their bearers will be animated by the same spirit that animated the bearers of the old standards.

One day, these signs will be venerable symbols of the memory of Germany's deep misfortune, Germany's boldest hope, Germany's hardest internal political struggles, and Germany's glorious resurrection! They shall be symbols of an immortal and eternal Reich, and the immortal and eternal German Volk!

The tasks posed to the men of the militant movement of the party in the fifteen years since 1923 have remained the same — indeed, they have expanded. Back then, the new ideal had to be proclaimed and implemented in Germany, and today this ideal has to be kept and deepened! The National Socialist movement shall be the school of the mind, the school of the will, but also the school of the body! And that is why the victors of our sport competitions are also standing among you this time. I greet you, especially, and I expect that these competitions will develop into a tremendous event, which will receive its final crown on the day that, just to right of the new Congress Hall, the colossal stadium of the German Volk is completed!

These two buildings, one of which you already see rising, will represent the synthesis of National Socialist education very clearly: the strongest spirit of faith and will, of confidence and persistence, and above all energy that delights in doing our duty, connected to a strong body, healthy and beautiful — that is how we want to shape our people for the future! That is how we want to educate it, never losing sight of this goal! We want to believe in its realization with the same boundless faith with which, fifteen years ago, we believed that these four banners would become those of all of Germany!

This Germany stands before us now, and we have the good fortune to live in it. Right now, other Germans are still denied this joy. But our hearts fly out to them — just as we know that their hearts are here with us now!

But we all feel only one duty: it has been said a thousand and a million times, and it lets itself be summarized with a single phrase, with one creed:

Germany — Sieg Heil!

TO THE SOLDIERS OF
THE ARMED FORCES

September 12th, 1938

Soldiers of the German armed forces!

As in past years, you have once again mustered in Nuremberg for the Reich Party Congress. For the first time now, you do so as soldiers of the Greater German Reich!

This dream of centuries has become a reality, and we ascribe this to two facts:

Firstly: the successful creation of a true German national community. This was necessary for the fulfillment of this dream.

Secondly: the reestablishment of our German armed forces, whose soldiers ultimately actualized this dream by marching in!

We can draw two lessons from this:

Firstly, we can recognize the necessity of the movement's existence. In less than two decades, it was able to lead the German Volk out of its condition of great internal confusion and to the unity we see today. The National Socialist Party and doctrine are the guarantors of this German national community!

Secondly, we have to realize how necessary it is to provide external defense to this national community, which has been brought into such good order internally. This defense exclusively depends on the strength of our own military, and of each individual serviceman himself.

No treaty, no convention, no agreement gave us the natural right to German unification. We had to take this right ourselves, and we could only take it thanks to you, my soldiers!

And so, both these great institutions of our people have to fulfill the same two tasks: National Socialism educates our people toward an internal national community, and the armed forces educate this same people to defend this community from the outside!

One of these was already entrusted to you in the new Reich, my soldiers. Your fulfillment of it has won you the love of the German Volk. It trusted you, and it knows it can trust its sons in uniform. For you have the best weapons that exist today, you are receiving the best training, and I know that you also have the best character!

You fit into the immortal front of German soldiery. I have had many opportunities in the past months to see for myself that this is so. I saw it on the maneuvering grounds, on the shooting ranges, on the training grounds, and I felt assured that the German nation could look at its soldiers with satisfaction!

I thank you for this!

However, we all do not serve for the sake of thanks, praise, or reward, unless this thanks, this praise, and this reward lies in what is most important for us in this world: in the German Volk and in our German Reich!

Germany—Sieg Heil!

THE FÜHRER'S CONCLUDING REMARKS AT THE 1938 PARTY CONGRESS

September 12th, 1938

National Socialists! Party comrades!

Fifteen years ago, on September 2nd, 1923, the first German Day took place in Nuremberg. It was truly the first, despite all previous events with similar names, because this rally had a greater significance than all previous similar conferences. On that very day, the militant groups of the National Socialist movement commandingly appeared for the first time. They left their impression on the whole rally. Nuremberg stood beneath the swastika. From this day on, it could no longer be ignored that a new political phenomenon stepped into the nation's political life, a phenomenon unfamiliar to the rest of the world and still strange to the world in the form of its emergence, in the composition of its followers, in its manner of propaganda, as well as in the image of its members' outward appearance. While the other so-called national associations and groups still mostly got their followers from bourgeois circles and recruited their militant organizations (such as they were) from these same circles, the National Socialist Party was even then emphatically a people's movement, meaning the greatest number of its followers was composed of the sons of the broad masses. Workers and farmers, small artisans and clerks made up the battalions of the SA. They formed the first cell of the party, and later still filled its regional groups.

Many of our fellow citizens, already cautious upon hearing the name "German Workers' Party," were utterly shocked when they first saw the rough characters that formed the movement's guard.

A national party made up of working people! They only understood the term "work" in the rarefied sense, which is the case with the bourgeoisie just as much as with the Marxists. For the National Socialist Party, the name "worker" was always a term of honor for all those who do honest work in the community, whether intellectual or purely material. Because the party was a people's party, it necessarily had more manual laborers in its ranks than intellectual workers, just as is the case within the people itself. This initially led to many misunderstandings. It was believed that a movement like ours, primarily made up of manual laborers, could never be suited for solving higher problems. In the eyes of our bourgeoisie, only the intellectual elite — who had gone astray in our bourgeois parties — were divinely ordained to address such issues. Marxism certainly immediately saw this movement as a despised competitor. They believed they could get rid of us; the National Socialist definition of the term "workers," in the sense of a conglomeration of all working people, was constantly decried in the public as a contradiction of the term "proletariat." Of course, this was true. The proletariat (or more accurately, the proletarian parties) had excluded the mental and intellectual workers from their ranks as much as possible. Of course, one cannot survive entirely without intellectual leadership, but this had been handed over to the Jews for decades.

The purpose of the communist and social-democratic parties was not to give the German Volk a better community or to educate it toward one, but to ruin the German national community and to create an unbridgeable chasm between the indigenous intellectual leadership and the Volk itself.

The worker was to be used as the battering ram against his own intellectual elite, until, through its destruction, the people would be handed over to an unnecessary class of Jewish intellectual literati and activists. Their goal was to establish a state like today's Soviet Russia, composed of 98 percent manual laborers and 2 percent Jewish commissars. This gives such an entity the right to call itself the "dictatorship of the proletariat."

It was understandable that the party of a new national community found no love from the Jewish wire-pullers of the proletarian world revolution. That the party recognized and saw through Jewry, and accordingly made its elimination part of its platform, also contributed to the hateful rejection the party received.

The bourgeois parties could not grasp the meaning and necessity of a new movement. Initially, they saw nothing exciting about the national organizing of workers, only something dubious. The two worlds had already separated from each other too much to be able to understand or trust each other. The bourgeois parties almost exclusively recruited and found members in the intellectual circles, and so they became at home in an atmosphere that was worlds apart from that of the proletarian parties. The rough outward demeanor, plus the not exactly formal clothes, aroused their aversion, or at least mistrust, especially after the November Revolution. All our fellow fighters will still remember with proud joy how the National Socialist German Workers' Party and its followers did not make a very presentable picture. Thus, it was no wonder that the thought occurred often in the bourgeois circles that this new National Socialist Party might represent an especially clever kind of property-stealing socialism.

This seemed more dangerous because, dressed up with nationalist explanations, those accursed socialist thoughts might be more easily smuggled past the Trojan gate of our bourgeois classes. The movement's name was suspicious, its clothing no less so; its demeanor likewise seemed dubious, and whatever one read in the press rounded out this picture.

Later, as the party fought for its place in public life and was then here to stay, this fundamental rejection was replaced by an urgent, though silent, hope. "Yes, a large party had formed; yes, it had won a place in public life—however, according to their name as a party of workers, and certainly according to their appearance, there is no way they could ever prove decisive in politics. Because to do so, it would have to be led. Because it was a party of workers, it must be without any intellectual leadership. You cannot rule without heads." Thus, this childish notion arose that this unstoppable force of the people could one day be intellectually sequestered in order to continue that clever politicking, which the bourgeoisie, lacking any of its own strength, should have given up long ago. They longed for the moment when the drummer boy (that was me!) could be replaced by the real statesmen (that was the others)! Who can be surprised, then, that the stubbornness with which the National Socialist Party fought for its goals and rejected all compromises gradually led its opponents to a deep hatred, so deep that our bourgeois parties were more ready to ally with Marxism than to express the quietest acknowledgment of the National Socialist Party, or to give it the slightest chance. More than once we experienced that shameful spectacle in the German Reichstag when a united front from the right to the left stood up against us. Back then, they talked so much about the necessity of considering the people's interests, the necessary struggle for freedom, but they acted against the only movement that was in a position to actually fight for and actualize these things, and which first and foremost was left alone to fight this battle with tireless effort and tremendous exertion.

My party comrades! We all still remember those days with pride.

Everything stood against us then.

To be a National Socialist meant to be ostracized and abandoned from all sides. Everyone hated us; everyone persecuted us. For every ten party leaders, in a year, there were hardly two who did not spend time in prison for their faith in Germany. The number of punished SA and SS men rose to the hundreds of thousands. Beyond this, they launched a bloody terror against the movement, which could be seen in the countless numbers of our dead, wounded, and crippled. And yet we look back at exactly this time with pride.

Today this time is doubly near to us, first of all because today we are among our fellow countrymen and citizens of the German Reich—the fighters of the old Austria, who have come out of a similar persecution of National Socialist men that lasted until very recently. What did they not have to endure? How many of their comrades were murdered, how many suffered loss of life or limb, how many were destitute year after year, how many tens of thousands of them were in prisons, penitentiaries, and internment camps?

But the second thing that lets us look back on this time with special intensity is the fact that what we experienced and endured within the nation back then is being almost exactly repeated on a global scale. And above all, our enemies today are ideologically the same as before.

As already mentioned, fifteen years have passed since the first German Day in Nuremberg. The organization of the National Socialist Party that marched back then has risen to lead and represent the German Reich. It is the acknowledged representative of our people. And in these few years—for what is a decade and a half on the scale of nations and world history?—it has accomplished a miracle.

If you could suddenly look back at September 2nd, 1923, and then let this image fade into today's Nuremberg, you would think yourself in a dream.

A crowd of fighters marched through the city then. They became a fighting nation. What was then the battle flag of companies and battalions is now the flag of seventy-five million people in this Reich alone. For seven days, all of Germany has once again marched with our movement through this city. We became aware, with special intensity, that the fragmentation of our nation has ended, and for the first time in history, we find ourselves with a united Reich, because we are a united people.

Fifteen years ago, the onlookers beheld the marching National Socialists partly happily, partly with concern; but today the onlookers and participants have melded into one spiritual unity. Only something has changed: if the National Socialist Party was seen as the movement of the broad mass, then today the National Socialist state has become the organization of the broad mass.

This party did not want to take only certain classes of our nation under its protection.

It pulled the German Volk back from the abyss when it seemed ready to fall. For, when we finally took power in 1933, our task was not to rescue a social class—that much even our bourgeois opponents have learned—but rather it was to save the German Volk as a whole. This was not a bunch of needy parties, but consisted of millions of unemployed workers, our farmers who stood to lose house and farm, our middle class that saw ruin before its eyes, and of course our intellectual workers, for whom there seemed no opportunity for skillful or knowledgeable labor.

When a movement is forced by circumstances to solve such problems, its first task has to be the organization of a real community. It cannot be denied that it was a colossal problem waiting to be solved. But everything depended on this solution. Our predecessors had failed.

It would only be overcome through the utmost exertion of our strength. First, this required the unified effort of all our countrymen. To arrive at this, the organization of our effort had to be prepared. This means: we had to forge unity between intellectual and manual laborers, and between the nation's political-economic leadership and the Volk that it led. This unity urgently required us to disconnect from a foreign body that could have never been integrated.

When we are still asked today why National Socialism fights the Jewish element in Germany so fanatically, why our movement insists upon its removal, then our answer can only be: because National Socialism wants to create a true national community. This community will only have a moral justification for its existence if ethnically and socially unassailable standpoints are instilled in the leadership and the people. Because we are National Socialists, we cannot tolerate having a foreign people that has nothing to do with us in any position of leadership over the German Volk. We know that the enormous tasks before us can only be solved with the strongest effort and strongest discipline—that is, only if the national community acts with the greatest determination to solve its problems. This, however, requires the absolute authority of the leadership. Forming such an authoritative leadership is only morally justified and bearable for a proud people if it is done without regard for the origin and status of the people's most capable sons. Thus, it is the National Socialist state's chief concern that it finds means and methods to ease and even the way for hard work, energy, vigor, insight, courage, and persistence.

Then there will never be antagonism between the leadership and the people. Then every farmer, every worker will always know that this leadership of all is also *his* leadership, because it is of *his own* flesh and blood.

Therefore, the strongest proof for the National Socialist movement's truly socialist attitude is its fight against a foreign leadership that has not grown out of the German Volk.

From henceforth, every worker's or farmer's son, if he is gifted and blessed, must be able to rise to the highest leadership of the whole nation with the help of our party organization and through the conscious leadership selection process. Conversely, even the greatest wealth and capital cannot open the doors of leadership to someone who does not belong to the German Volk.

This is the first requirement for setting up a real national community that will be anything more than a mere well-intentioned phrase.

Only by employing this organized community of our people were we able to succeed where our opponents had failed. Carried by the faith and strength of the German Volk's mass of millions, my comrades and I were able to not only lift us out of economic hardship in just a few years, but to also strip off the political chains that were meant to enslave the German Volk forever.

Thus, the German national community is no mere theoretical phenomenon, no dead issue, but is instead visibly alive as an organization. There were those who asked, especially after 1933, why National Socialism remained as a specific party after it conquered the state. This question is about as thoughtful as asking why the army still existed after instituting compulsory military service, since the thought of defensive preparedness has certainly been victorious and the problem has now been decided.

The formation and preservation of the German national community requires an organization to lead and educate it. The National Socialist Party is its solid core. It develops the national community's defensive capability on the inside. The party does not only build up individual organizations and place itself in leadership of them, but it raises and educates millions of young Germans year after year to be in this national community and integrates them into it. The organization of this national community is something colossal and unique. There is no German today who is not personally anchored and active in some formation of this National Socialist community. It reaches into every house, every workshop, every factory, every city, and every village. Beyond this, it embraces all the members of this Reich who find themselves in foreign lands, including them in this National Socialist community.

Thus, an enormous organization is forming, whose small branches begin in the families and make their way to the whole nation. But what this community has worked for these past six years and what it did and accomplished was all done in the interest of the German Volk, meaning the *entire* German Volk. This is the first time in our history that we have been able to form a movement whose roots and purpose lie in the German national community. Its duty is thus not to special interest groups, whether intellectual or manual laborers, great cities or rural towns, Catholics or Protestants, burghers or workers; it serves the interests of all!

Thus, the organization treats today's government as unconditionally sovereign.

It can also take the most unpopular measures, if these lie in the interest of the national community, because compared to *that*, they can be viewed as trivial. Thus, it is possible that a leadership exclusively responsible to the people can serve the worker just as much as the farmer. It is just as able to foster science and culture as it is on the other hand able to create the most tremendous welfare institutions. It can provide the most intellectually gifted the opportunity for practical application. On the other hand, it also prevents all harmful influences. The German Volk will always be the only constituent it serves—the German Volk as such, which it wants to see as a healthy, strong, and prosperous community.

And who wants to argue that these past six years have not provided impressive proof for the effectiveness of the new state and national organizations and their leadership?

We appear before the nation with calm confidence almost every year and ask them to judge. The most tremendous sign of approval that a government could ever have was received this year on April 10th. The Volk has acknowledged and confirmed that the new form of government and leadership is an institution that strives to be useful to the Volk with all its knowledge and strength, and to lead it back to freedom, to greatness, and to economic prosperity.

And despite this, we are experiencing on the large scale what we did within the nation in our decades-long struggle. A unified front of the rest of the world has stood against us since the day we took power. And as the capitalist democracy of our parliamentary parties went hand in hand with Marxism when it came to opposing National Socialism, so we still see the same conspiracy between democracy and Bolshevism to oppose the National Socialist community at the larger scale.

Perhaps the strongest evidence for the insincerity of our opponents during the National Socialist movement's struggle for power was that they formed a unified front against us in every crucial battle, whether they were bourgeois nationalists, capitalist democrats, or Marxist internationalists. By this, many of our countrymen became aware of how fraudulent the morals of a political fight must be, if they claimed to oppose us for nationalist reasons but had no qualms about allying with Marxist internationalists, or how untrue and treacherous the parties were who persecuted us — so they claimed — out of socialist motives, while unscrupulously joining forces with the staunchest advocates of capitalism. The Centrists opposed National Socialism as anti-church and for this reason decided to form a holy alliance with atheistic social democracy and even communism. And conversely, communists saw us — as they claimed then — as reactionary, but did not hesitate to band together against the National Socialists in the Reichstag with the real representatives of reaction.

It was a farce that, for all its limitless dishonesty, could only have an unsavory effect. But we have this same feeling today, too, when we see the so-called international democracies — which stand for freedom, brotherhood, justice, the right of national self-determination, and so on — joining hands with Moscow Bolshevism. It might be asked why we talk about the democracies so often and treat them so dismissively. We do so because we are forced to do so, for we are being attacked, and likewise because the behavior of these forces is so outrageous.

The dishonesty starts the very moment the democracies paint themselves as people's regimes and the authoritarian states as dictatorships.

I believe I can go ahead and say that, at this point in time, there are only two countries that, as great powers, have governments supported by 99 percent of the people.

What is called democracy in other countries is usually nothing but an infatuation of the public mind arrived at through the skillful manipulation of the press and of money, and clever exploitation of the consequences. Just how untrue the internal character of these democracies is can be seen in the attitudes they take to the surrounding world, depending on their needs at the time. We were able to see them venerate the really violent regimes of small countries when it fit their policy interests, even being ready to vouch for them and fight for them if necessary. On the other hand, they are silent about the greatest demonstrations of public support in countries that they do not agree with, going so far as to lie about these countries. And not only that: when it is politically convenient, these democracies even praise the Bolshevik form of government, even though the Soviet Union describes itself as a *dictatorship* of the proletariat. In other words: the real democracies find a way to describe countries whose governments have 99 percent of the people's approval as dictatorships, and to admire other countries (whose governments openly declare themselves as dictatorships, and that can only exist through mass shootings, executions, torture, and so on) as paragons of democracy. Is it not a macabre mockery of world history that this bloody representative of the most gruesome tyranny of all time moves around freely as a member in good standing among the upright proper democrats in Geneva? We experienced the same in Germany, when we saw the intimate connection between Jewish capitalism and theoretical communist anti-capitalism, just as the *Rote Fahne*, *Vorwärts*, and the *Frankfurter Zeitung* always went hand in hand — that is how it is all around the world. Moscow Bolshevism is the honored ally of capitalist democracy!

Is it surprising, then, that when regimes betray themselves like this, they have to reach for platitudes in countless other areas?

A democratic party congress — where the leaders can hardly be seen by their often so meager crowds of followers without being hissed at and booed, and that generally ends in a chaos of all against all — is presented as a wondrous demonstration and rally of the strength of democratic thought. But a National Socialist or Fascist congress, where a million or more take part with unequaled unity, only counts as a tragic sign of the dictatorship's brutality and a token of the collapse of freedom! Thus, they fight for the rights of the small nations and — if convenient — kill them. Thus, they always stand up for justice and try, if possible, to deny a people of seventy-five million its most basic rights. For fifteen years, Germany fought in vain for the most natural and rudimentary human rights.

They were denied the German Volk and the German Reich, even though that Germany was not led by Nazis, but was ruled by democrats and Marxists. When the National Socialist state, weary of this continued oppression and mistreatment, restored equal rights by its own power, they objected with the bitter hypocritical claim that this could have been reached via mutual understanding.

For fifteen years they bitterly worked against the most natural national interests — yes, against human dignity — handed down dictates and forced compliance at gunpoint, only to complain with hypocritical outrage in the end about the "unilateral overstepping" of sacred laws and the breaking of even holier treaties. Without the least concern for the natives, they forcibly subjugated entire continents. But when Germany demands its colonies back, they use the plight of the poor natives to explain that they could not deliver them to such a fate under any circumstances. At the same time, they do not hesitate to use airplanes and bombs to persuade their dear colored fellow citizens to tolerate their foreign rule. Certainly, these are *civilized* bombs, as opposed to the brutal bombs used by Italy in the Ethiopian War.

In these democracies they complain about the immeasurable cruelty with which Germany and now Italy are trying to handle their Jewish elements. All these great democratic empires only have a few people per square kilometer. In Italy and Germany there are over 140 per square kilometer. Despite this, Germany for many years let in hundreds of thousands of these Jews without a flinch.

Now that the complaints are too great and the nation is no longer willing to let itself be sucked dry by these parasites, they complain about it. But these democratic lands are not ready to replace their hypocritical complaining with a helpful deed; to the contrary, they coldly assure us that there is obviously no room in their lands! So, they expect Germany, with 140 people per square kilometer, to house the Jewish race without complaint, but the democratic empires, with but a few people per square kilometer, cannot take on such burdens. They offer no help, only moralistic lecturing!

As the National Socialist Reich, we are facing the same powers and forces that we did fifteen years ago. As far as the hostile attitudes of the democratic countries are concerned, we are unaffected. Why should it go any better for them than it did for the previous German state? Besides, I will say openly: I find it much more tolerable to bear the complaints of someone who can no longer rob me, than to be robbed and praised for it. We are being berated today. However, we are in a position — thanks and praise be to God! — to prevent every rape and pillage of Germany. The state before us was bled dry for almost fifteen years. However, this was recompensed with praise from the international community for being an "obedient democratic state."

But this pretense becomes intolerable the moment they fire off as threats against our countrymen a barrage of democratic phrases in a place where a large part of our people is left defenseless against shameless mistreatment. I am speaking of Czechoslovakia.

This state is a democracy, meaning it was founded according to democratic principles, insofar as the majority of people in this state was forced, without consent, to accept and add themselves to the fiction fabricated in Versailles. As a real democracy, they subsequently started oppressing the majority of the population in this country, mistreating them and depriving them of their rights. Gradually, they tried to convince the world that this state had a special political and military mission to fulfill.

The former French Air Minister Pierre Cot recently expressed it. According to him, Czechoslovakia exists to attack German areas and industries with bombs in case war breaks out.

This mission, however, stands opposed to the attitudes, interests, and wishes of the majority of that state's population. Therefore, the majority of that population is forced to remain silent. Every protestation against this destiny is an attack on the state's agenda, and thus is unconstitutional. Indeed, this constitution, since it was made by democrats, is not based on the national rights of the affected people, but on the political conveniences of the oppressors. This political convenience also required a construct that lent the Czech people sovereign supremacy. Whoever protests against this arrogation is an "enemy of the state," and is thus, according to democratic morals, considered fair game. The Czech people is thus appointed by Providence — which in this case looks to the interests of the framers of Versailles for guidance — to guard and ensure that this state purpose is not altered by anyone.

But if anyone from the majority of the oppressed peoples of this state should protest against this, then this person can be beaten down and, if necessary, killed.

If this were just a foreign occurrence that had nothing to do with us, then we would simply note it as an interesting illustration of democratic attitudes about national rights and self-determination. However, we Germans are very naturally interested and duty-bound to take part in this.

Among the majority of peoples being oppressed in this state are 3.5 million Germans, about as many people of our race as, for example, the total population of Denmark. These Germans are likewise God's creatures. The Almighty did not make them to be delivered unto a foreign power that despises them by a Versailles state-construct. And He did not make seven million Czechs for them to watch over and patronize 3.5 million, or to abuse and torment them.

But I can only tell these representatives of democracy that it is not irrelevant to us and that, if these tormented creatures can find no state and no help for themselves, then we will provide them with both. The deprivation of these people's rights must come to an end!

The conditions in this state are intolerable, as is generally known. 7.5 million people there are politically robbed of their right to self-determination for the sake of a certain Mr. Wilson. These people are being deliberately economically ruined, and slowly rooted out. These truths cannot be hidden from the world with platitudes, because the facts speak for them. The plight of the Sudeten Germans is indescribable. They want to destroy them. They are being inhumanly and intolerably oppressed and treated disgracefully.

When 3.5 million members of a people of eighty million cannot sing what song they like because the Czechs do not like it, or when they are beaten bloody only because they wear stockings that the Czechs simply do not want to see, or when they are terrorized and mistreated because they use a greeting that the Czechs find unpleasant even though they only greet each other this way and not the Czechs, or when they are hunted and chased like wild animals — then this is irrelevant to our esteemed representatives of democracy, possibly even agreeable, because it involves

3.5 million Germans. But I can only tell these representatives of democracy that it is not irrelevant to us and that, if these tormented creatures can find no state and no help for themselves, then we will provide them with both. The deprivation of these people's rights must come to an end!

I already expressed this clearly in my speech of February 20th. It was a very shortsighted construction that the statesmen of Versailles dreamt up when bringing the abnormal entity of Czechoslovakia into life. The task of abusing and mistreating millions of people of other nationalities could only be carried out as long as the brother nation was itself still suffering under the hard consequences of this general mistreatment by the world.

But to believe that such a regime could go on forever without limit would mean to be given over to extreme blindness. In my February 20th speech to the Reichstag, I explained that the Reich will no longer tolerate any further oppression and persecution of these 3.5 million Germans, and I ask the foreign statesmen to believe that this is no empty talk.

The National Socialist state has taken very heavy sacrifices upon itself for the sake of European peace, and very heavy national sacrifices. Not only did it not nurse any revanchist thought, but in fact it banned it from public and private life. In the seventeenth century, France gradually took Alsace and Lorraine from the old German Reich. In 1870 and 1871, Germany demanded and got these back in a difficult war that was forced upon it. They were lost again after the Great War. The Strasbourg Cathedral means a great deal to us Germans. Still, if we accept this as the final demarcation, then it is in service of European peace in the future. Nobody could force us to give up such ideas of revanchism if we did not want to give them up ourselves!

We gave them up because it was our desire to end once and for all the eternal conflict with France. The Reich has enacted similar measures and adopted the same attitude toward other borders as well. Here, National Socialism really proceeded from the highest sense of responsibility. We have willingly taken on the greatest sacrifices of abstinence in order to preserve peace for Europe and to do our part to open the road toward international reconciliation. We have acted more than faithfully.

No propaganda has been made against this decision in the press, in film, or on the stage.

In this same spirit, I have made offers for resolving European tensions, which were rejected for reasons that are still incomprehensible. We ourselves willingly limited our power in an important area, in the hopes that we would never again have to cross swords with the nation in question. This did not happen because we would not have been able to build more than 35 percent of their ships; it happened because we wanted to contribute to the easing of tensions and the calming of the European situation. Because a great patriot and statesman in Poland was ready to reach an accord with Germany, we immediately engaged with him and came to an agreement that means more for European peace than all the talk ever heard in Geneva's temple of the League of Nations.

Germany has peaceful borders on many sides, and is determined that these borders will count as definitive and thus give Europe a feeling of security and peace. But this self-limitation and self-restraint is apparently construed by many as a sign of Germany's weakness. Therefore, I would like to set this error straight.

I believe it does not serve European peace if there is any belief that Germany is not willing to express its interests in European questions, and especially that Germany could be indifferent to the suffering and lives of a sum of 3.5 million countrymen.

We understand when England and France take an interest in the whole world. But here I would like to assure the statesmen in Paris and London that there are also German interests, which we are determined to exercise under any circumstances. With this, I would like to remind you of a Reichstag speech of 1933, in which I made it clear for the first time before the world that there can be national issues on which our path forward is clearly delineated, and that I would rather assume any hardship, any danger, and any trouble than abstain from doing what is necessary.

No European state has done more for peace than Germany! No one has made greater sacrifices! But it must be understood that even these sacrifices have their limit at some point, and that the National Socialist state must not be confused with the Germany of Bethmann Hollweg or Hertling.

I explain all this here because in the course of this year an event occurred that forces us all to make a certain correction to our stance. As you know, my party comrades, after endless postponements of a national election, there were at least supposed to be community elections this year in Czechoslovakia. Even in Prague they were convinced of the untenable Czech position. They feared the unity of the Germans and the other nationalities.

Thus, they believed they had to take special measures in order to influence the election results through pressure on the voting process. The Czech government had the idea that the only effective measure would be violent intimidation. A demonstration of the weapons of the Czech state seemed well-suited for this intimidation. The Sudeten Germans were to be shown special Czech brutality in order to warn them to accept the Czech interest and to vote accordingly. In order to make this show of force seem plausible to the world, Mr. Beneš invented the lie that Germany had mobilized troops and stood ready to invade Czechoslovakia.

I gave the following explanation for this: the invention of such dishonest claims is nothing new. Around one year before that, the press in another country made up the lie that twenty thousand of our troops had landed in Morocco. The Jewish fabricator of this libel hoped to spark a war with this claim. At that time it sufficed to deliver a brief explanation to the French ambassadors to dispel this infamous slander for the world. This time, as well, the ambassador of another great power was immediately assured that there was no truth to the Czech claim. This explanation was repeated another time, and it was also immediately shared with the government in Prague.

However, the regime in Prague needed this fraud as a pretense for its terroristic extortion and election interference.

Here, after the fact, I can confirm that not a single German soldier more than those already serving there marched in, and not a single regiment or other unit marched toward the border. Indeed, not a single soldier was outside of his peacetime garrison in that time period. In fact, the order was given to avoid even the slightest impression of any move toward the border.

Despite this, that wicked campaign took place that organized all of Europe in the service of the criminal goals of a regime that intended to put the election under military pressure in order to intimidate its citizens and rob them of their voting rights. And in pursuit of this purpose, in its unscrupulousness, it did not hesitate to throw a great power under suspicion, because it needed a moral justification to alarm all of Europe and throw it into a bloody war, if necessary.

Because Germany had no such intentions, and was actually convinced that this regional election would confirm the Sudeten Germans' rights, our government did not do anything. But this was taken as an opportunity to claim that Germany shied away from doing anything due to the Czechs' firm stance and the interventions of England and France. My party comrades, you will understand that a great power cannot accept such wicked overreach a second time. Therefore, I have taken the appropriate precautionary measures.

I am a National Socialist, and as such I am used to hitting back against every attack. I also know very well that an implacable enemy like the Czechs will not be placated by indulgence, but would only be driven to greater arrogance. The old German Reich can serve as a warning here. Its love of peace turned self-destructive, and in the end it still could not avoid war.

In view of this, I have taken very serious measures on May 28th. Firstly, the previously announced increases of the army and the air force were greatly expanded by my order, and immediately implemented. Secondly, I ordered the immediate expansion of fortifications in the west.

I can assure you that since then, the most colossal fortifications of all time are in the process of being completed. For this purpose, I have given the Inspector General of German Road Construction, Dr. Todt, a new assignment. Through his organizational genius, he has completed one of the most impressive works of all time in connection with these fortifications. I will give you a few numbers:

- The German Western Fortification, which has already been under construction for two years, now has 278,000 workers of Dr. Todt's organization, another 84,000 beyond that, and another 100,000 of the Reich Labor Service and numerous pioneer battalions and infantry divisions.
- Aside from materials arriving by other means of transportation, the Reich Railway alone is delivering 8,000 railroad wagons daily.
- About 100,000 tons of gravel are being used daily. The German Western Fortification will be complete before winter. Its defensive capabilities are already fully assured. After its completion, it will include a total of 17,000 bunkers and tank traps. Behind this front of steel and concrete, which consists of three lines, and in some places reaches a depth of 4 lines or 50 kilometers, there is the German Volk at arms.

I have ordered this most enormous effort of all time for the sake of securing peace. But I will not, under any circumstance, sit idly by and watch the continued oppression of our countrymen in Czechoslovakia.

Mr. Beneš is being tactical. Following the Geneva pattern, he talks and wants to organize negotiations to solve this issue, while giving few concessions. This cannot go on for long! This is not about figures of speech, but about rights, and particularly injured rights. What we Germans demand is the right to self-determination that every other people has, not empty words.

Mr. Beneš has no concession to give the Sudeten Germans; they already have the right to determine their own lives, just like every other people.

But if the democracies are convinced, in this case, that the oppression of Germans has to be defended by any means necessary, then this will have serious consequences!

I believe I serve peace better if I leave no room for doubt about this.

I have not demanded that Germany be allowed to oppress 3.5 million Frenchmen, or that 3.5 million English be delivered to us; but I do demand that the oppression of 3.5 million Germans in Czechoslovakia stops, and that the right of self-determination is allowed to express itself.

It would be regrettable if this causes our relations with the other European states to be tarnished or damaged. But it would not be our fault. Besides, it is the Czechoslovakian government's responsibility to come to terms with the Sudeten German leaders and to come to an understanding one way or another.

My aim — our aim, my fellow countrymen — is to ensure that justice does not turn into injustice. For we are talking about German countrymen.

By no means do I want to let a second Palestine be created here in the heart of Germany through the diligent efforts of other statesmen.

The poor Arabs are defenseless and abandoned. The Germans in Czechoslovakia are neither defenseless nor abandoned. Understand that.

I believe I have to express this at the Party Congress, where we are joined by representatives of our Austrian district for the first time. They know best how painful it is to be separated from one's motherland. They will also best recognize the meaning of my remarks today. They will agree most joyfully when I state, before the whole German Volk, that we would not deserve to be Germans if we were not ready to take such a stance and to bear whatever consequences follow.

When we think of the audacity that even a small state has dared to show Germany in these past months, then we see that the explanation must lie in the unwillingness to recognize a state in the German Reich that is more than a momentary upstart.

As I stood in Rome in the spring, I became aware of how the history of mankind is seen too often in small spans of time and at correspondingly small scales. Thousands and thousands of years encompass only a few bloodlines.

Whatever becomes tired in that time can also pick itself up again. Today's Italy and today's Germany are living proof of that. They are regenerated nations, and can for that reason perhaps be called new nations, except that this newness is not grounded in virgin land, but historical land. The Roman Empire is beginning to breathe again. Likewise, though it is historically much younger, Germany as a political entity is also no new birth.

I have let the insignia of the Holy Roman Empire be brought to Nuremberg in order to remind not only our own Volk, but also the whole world, that there was a powerful German Reich over half a millennium before the discovery of the New World.

Dynasties have come and gone, and the outward forms have changed. The Volk has rejuvenated, but its substance has always stayed the same. The German Reich has slumbered for a long time.

The German Volk has now awoken, and it has placed its thousand-year crown back upon its own head. We who are the historical witnesses of this resurrection feel special joy and humble gratitude to the Almighty!

But this suggestion should also serve as a lesson to the rest of the world, as a suggestion to study history again from a higher perspective; it is a lesson not to fall into past mistakes.

The new Italian Roman Empire and the new Germanic German Reich are, in truth, ancient phenomena. You do not have to love them. However, no power on earth can remove them again.

Party comrades! National Socialists!

The first Reich Party Congress of Greater Germany ends this hour. You all are still filled with the tremendous historic impressions of these days. Our national pride and your confidence were strengthened by this demonstration of our people's strength and unity. Go home now, and carry in your heart that faithful trust that you have carried for almost two decades as Germans and as National Socialists.

You have the right to hold up your German head with pride, and we all have the duty to never again let it bow to a foreign will. Let this be our vow! So help us God!

ENJOYED THIS BOOK?

TO READ MORE, VISIT US AT

ANTELOPEHILLPUBLISHING.COM

www.ingramcontent.com/pod-product-compliance
Lightning Source LLC
Chambersburg PA
CBHW020430130626
46549CB00001B/65